Dissension and Tenacity

THEOLOGY IN THE AGE OF EMPIRE

Series Editor: Jione Havea

In this series, an international collective of theologians interrogate Christianity's involvement with empires past and present, trouble its normative teachings and practices whenever they sustain and profit from empire, and rekindle the insights and energies within the Christian movement that militate against empire's rapacity.

Titles Published

Religion and Power, edited by Jione Havea
Scripture and Resistance, edited by Jione Havea
People and Land: Decolonizing Theologies, edited by Jione Havea
Vulnerability and Resilience: Body and Liberation Theologies, edited by Jione Havea
Mission and Context, edited by Jione Havea
Dissension and Tenacity: Doing Theology with Nerves, edited by Jione Havea

Dissension and Tenacity

Doing Theology with Nerves

Edited by
Jione Havea

LEXINGTON BOOKS/FORTRESS ACADEMIC
Lanham • Boulder • New York • London

Published by Lexington Books/Fortress Academic
Lexington Books is an imprint of The Rowman & Littlefield Publishing Group, Inc.
4501 Forbes Boulevard, Suite 200, Lanham, Maryland 20706
www.rowman.com
86-90 Paul Street, London EC2A 4NE, United Kingdom

Copyright © 2023 by The Rowman & Littlefield Publishing Group, Inc.

All rights reserved. No part of this book may be reproduced in any form or by any electronic or mechanical means, including information storage and retrieval systems, without written permission from the publisher, except by a reviewer who may quote passages in a review.

British Library Cataloguing in Publication Information Available

Library of Congress Cataloging-in-Publication Data Available

ISBN 978-1-9787-1437-3 (cloth) | ISBN 978-1-9787-1439-7 (paperback) | ISBN 978-1-9787-1438-0 (ebook)

*Work on this book was supported by
Council for World Mission
through its DARE program
(Discernment and Radical Engagement)*

Contents

Preface ix

Chapter 1: "Take Away the Stone": Lazarus as (Tombed) Body
(John 11:38–44) 1
Jione Havea

Chapter 2: Call to Rise 13
Karen Georgia A. Thompson, Anna Jane Lagi, Aruna Gogulamanda, John Robert Lee, Chad Rimmer

PART I: TALKING BACK WITH NERVES, AGAINST BABYLON 25

Chapter 3: "The Lord Needs Them" (Matthew 21:3): The Gospel's Beasts and Sovereign Christ 27
Tat-siong Benny Liew

Chapter 4: Resisting the Economic Shitstem: A Postcolonial Filipinx-Korean Reading of Luke 16:1–13 with Mel Chen's Animacies Theory 41
Dong Hyeon Jeong

Chapter 5: Interrogating the Silence: Jesus' Response to a Mother's Cry, for a Daughter's Disability (Matthew 15:21–28) 55
Wendy Elson

Chapter 6: Translating Leviathan, Talking Back to God, Doing Public Theology from Below 71
Gerald O. West

Chapter 7: Sitting and Weeping by the Rivers of Babylon 83
Miguel A. De La Torre

Chapter 8: Lamentations as a Healing Response to Necropower at
   the Texas-Mexico Border   97
   Gregory L. Cuéllar

Chapter 9: *Tūturu Whiti Whakamaua, Kia Tina, Tina! Haumi e, Hui
   e! Taiki e!*: Defiance, Determination and Decolonisation! 109
   Te Aroha Rountree

**PART II: PERSEVERING WITH TENACITY, THROUGH
SHITSTEMS**   123

Chapter 10: RastafarI and Domestic Labour: Roots in Menstrual
   Taboos and Western Inequality   125
   Anna Kasafi Perkins

Chapter 11: Queer Arctivism: Talking Back to the Cis/tems   141
   Ana Ester Pádua Freire

Chapter 12: *The Bacchus Lady* as The Parable of "Promiscuous
   Care"   151
   Nami Kim

Chapter 13: Glimpses of God's Dis/Abled Domain: Rising Up
   against Empire in Small Steps / Huge Leaps   167
   Graham Adams

Chapter 14: Temporarily Abled or Permanently Differently Abled:
   Rising to Life with Disability   181
   Wanda Deifelt

PART III: UNENDING   191

Chapter 15: Rising to Life (John 11:38–44): Politics, Contexts,
   Illusions, Oxymorons   193
   Sainimili Kata Rockett

Chapter 16: Chant Down Christian Shitstems: Then What?   203
   Michael N. Jagessar

Bibliography   211

Index   225

About the Editor and Contributors   229

Preface

This book is one of two collections that were gathered from eDARE 2021,[1] which was hosted by Council for World Mission (CWM). The presenters included artists, poets, pastors, scholars, activists, and theologians, but not all of the papers are included in the publications out from eDARE 2021. Those included in this volume were reviewed and edited in line with the academic expectations and requirements of the publisher and the book series.

The subtitle for this first collection—*Doing Theology with Nerves*—reflects the determined ("nerves" as resolution) and daring ("nerves" as boldness) souls of the contributors, which ripple through the following chapters. These nerves are also conveyed by the title of the book—*Dissension and Tenacity*, and there are elements of dissension and tenacity in all of the essays.

FLOW OF THE BOOK

The first two chapters set the tone and locate the chapters in the flow of the book, over two main clusters of essays. The first cluster of essays are framed as "talking back with nerves, against Babylon," appealing to the spirit of *dissension and tenacity* among feminist (talking back to patriarchy) and RastafarI (chanting down Babylon) critics. And the second cluster of essays drives toward "persevering with tenacity, through shitstems." These two clusters are followed by two closing chapters that open up the conversation for further engagement.

Jione Havea (chap. 1) sets the tone of dissension with a rereading of John 11:38–44 in conversation with the artworks and poems presented at eDARE 2021. Jione's rereading dissents against the certainty and celebration of Jesus as having raised Lazarus from death. Was the dead man that came out of the tomb Lazarus? The text does not say. What was Jesus on about? Jesus walked away from the tombed man, leaving him at the narrative point of being stripped and unbound—what does that say about Jesus? And what about those who follow Jesus, away from the tombed body? Who cares, or should anyone care, for tombed bodies? These leading questions are footholds for locating the chapters.

In chapter 2, five of the poems presented at eDARE 2021 by Karen Georgia A. Thompson, Anna Jane Lagi, Aruna Gogulamanda, John Robert Lee, and Chad Rimmer are brought together as a collaborative "Call to rise." This kind of call has different connotations depending on location: it sounds different, for example, at places of worship in comparison to courts of law, sides of the road, and public squares. There is a "call to rise" in all those places, but for different purposes. In chapter 2, all of those purposes are evoked.

TALKING BACK WITH NERVES, AGAINST BABYLON

The first cluster of essays present dissenting readings of scriptural texts, and of the colonial bodies and traditions (read: Babylon, empire) that capital-ize upon such scriptures. This cluster flows from scriptures and theologies to borders and native peoples.

Tat-siong Benny Liew (chap. 3) argues that hierarchies among humans cannot be adequately analyzed until and unless we look at the difference and hierarchy constructed between human and non-human animals. Speciesism, in other words, provides a ready justification for some humans to discriminate against certain other humans—whether because of difference in race, gender, sexuality, dis/ability, etc.—as less than human, inhuman, more like animals, or simply beastly.

Starting with Matthew's odd depiction of Jesus's "triumphal entry" into Jerusalem on both a donkey and a colt (Matthew 21:1–11), Liew destabilizes the human/animal divide in Matthew's Gospel. As Jacques Derrida provocatively points out, the sovereign itself is often beastly, even or especially as sovereignty is established and reinforced on account of the sovereign's ultimate ability or power to exercise control over beasts and bestial forces. Our concern for life must not be limited to our own lives or even only human lives; it must also include lives of non-human animals.

Jeong, Dong Hyeon (chap. 4) offers a postcolonial reading of the baffling interaction between the landowner and his manager in Luke 16:1–13. First, after getting terminated for embezzlement, the manager resorted to reducing the loans owed by his master's debtors as his "solution" to his conundrum. Second, the landowner (or perhaps Luke) commends the manager's decision to lower his account receivables, even depicting such arbitrary decision as shrewd act that is worth emulating by others (v. 9). The passage further explains that managing dishonest wealth is not only inevitable but even necessary in preparing oneself to manage "true riches" (v. 11).

Jeong intersects the master's response with the postcolonially ambivalent relationship between Korean missionaries in the Philippines who own "mission centers" and hire local Filipinx as managers. Since the 1980s, many Korean missionaries to the Philippines erect mansions they call "mission centers." When missionaries go to their mission fields, they leave their mission centers with Filipinx managers. Miscommunications and misunderstandings happen quite often due to language and cultural barriers. The mission center owners become wary of their local managers for their savvy dealings, outsmarting their bosses in many ways. Such tension echoes the very definition of postcolonial ambivalence in which the mission center owners "hate" their local managers for their sly civility, and yet "love" or desire to be like them for their cunning methods.

Jeong offers an alternative reading that appeals to Mel Chen's animacies theory in which one finds life, the animating and the subverting, on more-than-humans. The manager resists and transgresses the economic *shitstem* by tapping into the animacies of (losing) more-than-human olive oil and wheat (vv. 6–7) as his affective resistance against the hegemonic grip of his master's unjust wealth.

Wendy Elson (chap. 5) offers a dissenting reading of the story of the Canaanite woman (Matt 15:21–28). When the Canaanite woman wailed her plea for her daughter's healing, Jesus offered no answer at all. This woman is not alone in her experience of silence as a response to her plea. What is the nature of this silence and how might a retelling from the perspective of the woman and her silent daughter bring healing for contemporary women and for the mission of the church? Elson enters the story from her experience as a mother to a child with disability. She explores the silence and the silencing of women, and entertains the possibilities for transformation. The Canaanite woman (Justa) finds healing for her daughter (Berenice) through lament, and her use of the liminal moment to focus on her daughter's need.

The Canaanite woman, shrewd, savvy, and full of sass, engages with Jesus around the nature and expansion of his calling, while refusing to be diminished in her personhood. Rejecting the marginalisation of "othering," she uses the silence / pause as a shelter as she regroups. Gathering her resources, she focuses on her goal as she courageously speaks her truth to power advocating for what her child needs in order to flourish.

Gerald O. West (chap. 6) draws on creatures from below, Behemoth and Leviathan, and uses exegesis and art to reflect on a form of public theology in which we publicly recognise and acknowledge God's complicity with injustice. "The crisis" that drives the poetry of the book of Job "is not about God's power," argues Bruce Birch. "It is about God's justice."

Job's interrogation of his friends' and God's theological conception of a just creation, provoked by his wife, forces God to admit to gaps in God's control of chaos and/as injustice. In his poetic protest Job catches glimpses of his likeness to Behemoth and Leviathan, but it is God who summons Job to be more fully like these monsters, talking back to God and forcing God to speak more truly of the world, of Job, and of God-self. Only then is God able to forge a collaborative alliance with Job and Job with God, as together they work for a more just order.

Miguel A. De La Torre (chap. 7) intersects the struggles of the poet in Psalm 137 with his own as a Cuban growing up in USA-Babylon. De la Torre relates to the poet's pain of being cast out of the land which witnessed his birth. Forever foreigners, sojourners who will never belong *aquí* (here) or *allá* (there). How can the psalmist, and people like him, find fulfillment *aquí*, when *allá* beckons for their return? How can they die in peace when their hearts were left behind, in the land of their parents? How can they forge an identity in exile?

Refugees, whether they be Jews or Cubans, are forced to deal with the incompressible pain of displacement. Judaism came into being in Babylon through the pain of questioning a God who would tear God's people from their homes and cast them into hostile land. Cubans also were forced to reimagine their identity, internalizing and naturalizing a false sense of belonging to overcome displacement and serve as protection from the pain of economic and psychological difficulties caused by uprootedness. Perhaps there can never be a return to one's native land, only fractured memories upon which it is recreated—a new way of (re)membering which conveniently forgets reality.

Gregory L. Cuéllar (chap. 8) turns to the book of Lamentations, especially its haunting and yet subversive example of how to lament in the traumas of imperial violence and colonization. Cuéllar harnesses the poetic response of Lamentations to postcolonial trauma as a way to lament in death zones like the Texas-Mexico border. Resourcing this task is a different reading of Lamentations that takes cues from Achille Mbembe's mapping of "necropolitical power" as well as his notion of the sacred "as power of therapy and hope." From this counter vantage point, Lamentations emerges less as melancholic literature than activist poetry that bears witness to the murderous depths of imperial power against those deemed its enemy.

The essay turns to the necropower afforded to the border security and cartel to render the Texas-Mexico border a death zone for migrants. Among the question that Cuéllar addresses are: How might the artistic mapping of imperial violence in Lamentations serve as a radical lamenting strategy for marginalized people coping with the deadly effects of necropolitical power? How might this proposed reading of Lamentations point racialized readers to modes of lament that reconstitute their lives as worthy of human existence while also exposing the multiple ways in which deadly forms of racist power operate?

Te Aroha Rountree (chap. 9) winds up this first cluster with a call for Māori to be defiant, (self)determined, and decolonise. *Defiance*: As native peoples, Māori are defiant. The whitewashed history of colonisation and the romanticising of missionary impact in Māori and Pasifika contexts aim to assimilate native peoples into dominant western Pākeha (white, European) society. We are defiant and we exercise our capacity to resist, to push back against the expectations to conform and to compromise.

(Self-)*Determination*: As native peoples we fight for what all peoples desire—the right to determine our own ways of knowing and being in the world. There exists persistent and pervasive systemic and institutional racism founded on colonial pre-conceptions of white supremacy. We seek to dismantle those oppressive structures, processes and ideologies, for they exclude Māori from self-determining power.

(Road to) *Decolonisation*: As native peoples we evoke story-telling and truth-telling for justice, for *whenua*, for *moana*, for *iwi*, and for all creation. In our quest for freedoms for ourselves our vision must extend beyond ourselves to *Papatuanuku me Ranginui* (earth and sky personified), to the realms of *Tane and Tangaroa* (forest and sea manifest).

PERSEVERING WITH TENACITY, THROUGH SHITSTEMS

The essays in this second cluster testify that shitstems do not have the final word. Perseverance is possible, and it requires tenacity.

Anna Kasafi Perkins (chap. 10) turns to RastafarI, which emerged in colonial Jamaica as outcasts from the society due to their Afro-centric religio-cultural challenge to Babylon. This outcast status has changed significantly, and RastafarI has become secularised. However, many Rastas resist secularisation and one of the areas in which they remain separated from Jamaican society is in their refusal to work in the Babylon shitstem, expressed in their emphasis on self-sufficiency and eating from the earth. Both family and communal life are organised to reject ways of understanding work in the larger Jamaican society, which maintains distinct spheres for females and males, though even that is changing, slowly. Nonetheless, in family life, Rastamen generally remain distinctive; they take a more active and affective role in domestic labour than their non-Rastafarian counterparts while maintaining patriarchal norms of male headship and female inferiority.

Perkins explores the question of domestic labour within the Rastafarian community, specifically the domestic roles in the Rastafarian family. She argues that the distinctive role of Rastamen within the household is the direct result of both the importance of the children ("yootz") and Rasta biblically based menstrual taboos. The Rastaman's woman ("daata") is relegated during her menses and so is not allowed to cook or mingle with the men. Perkins concludes that Rastamen have internalized unequal gender viewpoints from the Bible and Western bourgeois notions of male as the head of the household/nuclear family with his wife and children dependent on his wage, guidance, and teaching. She proposes insights from female Rasta scholars as part of the process of "imparting" (contributing and impacting) domestic labour in RastafarI.

Ana Ester Pádua Freire (chap. 11) highlights art as an instrument of human emancipation. Art is an important political language of resistance as well as a community's expression of its own experience. Freire explores the trans-conceptual encounter of art, religion, and politics by a case study of the Metropolitan Community Church of Belo Horizonte (MCC BH) and its participation at the March Against LGBTphobia in Belo Horizonte, Brazil. MCC BH is a member church of the Universal Fellowship of the Metropolitan Community Churches (UFMCC), the first inclusive denomination in the world.

MCC BH developed, through Queer Theology, a *sui generis* arctivism exemplified by the performances of the drag queen, Simone Star. Through the lens of the trans-conceptual construction of a religious and a political liturgy, Freire examines the use of arctivism by MCC BH as a social language, which challenges cisgender and heteronormative systems. The case study reveals that the active use of liturgy, as a ritualistic way that this faith community identifies itself, is a fundamental mechanism to experience the world, while subverting the precariousness of being sexual and gender dissidents. As a result of that, Freire shows that religion and politics can be found in the religious temple, and on the streets, through art as an emancipatory activity that resists the cis/tems.

Nami Kim (chap. 12) reflects on the experience of "Bacchus ladies"—women who sell the Bacchus, a popular energy drink, to elderly men in public places (e.g., park, plaza) in South Korea. The Bacchus ladies also "sell sex" to elderly men in those public spaces; they prostitute in their "old" age for daily survival in a society where elderly people with no resources and safety net greatly suffer. The Bacchus ladies are "despised," and the men who buy their sexual services are also considered filthy, vulgar men who shamelessly "buy sex" in their "old" age. The women pejoratively called the "Bacchus ladies" do not fit the image of respectable "grandmothers" who are "properly" aged, care for their grandchildren, and do not engage in sexual acts. The Bacchus ladies perform counter normative acts as elderly women and are subject to being humiliated, scrutinized, policed, and arrested by the state if they get caught for prostituting. Their counter-normative acts and lives show that they are positioned outside of the category of normatized, decently aged cis-gender, heterosexual, monogamous women who conform to socially prescribed gender roles and relations.

Through analysing "The Bacchus Lady" ("A Killer Woman" in Korean), a film that closely follows a Bacchus lady named So-young, and the people whom she encounters and engages, Kim proposes ways in which feminist theology can open up a counter-normative space in which the normative understanding of aged women as respectable and virtuous, and of the family as a heterosexual nuclear unit, are contested. Drawing from Cathy Cohen, Marcella Althaus-Reid, and other queer scholars, Kim shows how feminist theology paid little attention to "indecent" women who live "(un)holy" lives as aged sex-workers. "Decent" theologies that conform to the normative understanding of gender, sexuality, age, and family, reinforce structural and social inequalities under the guise of some normal and natural order to life, and are inherently harmful to women regardless of whether they fit or not such normativity in a heteropatriarchal, classist, misogynist, transphobic, xenophobic, and ageist society.

Graham Adams (chap. 13) turns the attention to dis/abled bodies. Even where the shitstem offers support to people, specifically children, with disabilities, it does so on the basis that they "cannot" do certain things, that they "do not" meet particular developmental benchmarks, and that they "will not" function as independent (economic) actors. In other words, it "sees" their identity, dignity, and agency in terms of deficit—that which "cannot" be seen.

Adams's nephew, Simeon, has a genetic condition causing "global developmental delay" and this is the systemic culture in which he is growing. While the shitstem views his achievements as small steps, the *truth* is that they are huge leaps. How, then, might we alternatively view such identity, talking back to the deficit model, to glimpse more fully what Simeon is revealing to us?

Part-way through the man's healing in Mark 8:22–26, he glimpses others as "trees, walking," so perception is inverted: the dis/abled person exercises agency to (mis)perceive able-bodied people in objectified terms. What can we learn? A) Dis/abled people lead the way to God's realm, leaping in small steps—and a theology of "chaos theory" reaffirms the power of small events, destabilising how the empire sees, thinks and acts; B) "Able"-bodied people should "receive God's realm" as dis/abled people, alert to the objectification of others, queering mis-perceptions; and C) As Jesus tells the man not to return to the village, so we should not revert to sites of objectification, but identify how God's alternative horizon both exposes the shitstem's limited vision and enables and inspires us, alternatively, to see and celebrate each other's dynamic humanity.

Wanda Deifelt (chap. 14) interrogates the idea of bodily perfection (even if this is an unattainable ideal), promoted by fields as diverse as advertising, physiculture, plastic surgery, diet programs, or medicine. The notion of what a normal body does and looks like has become normative and falls under constructs of modernity, often emphasizing the dichotomy between body and reason. It also perceives the body as a machine made of bone and flesh that responds to the will of the brain.

But what happens when this "machine" does not comply? How does bodily expectation of normalcy reconcile with the reality of its limitations? What are the consequences of labelling a body as disabled? What are the epistemological shifts engendered by centering theological discourse and practice from a perspective of disability? Does our approach to our own bodies change once we realize that there is no perfect body? How does our understanding of embodiment (the multiple bodies we inhabit: personal, social, ecclesial, ecological, etc.) shift once we no longer assume perfection but accept limitation and embrace vulnerability? What are the consequences for ethical engagement if the starting point is not independence and autonomy but the fact that we are only temporarily abled?

UNENDING

The collection closes with two essays that invite further engagement with, and interrogation of, the dissensions and tenacities that ooze through the previous pages.

Sainimili Kata Rockett (chap. 15) problematizes the preference for "rising to life" that runs through this collection. What is the big deal, seeing that the life into which the dead (will) rise is shits(tems) and sods? And why would anyone want to rise to life, only to die a second time?

Michael N. Jagessar (chap. 16) invites further engagement with the "so what" and "what's next" questions. As long as there are empires, and as long as shitstems are all around, *dissension and tenacity* are *unending*.

NOTE

1. eDARE: "e" because the DARE conference took place virtually, and DARE stands for "Discernment and Radical Engagement," a program of CWM.

Chapter 1

"Take Away the Stone"

Lazarus as (Tombed) Body (John 11:38–44)

Jione Havea

> We need to help our sisters
> Selling skin for recognition
> That carries only until sunrise
> Breaking their dreams into pieces
>
> (Anna Jane Lagi, "What I See, Hear, and Understand"; see chap. 2)

The Taliban officially returned to Kabul on 15 August 2021, marking the end of the invasion by the American empire—the USA, which by the way continues to occupy (is)lands in Oceania: including Hawai'i, Tutuila, Guam, and Mariana. One (foreign) empire departs, and another (local) empire returns. Both empires may be noble in the eyes of their respective powerbrokers, but both are dis-respective savages in the eyes of their victims.

Shortly after the changeover between the two empires (read: noble savages), more Afghan families sell their daughters in order that *they* survive: the innocent, young daughters survive by being adopted by wealthier families that can provide care and security; the unemployed, unpaid parents receive money (bride price) to feed the rest of the family; the desperate grandparents, uncles and aunties are free to seek asylum in other places after they sell their orphaned granddaughters and nieces; and so on.[1] Those daughters and families did survive, but not for long. The relief lasted the night . . . "until sunrise / Breaking their dreams into pieces" (Anna Jane Lagi). And as the dusts begin to settle over Kabul, "a staggering 95 percent of the [Afghanistan] population is not eating enough food."² There were many other atrocities, in Kabul and across Afghanistan, but the picture is clear—pandemonium.

Fast-forward, six months later: on 24 February 2022, the Russian empire (which by the way invaded Afghanistan at a previous time) invades one of its neighbors—Ukraine. Russia's president claims that this was a "special military operation," and his allies refuse to call it a "war." Notwithstanding, this invasion has been ongoing since 2014 with the Donbas war and the annexation of Crimea, at the shores of the Black Sea—one of the passageways between Europe and Asia. At the time of writing (five weeks after the invasion), many lives—of humans—including babies and children—animals, plants, and countless innocent creatures of the air, earth, and sea—have already been lost and displaced in and from Europe, the cradle of whiteness. The Russian invaders are better equipped, and no less ruthless than the Taliban. I count the Russian powerbrokers and invaders among history's noble savages.

Between Kabul and Kyiv, cornerstones are shaken, walls and buildings fall, and the wreckages bury bodies and memories. Livelihoods and aspirations—targeted and bombed. Pasts and futures—exploded. Orphans and widows—dispersed. These scenarios are common when empires raid, within and across their borders.

Outside of Afghanistan, America and Europe, the list of modern empires includes Israel, Ethiopia, Indonesia, Myanmar, and many others. As empires raid, lives burn, stones fly, and questions ricochet: Who will receive the refugees? Who will bury the victims? Who will pick up the rubbles? Who will rebuild after the invasion, occupation, and destruction? How will peace be regained? How will justice be established? And how will creation heal?

I imagine those kinds of questions being asked by the golden-brown faces in Maxime de Palm's "Reperations for the Caribbean," the artwork on the cover of this book. De Palm—a Caribbean woman artist and activist who has migrated to the Netherlands—presents golden-brown faces, and the positioning of the hands are revealing. Some hands clasp their cheeks, suggesting that they are surprised. Or are they covering their ears? Some hands screen their eyes, as if they do not want to see. Or are they squinting, trying to see clearly? And some hands cover over their mouths, as if they are lost for words. Dumbfounded. Stunned. Silenced. Unwilling to talk back.

What might the golden-brown faces in de Palm's artwork see, hear, and feel in the raids by modern empires, and their aftermaths? How might we see, hear, and feel the world around us through the golden-brown faces in de Palm's artwork? These questions are difficult, but they need to be raised because, to borrow the words of Karen Georgia A. Thompson:

> we struggle with what we see
> witnesses to the resident brokenness of life

our hearts ill at ease
as we question who we are
in the presence of this sea
of misery and suffering

(Karen Georgia A. Thompson, "testify"; see chap. 2)

STONES

"Take away the stone," said Jesus—who was "greatly troubled"—when he came to the tomb of Lazarus (John 11:38–39).[3] Rewind, several verses earlier: Jesus took his time to come to Lazarus who, according to Lazarus' sisters (11:3), Jesus loves. Jesus did not rush back to be with his beloved, during his time of need. What's up with Jesus?

Lazarus?

That Jesus was "greatly disturbed" may have been, on first reading, because he did not expect Lazarus to die seeing that, upon hearing the news from Martha and Mary, Jesus responded—"This illness does not lead to death" (11:3–4). He stayed on for another two days. He expected Lazarus to live. Or did he not really care for Lazarus? Later, Jesus somehow knew that Lazarus had died. He then led his disciples back to Judea, so that he would "awaken" Lazarus "their friend." His disciples were reluctant, but they ended up going, upon a final push by Thomas: "Let us also go, that we may die with him" (11:16).

When Jesus and his disciples arrived, Lazarus had been in the tomb for four days. Dead, and buried. And people—"the Jews"—were gathered at the family home, to console Martha and Mary. Martha came first to meet Jesus, and then Mary and the Jews came. Their weeping "greatly disturbed" Jesus "in spirit" and he was "deeply moved" (11:33). For some of the Jews, Jesus' emotional response showed how much he loved Lazarus. But some were sceptical: "Could not he who opened the eyes of the blind man have kept this man from dying?" (11:36). In other words, where was Jesus all this time? Why didn't he do something?

"Take away the stone" announces the beginning of Jesus' special operation. Against Martha's concern that opening the cave will bring shame to her family and to the community, for she expected that there would be a stench— from the body of her brother, or from other buried bodies—in the cave, Jesus pushed on with his special operation. He showed off how close he was to *the*

Father, with a prayer, and then with a loud voice he called, "Lazarus, come out!" At this point, the text is clear:[4] "The dead man came out, his hands and feet bound with strips of cloth, and his face wrapped in a cloth. Jesus said to them, 'Unbind him, and let him go'" (11:44).

Amazing.

But was he Lazarus?

The text does not confirm. Instead, the text turns to the Jews who were having issues with Jesus—presumably they are the ones who wanted to stone Jesus earlier (11:8), and to whom Thomas was alluding (11:16)—and left the dead man to be unbounded outside the cave. The dead man was called out, and then he was left stranded. What might the golden-brown faces in de Palm's work see, hear, and feel in Jesus' special operation? Would they turn with the text to the Jews, or stay with the dead man who has been called out of the cave?

Jesus!

Jesus was determined. He planned a special operation, and nothing was going to stop him. Not the Jews, who earlier tried to "stone" him (11:8; λιθάζω). Not Martha, who warned Jesus of the domino effect of his special operation. Not Mary, whose tears deeply touched Jesus' nerves. And not even death, nor the stench of death. Jesus was undeterred, like a beastly sovereign (see Tat-siong Benny Liew, chap. 3).

"Take away the stone" (11:39; τὸν λίθον) was directed at many "ears": the disciples, the Jews, the crowd, as well as the stone (λίθος) that was laid against the cave in which Lazarus was laid to rest (11:38). "Take away the stone" would have rung in the ears of those in the vicinity: seize the moment, it's showtime. At stake was the "glory of God" (11:40) and the status of Jesus as the one sent by God (11:42). Lazarus was collateral; his sisters were pivots, to accentuate Jesus' humanity (the weeping Mary touched his nerves, 11:32–33) and divinity (the caring Martha drew Jesus to the Father, 11:39–42). The Jews were the foes, and "Take away the stone" is directed at them also—Jesus' words thus bring to mind the stoning (λιθάζω) that the Jews wanted to give Jesus (11:8). "The stone" in Jesus' words was, so to speak, thrown at several birds—including the family, the Jews, and death. Put another way, Jesus' words were aimed at multiple faces.

FACES

Emmanuel Garibay, a Filipino activist theologian, figuratively throws stones at the multiple faces of theology with his work titled "Teolohiya" (Tagalog

Figure 1.1. Emmanuel Garibay, "Teolohiya" (2021)

for "theology"; see Figure 1.1). The human figure in this work represents Teolohiya (theology, theologian), who carries an image of Jesus in the right hand and a book in the left hand. The image is much larger than the book, even though the book is the source for the image. Garibay here throws stones at theologies and theologians for pumping up the book (word, text) into their inflated image (theology). On that note, which theology or theologian does not pump up their source-book?

Teolohiya hides behind the stone-like image of Jesus, using the image as a (partial) mask. The eye of the image is close, as if it is frozen. Or asleep. Even dead. The inflated image does not see. It is blind. Teolohiya hides with an open eye, but the eye is hollow (like a cave). And it is empty. The mouth is sealed (like a tomb). Teolohiya does not see, and it does not speak. It is stone-like, thus it mimics the image that it holds. At the same time, the image also reflects Teolohiya. Teolohiya holds the image and the book, and gives the impression that it is innocent.

Book

The story of Jesus raising a dead man (who could be Lazarus) is one of the stories from the book that theologians pump up. So did my Sunday school teachers, who convinced me and my peers that it was a miracle. A special operation. Awesome. My Sunday school teachers were faithful readers. They celebrated the miracle, and then carried on with the narrative (book). They too abandon the raised dead man, at the point of being unbound.

On this occasion,[5] i pause with the golden-brown faces in de Palm's work. I resist the flow of the narrative (book), opting to linger with the dead man whom Jesus called out of his state of rest. Jesus gave instructions to the crowd—first, to take away the stone and second, to unbind the dead man— and in describing the dead man the book draws my eyes to specific body parts: "his hands and feet bound (δεδεμένοςδέω) with strips of cloth, and his face wrapped (περιεδέδετο) in a cloth" (11:44a). I assume that the other parts of his body were also bound and/or wrapped, but the narrator limits me to his hands, feet, and face.

How one renders δεδεμένος (root: δέω) compared to περιεδέδετο (root: περι-δέω), is a matter of choice. The Tongan Bible uses *ha'i* for δεδεμένος ("bound" in NRSV) and *tākai* for περιεδέδετο ("wrapped" in NRSV). The term *ha'i* suggests that force has been applied, as when one ties up firewood, a canoe, an animal, a prisoner, or a slave; the Tongan Bible thereby gives the impression that the hands and feet of the dead man were tied up to stop him from reaching out (to untie himself) and walking away. He was *ha'i* so that he stays put, "bound" to stay in the shut up, secured with a stone, cave. On the other hand, the term *tākai* expresses care and tenderness: *tākai* refers to the applying of oil to a body, so it connotes a gentle "wrapping"[6] of the face with the cloth. *Tākai* is what Tongans do, with oil, to the face and body of the dead. On the one hand, the choice of words makes the narrative meaningful for Tongan readers. On the other hand, the Tongan Bible inserts Tongan cultures into the book. In other words, the Tongan Bible "blows up" (inflates) the source-book. "The book" (á la Garibay) is therefore inflated for Tongan readers.

While I agree with Garibay that theologians—including myself—inflate biblical texts (book) with our theologies (image), I here add that "the book" is not set in stone. As the Tongan Bible inflates, blows up, its source-book, so do I suspect with "the book" (version, translation) in the languages of the Philippines (for Garibay) and the Caribbean islands (for de Palm). Because languages—ancient and modern—are dynamic, translations will involve both *ha'i* (aiming to fix the meanings) and *tākai* (aiming to make the book meaningful in the local language). This is true of all versions (translations) of the same source-book, and also with regard to the so-called original version of the source-book itself. In whatever language, ancient—Aramaic, Greek, Hebrew—or modern, the book blows things (including itself) up. The book is not set on stone, and it is not innocent.

Image

Teolohiya (theologies, theologians) too, modern and ancient, are not innocent. Some Teolohiya *ha'i* the book up with their images, and some *tākai* the book with theirs. Whether *ha'i* or *tākai*, but realistically it's a combination of both, Teolohiya are not dumb or blind—even if they pretend to be objective and stone-faced.

When Tongan theologians and Sunday School teachers inflate, blow up, their book, they appear to have (unconsciously) learned to do what the book does. Lest I be mistaken, I am suggesting here that the saying "monkey see, monkey do" applies to Tongan theologians and Sunday School teachers. But this is not unique to Tongans; theologians and Sunday School teachers outside of Tonga are in the same boat.

The closed and empty eyes in Garibay's work take me back to the white eyes in de Palm's *visual* artwork (on the cover of the book). De Palm depicts golden-brown faces whose eyes have been whitewashed, so that they *see with white eyes*. This is one of the legacies of the Christian mission in her Caribbean and Dutch placements. Seeing with white eyes is as true for the natives in the Caribbean and Philippine islands as it is for natives in other (is)lands in the mission field: owing to the Christian mission, natives were—not just threatened, but actually—stoned, to the point that their eyes became white.

As it was back then, so it is nowadays: coloniality is alive. As such, the key challenge of de Palm's work is for we who are daughters and sons of parents whose eyes were stoned-white learn to see things in our native ways, with our golden-brown eyes.

BARS

The whitewashing and eye-whitening of natives was strong during the Atlantic slave trade—which enriched Christian mission bodies and funded "church theologies" (see Gerald O. West, chap. 6). The slave trade is the inspiration for Neil Thorogood's work, "There Must be a God Somewhere" (see Figure 1.2; see also Michael Jagessar, chap. 16).

"There must be a God somewhere," but it is not clear how that God was among the black African people who were baptized and then shipped across the Atlantic, as commodities in the slave trade—for someone else's profit, somewhere else. There was a God that (according to my Sunday School teachers) responded to the prayer and demands of Jesus in John 11, but not to the prayers of thousands of African slaves whose howls and weeping were drowned into the middle passage, across the southern part of the Atlantic Ocean (see also Miguel de la Torre, chap. 7). There was a God that responded to the removal of the stone in John 11 (in my Sunday Schooled ears), and thus made Jesus look good in the eyes of the crowd (see also Sainimili Kata Rockett, chap. 15), but not to the thousands of victims at borders of

Figure 1.2. Neil Thorogood, "There Must Be a God Somewhere" (2021)

empires from Afghanistan to Russia, and to the Americas (see also Gregory L. Cuéllar, chap. 8).

Borrowing the critical observation that Thorogood raises, this collection of essays asks—What need to be done so that the God who must be somewhere comes through the bars to embrace the enslaved, the persecuted, the invaded, and the minoritized (on account of their location, age, gender, body, orientation, race, color, dis/ability)? And how do we who are in the businesses of Teolohiya "blow up" (remove) the bars, and call on the God who must be somewhere to be where it matters? In my humble opinion, to have a chance at what those questions seek, requires dissension and tenacity.

Dissension

> rise like silver flying fish over clean waters of living oceans
> like scissor-tailed sea birds over life-giving heritage
> rise up over our ravaged, sorry earth
>
> (John Robert Lee, "Uprising"; see chap. 2)

The artists, poets, and authors (lest I be mistaken: they all are theologians in their own, various, creative ways) who contribute their works to this collection talk back and push back against the usual, mainline readings and theologies. In different ways, these daring theologians "take away the stone" and unbound the subjects whom they have called to "come out." AND they do not walk away, following the narrator and faithful readers of John 11, who are more interested in Jesus than in the tombed Lazarus (who may have been the dead man that came out of the cave). To the contrary, based on the bits and pieces that i know about them, the theologians who contribute to this book prefer to stay, in their contributions and in their practices, with the tombed bodies, tombed books, tombed theologies, tombed images, tombed missions, tombed whatever, that they call out. They prefer to stay because they were, and are, among the tombed. They prefer to stay because they are confident that, like silver flying fish and scissor-tailed sea birds, the tombed can "rise up over our ravaged, sorry earth" (John Robert Lee, chap. 2). In the context of this reflection, *staying with the tombed* is an expression of dissension.

To be fair, dissension was part of Jesus' special operation. His demands were against the usual way of doing things. He demanded that the stone be taken away, even though he did not bring a dead body to bury. He called a dead man to come out, even though he did not come in time to say goodbye to him or to comfort his sisters. He demanded that a dead body be unbound and unwrapped in the eyes of the crowd, despite the expected shame. Thankfully, he demanded that they untie only the legs, feet, and face, rather than the whole body. That would have been awkward, especially for the sisters. In his demands, Jesus talked back against the usual, mainline ways. However, he talked but did not touch. Then he moved on with his crowd. There is no textual sign if anyone stayed with the tombed man.

When the US empire left, moved on from, Afghanistan in August 2021, the situation became worse for the locals. In such a context, I wonder what the John 11 story might turn into if Jesus and the book (à la Garibay) stayed with the unwrapped tombed body. My query is speculative, and it is against the grain of the book, but it joins the chorus of those who, to borrow reggae speak, "chant down Babylon." Babylon is a figure for empires, and chanting is done with words and stones. The young people who join climate marches and strikes, or who demonstrate against the junta at Myanmar, or who throw stones and marbles at Israeli bulldozers, are among those who rise up to chant down Babylon. Chanting down Babylon embodies dissension.

Three ripples of dissension and the courage to chant down Babylon flow through the pages of this collection. First, Jesus, God, and the book are called out. Jesus is shown to have been a beastly sovereign (see Liew, chap. 3), and an uncaring Jew (see Elson, chap. 5), and God is shown to be unjust (see West, chap. 6). And "the book" is called out for its place in impoverishing and disempowering natives in the mission field (see Jeong, chap. 4).

Second, mainline readings and theologies are called out in the interests of migrants and refugees (see De La Torre, chap. 7), bordered bodies (see Cuéllar, chap. 8), native bodies (see Rountree, chap. 9), bloodied mad hired bodies (see Perkins, chap. 10), queer bodies (see Freire, chap. 11), promiscuous bodies (see Kim, chap. 12), and dis/abled bodies (see Elson, chap. 5; Adams, chap. 13; and Deifelt, chap. 14).

Third, the "normalized" and "normatized" forms and formats of doing theology are opened up to the courage, imagination and wisdom of artists and poets (see Thompson, Lagi, Gogulmanda, Lee, and Rimmer, chap. 2). Doing theology is not a privilege only for authors, and it is not necessary to always tie things up. Hence, at the end, this book is unending, interrogating the politics of "rising to life" (see Kata Rockett, chap. 15) and initiating the next—"then what?"—conversations (see Jagessar, chap. 16). In this collection, dissension is not limited to the book and the inflated images (à la Garibay). Dissension is also thrown at the business of doing theology.

Tenacity

> Yours is the strength of fragility
>   Refined in the knowledge of love that will topple
> temples of resolve
>
>   (Chad Rimmer, "Strong"; see chap. 2)

Surviving is needed when one faces abuse and negligence; surviving is a form of resistance. But survival on its own does not stop, nor prevent, abuse and negligence. Calling out the *shitstem* (to use reggae speak) that enables and justifies abuse and negligence is also needed, and this is a dish best served with tenacity. But in the face of invasions and slave trades, and raiding empires, surviving and / with tenacity are difficult.

One may have a small voice, a gentle spirit, an agile hand, yet what that one says and does are revolutionary and have lasting effects—people with those gifts are tenacious in their "fragility" (Chad Rimmer). Put another way, tenacity is not just about what one does but also about the effect of what one does. In the face of empires, tenacity is not just what one does (e.g., with a loud voice and strong arms). Tenacity also has to do with the upshot of what one does (e.g., being a pest in the face of empires). One may do something simple, but it has pestering effects; that simple act is a testimony to the "strength of fragility [. . .] that will topple temples of resolve" (Chad Rimmer).

Ash Dahlstrom, an indigenous Australian, twitted on 26 Jan 2022: "My favorite beverage is the tears of colonisers who are mad that we exist."[7] Every year—26 Jan is "Australia Day," a national holiday to commemorate the landing of the First Fleet at Sydney Cove in 1788. But for indigenous Australians, 26 Jan 1788 was "day one" of invasion and dispossession. That indigenous Australians continue to survive is befitting of celebration. Truly. Amazing. Their survival, appealing to Dahlstorm's words, makes the British colonisers cry. I take this impact on the colonisers to be the outcome of *tenacity*, from the side of indigenous Australians. What indigenous Australians have done was to (simply) survive, and their survival makes the colonizers mad. Similarly, the survival of Māori natives (see chap. 9) and Cuban migrants (see chap. 7) also make their colonizers mad. Turning back to de Palm's artwork, what might the golden-brown faces see, with their white eyes, in the tenacity of black and brown folks?

UNENDING

> She was told
> that she was dirt,
> She was filth and
> in this sacred land of thousands of goddesses
> she is called a Dalit.
>
> (Aruna Gogulamanda, "She was told!"; see chap. 2)

The teaching that dead bodies are unclean is shared across cultures and traditions, books and theologies. In Judaism and Christianity, "Those who touch the dead body of any human being shall be unclean seven days" (Num 19:11). A similar position is held in Hinduism, in which cremating dead bodies is among the menial duties assigned to Dalits.

Dalits are *beneath* the Hindu caste shitstem, which is defined and legislated by "the book" (á la Garibay). In fact, Dalits are not even subjects of the book. Dalits symbolize defilement par excellence, as the old English label "Untouchables" convey. They are not to be touched. They do all the dirty, filthy work. And they are not privileged to the cycles of reincarnation. Once a Dalit, always a Dalit. They are always dirty, and filthy.

The dead man who was abandoned outside the tomb—when Jesus and the book moved away—is a figure for the Dalit. No one told him that he was dirty and filthy, but those who moved away from him—Jesus, the disciples, the Jews, the narrator, the book, and some Sunday School teachers and theologians—treated him as such. Would the Dalits of India, and of the world, abandon him? If they opt to stay with him, what would they do? These questions too are speculative, but their call is simple: stay with tombed bodies, especially if you called them to rise.

In the presence of de Palm's golden-brown bodies, and through Thorogood's bars, the call behind this reading is for our Theolohiya to dissent, with nerves to stay with the so many tombed bodies—of humans, animals, plants, and other creatures of the land, the sea, the air, and the underground—around us. Dissent tenaciously with hope, that Jesus may one day come back to learn something from the Dalits.

NOTES

1. See Anna Coren, Jessie Yeung, Abdul Basir Bina, "She was sold to a stranger so her family could eat as Afghanistan crumbles." *CNN* (01 Nov 2021; https://edition.cnn.com/2021/11/01/asia/afghanistan-child-marriage-crisis-taliban-intl-hnk-dst/index.html).

2. Ruchi Kumar, "In Afghanistan, 'people selling babies, young girls to survive.'" *Aljazeera* (31 March 2022; https://www.aljazeera.com/news/2022/3/31/afghanistan-faces-hunger-crisis-of-unparalleled-proportions).

3. All biblical quotations are from the NRSV, unless indicated otherwise.

4. Prior to this point, however, the text is not clear regarding who removed the stone, and whether Jesus spoke into an opened or still closed cave. Several details of this special operation are ambiguated.

5. I offered another reading with "Lazarus troubles," in Ken Stone and Holly Toensing (eds.), *Bible Trouble: Queer reading at the Boundaries of Biblical Scholarship*, 157–73 (Atlanta: SBL, 2011).

6. Without the accent (indicating long ā-vowel), *takai* means "encircle, around."

7. I learned this from Brian Kolia, an Australian-Samoan colleague.

Chapter 2

Call to Rise

Karen Georgia A. Thompson, Anna Jane Lagi, Aruna Gogulamanda, John Robert Lee, Chad Rimmer

To the lives at the underside of Empire, this chapter issues a *call to rise*. Herein, verses come together to testify (Thompson); to affirm that it's important to see, hear, and understand (Lagi); to interrogate what one's people have been told by cultural and religious traditions (Gogulamanda); to spark uprising against shitstems (Lee); and to be strong through all of those (Rimmer).

As a means for doing theology, poetry is hospitable. It provides room for the wild and invites theologians to slow down, to ponder . . . and to also testify, explain, interrogate, uprise, and be strong, in the doing of theology. These verses are offered here in preparation (as in the "call to rise" in courts of justice and places of worship) for the reflections that come in the pages of this book.[1] Readers are encouraged to hear these verses in their own pace, and for their own interests; and where helpful, consult the explanations that the poets provide for the inspiration for the following calls to rise.

Testify

Karen Georgia A. Thompson

testify begins as a play on words built on the double meaning of the word. Testify means to bring evidence as a witness in a court of law. In this regard, we are all witnesses to the atrocities that we see among us. We cannot be silent onlookers. As witnesses, we must testify given the discomfiture created by injustice and the struggle we experience watching others suffer. We testify not only for ourselves. We testify for ourselves and for others telling the stories and demanding justice in the land on behalf of those who are oppressed and marginalized.

There is also a church related meaning here. In some church traditions there is "testimony time" which is an invitation to talk about the goodness of God. When one testifies in this way, it is about the experience of God. How has God shown up in your life? What has God done? As one provides testimony, the gathered company might shout: "Testify!" This is sent and received as a word of encouragement to the story or event being recounted; it is also a sign that the audience is listening, hears and affirms God present and active in the world—even as God is active in the life of the individual providing testimony. Testimony is necessary to bring about change, and yet, words are inadequate. Action has to accompany the testimonies brought to church and society appealing for a world in distress and in need.

> we struggle with what we see
> witnesses to the resident brokenness of life
> our hearts ill at ease
> as we question who we are
> in the presence of this sea
> of misery and suffering
>
> faces radiating hunger and poverty
> confront us on busy streets
> hearts consumed by loneliness
> stand next to us
> beating the rhythm of life
> transcending time
>
> we struggle to comprehend the wicked
> consumed and driven by their greed
> the raging pursuits of the one percent
> outpacing the rights of those in need
>
> with eyes open we witness
> changes to earth and sky
> the waters of the earth are rising around us
> calling out the chaos of our times
>
> we are silent onlookers
> surveying the carnage of centuries
> eyewitnesses to the bruising of hope
> our lips mouthing words
> inadequate to describe the breaches we see
>
> troubled waters surround us
> pools created from our tears
> their depths teeming with fear
> holding the wreckage of broken hearts and lives
> scarred by trauma and marred by distress

what say we to the millions who died?
their memories archived as statistics
victims of pandemics
their voices rising in unison
crying in protest to the lies they hear in our silence

we are not well
the festering of dis-ease a sign
our restlessness a condition calling forth
new language for creating a new world
one where all will live well and flourish

we listen for god-talk to inspire
words of power to call into being a new creation
the eighth day where righteousness prevails
when justice will flow as sweet rushing waters
to cleanse and to heal all brokenness

instead death visits daily
multinationals stealing waters and deforesting lands
food deserts overtaking the health of the poor
their blinding dry sands
filling the mouth and bellies of parents crying for justice
while begging food for their children

necropolitics dictating the fate of them
labeled as marginalized
while dispensing life to the rich
crushing under foot lives resistant to control
attempting to maintain semblances of an exclusive normal

we testify
to vindicate the innocent
their lives taken before their potential materialized
to the shameful greed producing suffering
to the scandal of excess
to the hoarding of wealth and resources
to the near extinction of hope and possibility

our words are not enough
an inadequate offering proffered
to those robbed of their dignity
deprived of respect
rendered unable to flourish
we offer god-talk in a language obsolete to the masses
words no longer understood by those in need of hope

in this pandemic laden world
where disease flourishes
snatching lives from the innocent
uncovering the lies we told ourselves
we witness death as we hold our words

the waters are rising among us
waters teeming with hatred and fear
waters overwhelming as they carry the silt and sediment of histories
long forgotten
stories presumed buried
their characters preying on the innocent
we watch

we dream we are awake
an awakening contrived from visions
of ourselves as makers of change
illusions of our salvation and safety
shrouding the reality of our times
we are called to god-action
gushing like new wells in dry places

these living waters bring new hope
quenching parched souls
needing healing from their fragility
the repaired turned repairers of the breach

17 October 2021
4:29
KGAT
Olmsted Township, OH
© Copyright 2021 Karen Georgia A. Thompson

What I See, Hear, and Understand

Anna Jane Lagi

"What I See, Hear, and Understand" was inspired by the young women and students that participated in the Pacific Girl Webinar in 2020 (in Fiji). I remembered what it was like to be in high school, trying to find out who I was and what I wanted to stand for. And I could easily imagine these young women set out into a world full of possibilities for change with so much energy and passion but not knowing where or how to start. This poem was a reminder that no matter what issues we are advocating, or problems we are seeking a solution for, it is and always will be . . . about people.

They said I do not listen
In one ear and out the other
That I disregard their advice
And disrespect our culture

Simply because I refuse
To stretch my soul into a canvas
They can paint on their instructions
And deliver to the masses

They said I do not see
Or understand the bigger picture
But all I see is inhibition
Of what could be a better future

I also want to bear our flag
And parade it in the light
But we need to invest
In what will also glow at night

We need to see that a child
Is a gift and not an item
That we decorate our shelves with
But needing heart and soul investment

We need to help our brothers
Buckling underneath the pressure
Of a role they were assigned
But never properly prepared for

We need to help our sisters
Selling skin for recognition
That carries only until sunrise
Breaking their dreams into pieces

We need to see that disability
Need not a segregated community
But rather seeing a new window
To understanding our humanity

They said I do not listen,
So listen, I shall not
To the judge who fights for no one
Unless it regards his lot

They said I do not see
And therefore I shall not
Even try to understand
The apology for getting caught

I will only ever listen
To the child crying out
Desperate for sweet freedom
From the chains of a mind cult

I will only ever see
Doors that can be opened
For my brother to walk through
And claim the treasures laid up for him

I will only ever understand
The purpose of my fight
For my sister who is priceless
And worth her throne in the sunlight

I see freedom and ability
I hear "Yes" and "Amen"
My seeds of hope will produce a harvest
This I believe
This I understand

She Was Told!

Aruna Gogulamanda

We are told many things, by and through our cultures and religions, which are oppressive. Yet we honor those words, because we have been raised to do so. And not ask questions. This poem names some of those suppressive words, told to Indian Dalit women. Naming those here comes with an invitation—to rise up from under the burdens of those words.

> She was told
> not to wear a blouse
> To allow every male
> watch her as a device.

> She was told
> to bend her back, not walk straight
> to fill the tender tummies, keeping herself a bait.

> She was told
> to toil all day long in the fields
> as a human machine
> deprived of food and water.

> She was told
> to swallow the pain of not feeding her baby
> though her lactating breasts pine to sate its hunger.

She was told
to take the insults, jeers, beatings and assaults,
for being born a woman in a cursed clan.

She was told
to take the daily thousand cuts
of sexist remarks, acts and assaults
of her man and master.

She was told
that she is bad omen,
a bloody sanitary pad, useful but a disgusting topic.
The relentless sun beats on her
her dreams, beauty and youth
sacrificed in the service of the land, the hut, the master.
Her eyes, two dry hollows bear silent witness
to hundreds of deaths of her mothers, daughters, sisters
their dreams, respect and their bodies.
Her calloused hands, her unkempt hair
her cracked heels, her wrinkled hair
yell the tales of living through fears and years
of centuries and millennia of violations and deaths.

She was told
that she was dirt,
She was filth and
in this sacred land of thousands of goddesses
she is called a Dalit.

Uprising

John Robert Lee

This poem addresses the theme "Rising to life" (of eDARE 2021 Conference). At its centre is the concern with the desacralisation of the earth, an ecological focus, that looks in particular at the blue economy and what is happening with our oceans and their life. The poem calls us to rise from the world as it presently is, with its desecrations and destructions, aimed at enriching the few wealthy, to rise to the better world God calls us to, where earth's creation is respected and cared for. Humans have been made the steward, the caretaker of the earth. And they will be held responsible by God for what they have done or failed to do. The prophetic voice in the public square is emphasized in the poem's epigraph which comes from Jeremiah.

    The metaphor of the degradation of the oceans also applies to other forms of exploitation and suffering, including humankind's denial and repression of its own sacred calling to represent the Creator. The poem calls us to rise to the "grace we were gifted," to take up our God-given responsibilities for our earth and each other, to repair "our ravaged, sorry earth." It is a theological call into the public square of our daily lives. The poem calls us to an uprising.

> "O earth, earth, earth,
> *Hear the word of the Lord*"
>
> —Jeremiah 22:29
>
> Like our garbage throttling oceans, the barrage
> of horrendous news from every corner of this fatigued planet
> deadens us to suffering life in war zones, famine-plagued villages,
>
> race-baiting sidewalks, grief-stricken ICU wards, streets of homeless children
> & aging dementia, numerous catalogues of pain
> to which we have grown numb, dumb & frankly, bored —
>
> hearts & minds are choked with junk, vain
> matter on which we feed neglected souls,
> desacralized spirits, if you allow me to invoke imago Dei,
>
> the sacred space made for holy, holy, holy—like deep-sea
> coral, pearl-making oyster, supple divine dolphin,
> fluting whales, all that depth-diving aqua-marine multitude
>
> that we throttle with careless plastic capital —
> we need, we need to rise to life, rise to see our fall
> from the grace we were gifted, rise with hearts leaping to do right,
>
> rise like silver flying fish over clean waters of living oceans
> like scissor-tailed sea birds over life-giving heritage,
> rise up over our ravaged, sorry earth.

Strong

Chad Rimmer

"Strong" highlights the nexus between theopoetics and process theology. Rising is about our becoming, and becoming is about our being. There are many philosophies about what it means to be, to become, and the power that is required for us to be. But this is not an academic question; it makes all the difference in the world for how we Rise Up, or Fall. Dating at least back to the conflict between the Greeks Heraclitus and Parmenides, there are those who think that our being happens in a closed system of individuals who have to learn to get along or struggle and compete to climb a ladder of becoming. Domination and power-over are usually a hallmark of these social, biological, religious, economic and political systems. But there are those who prefer to see life as an open system, where becoming is interdependent. Being is predicated on a whole ecology of social, spiritual, and natural relationships. Ubuntu philosophy proclaims "I am because we are." Process and feminist theologians know the truth that we are because of a creative life giving power-with. This life giving power of synergy begins in the Holy Trinity that is a diversity in a perfect communion of love, and reflected in the eco-kinship of creation that resounds the voice of Holy Wisdom.

Rising to life must be a co-rising. And this creative power is inherently a non-violent power. Even among the ambiguities of our natural creaturely condition (disease, predation, natural disasters and accidents), the un-natural injustices of life usually result from a belief that we are part of a closed system where domination is the goal of a dominion of power-over, where grace has no place.

We expect to find this logic of hierarchical, closed systems operating in the world of real-politik, patriarchal social and religious systems, even in the natural sciences among those who believe that nature is "red in tooth and claw." But this poem reveals my shock to find that this logic of domination colonizes even our approaches to healing. During the course of my wife's cancer, there were many who valorize the "battle" of defeating cancer and not letting cancer "win." Besides the failure to understand what cancer is and the inherent violence of the treatments themselves, this interpretation of power not only underestimates the reality of the aggressive cancers that many like my wife have, but such exercises in power divert spiritual, psychological and immunological resources that are needed for resilience in the path to true healing. Rising from the ashes of such injustices must follow a long path of love, grace, light and peace. This is true power.

There are forces that cannot be destroyed. Battles may be won and must be. But history has shown that the only thing that has ever transformed the world is non-violent love. Those that are acquainted with suffering, fear and pain know what Elijah discovered. God is not in the fury, but in the silence. God is in the ecological wisdom that is woven into the fabric of creation. The open synergy of power-with subverts the patriarchy of power-over and exposes the logic of domination for the weakness that it is. In the end, those who have fought the good fight have seen the way to healing and overcoming. True power is revealed in the story of Samson and Delilah. It is the same truth that was revealed from the cross. It is the same truth that is known by every person who suffers from disease, or under the weight and injustice of systemic oppression. There are seasons for battles, but this poem "Strong" reminds us that rising up to healing and transformation (salvation!) is known by those that drink deeply from the quiet soulforce that unites us in this open system of our gracious becoming.

Like Delilah, I shaved your head in secret.
Like Samson, you emerged from the night shorn
    yet miraculously your power was intact.
Your power to break the chains of pain after each cycle
    and rise up under the weight of each test
        to topple pillars of uncertainty
        with some indefatigable energy.

Like Samson, there are those that watch you in awe,
    and yearning to confirm some myth of the human will,
    they pay pious homage to your rock-hard core,
    bow to a fierceness
        that spites the boatman
        though he already received an advance on the crossing,
    They worship a war they think you are waging.

But the secret of Samson was misunderstood.
He was confused from whence strength came,
    and they are, too.
Samson sought strength
    In the death of the death-dealer,
And in the end, the vengeance killed him.
Coming in hot destroyed him.
A rock hard core was his demise,
    not his strength.
And neither is it yours.
To see the source of Samson's strength,
They must not look to the Rock,
They must look to the stream beneath it.
En-hakkore empowered him.
"The Spring of the One who called him to life."
See the gentle source!
The cool, clear font of Life
Nourishes, and never annihilates.
Don't they know they must do the same to find yours?
They watch your shorn crown in awe of your enduring
    strength.
But like Samson, they misunderstand the source.
It is more profound than they are willing to look,
    More real than the rock they want to see.
You are no rock,
    For your bones have been broken.
You are not fierce,
    For you weep to know the tender touch of another day's
    dawn.

You are no warrior,
> For you pray peace to be restored to the rebellion in your body.

You know, far more than they,
> That warring only ever depletes.

As one familiar with suffering,
> You dare not valorize violence in pursuit of hope.

Because yours is the Power perfected in weakness.
Yours is the strength of fragility
> Refined in the knowledge of love that will topple temples of resolve
>> By breaking foundations of fear
>> With a gentle trickle of hope
>> That erodes the ramparts of hollow shibboleths
>
> Destined to echo meaningless clichés about strength and power
>> By those who have never suffered want of anything
>> and reveals that bare truth about the gentleness of life
>> and the limits of human ability
>> that is known by all who have suffered
>>> the blessed resignation
>> in which the true power of Grace becomes known.

No, if they really want to see your strength,
They must not look to the rock that stands before them,
But the daisy which grows out from under it,
> nurtured by the stream.

It will never seek to destroy the rock that looms above it.
It will simply,
> Persistently,
> Wonderfully,
> Gently,
> Kindly,
> Justly,
> Beautifully,
> Peaceably

Grow.
Not lashing out tendrils to crush,
But sending its roots
> down,
>> To places
>>> unseen,
>> To drink
>> deeply

                    Of the Spring
                        of the One
                            who calls
                                her
                                    to
                                    Life.

NOTE

1. The following essays refer to these poems, and thus placing them in the same chapter helps readers find them.

PART I

Talking Back with Nerves, against Babylon

Chapter 3

"The Lord Needs Them" (Matthew 21:3)

The Gospel's Beasts and Sovereign Christ

Tat-siong Benny Liew

Even from its very beginning, Matthew's Gospel distinguishes Jesus as one with regal pedigree and status. As if introducing Jesus as "the son of [King] David" (1:1; cf. 1:6) in Jesus's genealogy is not enough to signify his royal connection, Matthew adds in the birth narrative that Jesus himself "has been born king of the Jews" (2:2) and moves the plot immediately into a duel between sovereigns, in which King Herod dies after failing to eliminate Jesus (2:3–20). As the Gospel concludes, Matthew's resurrected Jesus will declare majestically that "[a]ll authority in heaven and on earth has been given to [him]" (28:18). It is not an exaggeration to suggest that Matthew's Jesus is a sovereign Christ.

Perhaps surprisingly, Matthew's sovereign Christ also compares himself to animals; in fact, he presents them as faring better than he himself: "foxes have holes, and birds of the air have nests; but the Son of Man has nowhere to lay his head" (8:20). While Martin Heidegger has famously made distinctions among the "worldless" stone, the "poor in world" animal, and the "world forming" human,[1] Matthew's Jesus is emphasizing here his own homelessness, which may be related to his experience of being hunted by his opponents like a prey. Homelessness or not feeling "at home" for a thinker/philosopher, according to Jacques Derrida, is comparable to Heidegger's assumption that animals lack attunement to the world in which they exist.[2] Derrida does this in the final seminar that he offered before his death—titled *The Beast and the*

Sovereign—where he critiques the long and pervasive philosophical assumption that differentiates humans and animals, as well as faults the "Greco-Judeo-Christiano-Islamic" tradition for denigrating animals.[3] Arguing that an emphasis on human sovereignty and superiority over non-human animals has led to not only the hurting and the domesticating of animals but also the dehumanizing of other humans (particularly women, slaves, children, and indigenous people or foreigners),[4] Derrida proceeds to question what humans tend to assume about themselves, including the rigid difference between humanity and animality, and points to the need for humans to rethink our relations with other living creatures. With the seminar taking place shortly after 9/11 in 2001, one can also see Derrida trying to think and talk about sovereignty in these pages in relation to the military aggression of the United States against Iraq. Since Derrida also suggests that a particular strong understanding of sovereignty is "theological," I will interrogate in this paper how Matthew's sovereign Christ relates to animals, animality, and ipseity (or the power of one's self-identity as an autonomous, self-determining subject). Following Derrida and the public conversations that his work has helped bring about, my purpose in doing so is to critique anthropocentrism and to assert the value of animal lives, especially in a time when the anthropocene has led to the ongoing mass extinction of species—what scholars have called the "sixth extinction." For Derrida, a better way to do so is not to deny the difference between humans and animals but to multiply differences that exist among humans and among animals.[5] Most of all, he does so by challenging if humans "can ever possess the *pure, rigorous, indivisible* concept" of sovereignty.[6]

Incidentally or not, questions of animality appear right after Matthew told us about Jesus's birth, his being taken to Egypt, and his new home in Nazareth after Herod's demise in Matthew 2. In Matthew 3, John the Baptist shows up in the wilderness to "prepare the way of the Lord" (3:3) by announcing God's judgment and calling the people to repentance. What is intriguing in light of Derrida's seminar is the Baptizer's appearance, diet, location, and vocation. Wearing "clothing of camel hair with a leather belt around his waist" (3:4). Dressed in animal hair and animal skin, in other words, John the Baptist comes across as a savage, or a man in an animal state. While "locusts and wild honey" (3:4) are in keeping with Jewish purity laws, they are, for lack of a better term, "raw food" that put John closer to non-human animals, especially given his whereabouts. The presence of the Baptizer in the wilderness and around the Jordan, both indicators of geographical and symbolic boundary in biblical literature, puts John on the verge between humanity and animality, but John is also presented as someone who has a special relationship to God's salvation.[7] Most significant for our consideration is the fact that Matthew's Jesus, in the words of the Baptizer, "com[es] after" John

(3:11) and comes to this boundary region to be baptized by this animal-like prophet, and received the Holy Spirit descending and alighting on him "like a dove" (3:13–17). Matthew's Jesus comes out of his water baptism, then, with a bird—a non-human animal—attached to him. Then he is led by the Spirit—still in the form of a bird?—further into the wilderness to be tempted by the devil (4:1)—yet another contest of power or struggle for sovereignty for Matthew's Jesus?—before he begins his proclamation, calls his disciples, and heals the sick (4:12–25).

Before the publication of Derrida's seminar on *Beast and the Sovereign* in two volumes, his interest in questions about humanity's relations with non-human animals has already become obvious in *The Animal That Therefore I Am*. As is well known, the French title of this earlier book by Derrida can be translated also as *The Animal That Therefore I Follow*. In the book, Derrida reads the creation stories in Genesis 1–2, pointing out particularly that the human who names the animals was actually created after the animals and asking if priority is given to the human or to the animals in these chapters.[8] In fact, Derrida recounts in this book his experience of being seen naked by his cat and how the gaze of this animal in this unexpected encounter embarrassed him by making him aware of his nudity.[9] If, as humans have long assumed, animals are different from humans because they don't know their nakedness and hence have neither feelings of embarrassment or shame nor need for clothing, Derrida wonders what being human means if it's the cat that brought about his humanity by causing him to have these supposedly human realizations of nakedness and feelings of shame.

I am suggesting that something similar is going on with Matthew's sovereign Christ. He follows both a beastly John and a bird-like Spirit into a liminal space to prepare and get himself ready to assume his kingship, lordship, and sovereignty. Animality in these early chapters of Matthew appears positively as a herald and a guide; it is something close to the divine, close to holy, or simply is divine and holy. "Famished" after fasting for "forty days and forty nights" (4:2) in the wilderness, Matthew's Jesus himself seems to be in an animal state. He has no home, no food, and no one to converse with besides the devil. At the same time, he begins to demonstrate his sovereignty in the wilderness. Should or could we say that animality is a requirement or a kind of preparation for Matthew's Jesus before his assumption of sovereignty?

Rejecting the devil's three proposals, Matthew's Jesus shows that he is not controlled by rapacious appetites as animals are often assumed to be (though we know that animals, even the most ferocious kind, may give up their prey to avoid dangers that they are able to perceive). Instead, he can govern his appetite, his aspiration, and his ambition to retain his freedom from the devil (4:1–11). Rather than using his mouth to consume food when he is in extreme hunger (4:2–3), Matthew's Jesus uses his mouth to cite scriptures and speak back to the devil (4:4–10) and, after emerging out of the wilderness and moving to Capernaum, to proclaim repentance in light of the coming kingdom of heaven (4:13–17) and to call disciples (4:18–22).

Seeing what he calls "interiorizing 'devourment'" and "exteriorizing 'vociferation'" as complementary rather than contradictory, Derrida points out that *apophantics* (the language of declaratory assertion or discourse of judgment) is understood by many philosophers as absent from animals but characteristic of sovereignty.[10] If so, then the sovereignty of Matthew's Jesus seems to be firmly established by his Sermon on the Mount in Matthew 5–7. From his pronouncements of beatitudes to his repeated uses of the "you-have-heard-that-it-was-said . . . but-I-say-to-you" formula to render judgment on various topics, Matthew's Jesus comes across as one who knows and makes things known. Matthew's Jesus is, of course, known for delivering five long discourses (5:1–7:27; 10:5–42; 13:3–52; 18:1–35; 24:4–25:46) to rival the Pentateuch that has been attributed to Moses;[11] in that sense, one can even say that Matthew's Jesus is the sovereign who lays down the (new) law. He also announces that what he says will take place, and that, unlike heaven and earth that will pass away, his words will not (24:34–35). Although Gunther Bornkamm only looked at Mark 4:35–41 and Matt. 8:23–27 in his short article that effectually began what we now know as redaction criticism, he was on good grounds to argue that the disciples in Matthew no longer see their Jesus as a mere "teacher" (as the disciples do in Mark 4:38) but as "Lord" (Matt. 8:25).[12]

In his authoritative discourses, Matthew's sovereign Christ frequently employs parables, which basically make up one of his five long discourses (13:3–52). In *Beast and the Sovereign*, Derrida mentions how "the essence of political force and power" often "passes via fables, i.e., speech that is both fictional and performative."[13] The parables of Matthew's Jesus may well be understood as fables under this definition, especially as he tells them to establish his identity as a sovereign. Some of these parables also portray an imperious household lord or master with absolute power over his slaves (e.g., 13:24–30, 44–52; 14:45–51; 25:14–30). Plutarch, who was a vegetarian, had famously compared treatment of slaves to treatment of animals.[14]

Readers of Matthew should notice how animals are often woven into the texture of the *apophantics* of Matthew's sovereign Christ. He talks about not giving something that is holy to dogs and not throwing pearls before swine (7:6), for instance, and he affirms that a human being is more valuable than a sheep (12:11–12). He repeats this affirmation by telling his twelve disciples that they are more valuable than "many sparrows" (10:31), because these "birds of the air [. . .] neither sow nor reap nor gather into barns" (6:26). Whether birds really do not do these things or if this falls into the category of what Derrida calls "the fabular" as "a simulacrum of knowing,"[15] I am not able to tell. Instead, I will focus on Derrida's repeated arguments in his seminar that, since difference between humans and animals justifies cruelty against animals, "in the place of the beast, one can put, in the same hierarchy, the slave, the woman, the child."[16] If the household lord in the parables we mentioned above is referring to Matthew's Jesus, does it mean that his followers are slaves who can be treated as animals? We know that Matthew's Jesus tells his disciples that they must "become like children" to enter the kingdom of heaven (18:3). While humility and not animality (e.g., deficiency in understanding) is highlighted as "becom[ing] like children" (18:4), Matthew's Jesus does use animal imagery to talk about not only himself but also his followers. When he sends his disciples out in his discourse on mission, Matthew's Jesus says he is sending them out "like sheep into the midst of wolves" so they have to be "wise as serpents and innocent as doves" (10:16). While Thomas Hobbes is known for using the wolf to talk about threats between humans, Derrida points out that this was perhaps first done by the Roman playwright of the third and second century BCE, Plautus, and that while fox, wolf, and lion all tend to appear in political discourse, wolf is the animal that appears most extensively.[17] Matthew's Jesus further stresses these subtle threats between humans by telling his followers to be aware of false prophets, who "come to you in sheep's clothing but inwardly are ravenous wolves" (7:15). When he affirms that his disciples are more valuable than "birds in the air" (6:26) such as sparrows (10:31), he is in effect promising them the protection and care that they should both desire and require. Elsewhere, Matthew's Jesus will once again refer to Israelites, including his followers, as leaderless or lost sheep and to himself or to God as a shepherd (9:36; 18:10–14). In other words, the imagery of sheep underscores the importance of Matthew's Jesus and/or God to people/disciples who are needy and vulnerable. The subordination of sheep to shepherd functions analogically to the subjection of slaves to household masters or the reliance of children on adults. Not to be missed in these imageries is the not-so-subtle alignment of the sovereignty of Matthew's Jesus with the providence of God. This exaltation of God's providence brings us back to what Matthew's Jesus says about birds. If he is bringing in the birds as an object lesson for his disciples to learn, is he indirectly asking the disciples to become (like?) birds by not worrying about tomorrow, especially if one of the assumed differences between humans and animals is the latter's lack of foresight (such as the possibility of death)?[18]

Immediately before this discourse on mission, Matthew lists for us the names of the twelve disciples: they are all men. Does Matthew's Jesus think that women would hamper his sovereignty? Is that why he talks about making oneself a eunuch "for the sake of the kingdom of heaven" in a conversation about marriage and divorce (19:3–12)? While the same discourse also characterizes Israelites to whom the disciples are sent as sheep, Matthew's Jesus uses the same imagery to talk about the people of Israel when a Canaanite woman asks him to cure her daughter. When the woman continues to ask him for help, however, Matthew's Jesus makes a change to refer to the Israelites as "children" and employs a different animal imagery for the Canaanite women: namely, dogs (15:21–26). Perhaps Matthew's Jesus is being consistent with his earlier statement about not giving something holy to dogs (7:6), he tells the Canaanite mother that food should be reserved for children and not given to dogs. Despite being denied of her and her daughter's humanity, the Canaanite mother willingly plays a servile role and turns herself and her daughter effectually into domesticated dogs. "Yes, Lord," she says, "yet even the dogs eat the crumbs that fall from their masters' table" (15:27). Judging from these passages, animality does not preclude inclusion in the community of Matthew's Jesus, but it certainly helps institute the structural sovereignty of Matthew's Jesus in the community. Calling other people animals, be it sheep or dogs, is not only powerful but also performative when it is done by Matthew's Jesus.

So far, I have been arguing for the importance of animality for the emergence of Matthew's Jesus and the establishment of his sovereignty. Now I want to propose that animality is also crucial for the continuation of Jesus's sovereignty in Matthew, because his sovereignty is in many ways beastly. As I have pointed out in the discussion of his encounter with the Canaanite mother, calling people animals is an injurious and insulting form of dehumanization. Derrida connects the sovereign with beast because both imply force and brutality. More specifically, Derrida discusses how sovereignty rules by emphasizing fear and threatening violence.[19] It is rather telling that each of the five long *apophantic* discourses by Matthew's Jesus ends by promising reward to those who obey or punishment to those who don't (7:24–27; 10:40–42; 13:47–52; 18:23–35; 25:31–46). I will focus on two endings that assume the power of humans over animals to elaborate on what seems to be a carrot-and-stick approach of Matthew's Gospel, but let me just mention that, among the three endings that I will not take up, one features the power of a king over his slaves (18:23–35). The very last parable in the discourse of parables promises that "at the end of the age," bad fish that have been caught in the net of the kingdom of heaven but do evil will be fished out and separated from the good fish and thrown out into the "furnace of fire" (13:47–52). At the end of the apocalyptic discourse is the well-known parable of the sheep and the goats, where Matthew's Jesus is presented as a shepherd as well as someone who sits on the throne and judges all the nations. Depending on how they treat "the least of these," some (the sheep) will inherit the kingdom and receive eternal life while others (the goats) will be sent away into eternal punishment (25:31–46).

Both of these parables are about inclusion and exclusion; they also make clear that current inclusion in the community of Matthew's Jesus is not necessarily permanent, since everything cannot be known until a time of future judgment. Furthermore, exclusion is not its own punishment; instead, exclusion implies ongoing pain and total destruction. The choice is therefore either be wiped out by Matthew's Jesus or be included as his faithful slaves or domesticated animals. The dynamics becomes even more difficult, because Matthew's Jesus shows that the final judgment will overtake people by surprise. In his apocalyptic discourse, Matthew's Jesus states that the final judgment will come "at an unexpected hour," and that no one except God will know "on what day your Lord is coming" (24:36–44; cf. 25:1–13). Derrida begins the very first session of his seminar on *Beast and the Sovereign* by referring to the stealth movements of a wolf: "to walk without making a noise, to arrive without warning, to proceed discreetly, silently, invisibly, almost inaudibly and imperceptibly [. . .] to surprise a prey, to take it by surprising what is in sight but does not see coming the one who is already seeing it, already getting ready to take it by surprise, to grasp it by surprise."[20] Derrida's description of the wolf here seems to me to be applicable to Matthew's Jesus. The shepherd who is supposed to protect the sheep from the wolves turns out to be another ravenous (male) wolf in disguise (cf. 7:15) who will not hesitate to consume some of those under his charge by separating them out as goats or as bad fish. Is he protecting the sheep from other wolves to save the sheep for his own devourment? Or is he eating them so no sheep will develop into a competing wolf or a rival sovereign? Matthew's sovereign Christ is in this sense also a beast indeed: his sovereignty can be base and brutal.

Two more animals appear in Matthew in a passage that also implies the beastly sovereignty of Matthew's Christ. Before what has traditionally been known as his triumphant entry into Jerusalem, or what can be seen as a great and public celebration of his sovereignty, Matthew's Jesus sent two disciples to fetch a donkey and a colt (21:1–2). In a way that is rather mysterious or perhaps appropriately majestic for a sovereign, he tells the disciples to just untie and take the animals without asking anyone for permission. He does, however, add that if anyone asks what they are doing, they should simply say, "The Lord needs them," and then they will be able to carry out what he wants them to do without obstruction.

One of the reasons why Derrida connects beast with the sovereign is their outlaw status. While animals are often viewed as below the law, the sovereign is above it.[21] Here we see once again that the words of Matthew's Jesus come across as their own laws. He can take without asking, and his words can stop anyone from getting in his ways (even or especially when those words do not actually explain his or his disciples' action). If might is right and the sovereign can break the law whenever he sees fit, then it is rather apt that

Matthew's sovereign Christ ends up being crucified between two criminals as "the king of the Jews" (27:29, 37–38; cf. 26:55).

After successfully bringing the donkey and the colt to Matthew's Jesus, the disciples use their cloaks to provide a kind of padded seat for Matthew's Christ to ride into Jerusalem. A large crowd blanket the way before him with their own cloaks and tree branches, praising him out loud as one who is coming in God's name, as Matthew's Jesus performs a circus act by riding on two different animals simultaneously (21:6–9). This passage in Matthew has been much discussed by scholars because, as many have pointed out, Matthew does not seem to understand that the Hebrew scripture that he cites to underscore that his Jesus is the fulfillment of God's promises in Hebrew poetry. Since Hebrew poetry works by parallelism and not by rhythm, Zachariah 9:9 should not be taken literally as referring to two different animals.[22] Instead of reading this passage as a mistake, I will argue that the passage is revealing how Christ's sovereignty is dependent on animality. As Niccolò Machiavelli suggests in *The Prince*, the sovereign, in addition to keeping his promises as a human should, must also have the strength of a lion and the cunning of a fox. That is to say, a sovereign is not only a human-and-animal hybrid but also a chimera animal.[23] This is precisely the picture of Matthew's sovereign Christ as he rides on two different animals in this crowning or clowning scene. Matthew's Christ in this scene is what Derrida calls "the spectacle of a spectrality," because it literally shows the "haunting of the sovereign by the beast and the beast by the sovereign, the one inhabiting or housing the other, the one becoming the intimate host of the other [. . .]. In the metamorphic covering-over of the two figures, the beast and the sovereign, one therefore has a presentiment that a profound and essential ontological copula is at work on this couple."[24] In other places, Derrida will use the language of prosthesis or that of grafting to describe this coupling of or copula between the beast and the sovereign.[25] Let me, however, emphasize the adjectives used by Derrida in the sentences I cited. The "profound and essential" coming together of beast and sovereign is perfectly and openly confessed by Matthew's sovereign Christ when he says in reference to himself and the two animals: "The Lord needs them."[26]

If his celebratory or crowning entry into Jerusalem turns out to be a disappointment, Matthew's Jesus will secure his sovereignty through his death and resurrection. If one follows the distinction that Heidegger makes between human dying and animal perishing (because animals, according to Heidegger, lack anxiety and fear of death that humans have),[27] then the episode of Matthew's Jesus in Gethsemane may be read as a proof of the distance between Matthew's Jesus and animality (26:36–46). Following Heidegger to argue against Heidegger, Derrida proposes that anxiety may have a benumbing effect that highlights the animality of humans, since benumbment is an animal characteristic for Heidegger.[28] Matthew's Jesus is clearly struggling in the prospect of death, asking God three times if he may bypass the cross. What I want to point out is how this anxiety causes Matthew's Jesus to feel torn and ambivalent not only about God's will (he wants to do God's will and his thrice-repeated prayers suggest that he is not sure if the cross is really God's will for him) but also about what to do with his disciples. In Gethsemane, Matthew's Jesus seems to both fear and desire solitude, which is, as it has often been pointed out, a characteristic or a cost of being a sovereign.[29] Taking his disciples to Gethsemane, he leaves them but go on further with Peter, James, and John. He will then go away from these three disciples to pray and return to them three times as if he cannot decide if he wants to be alone or if he wants their company. Matthew's Jesus, even if it is only for a short period of time in Gethsemane, seems dazed and confused by anxieties and fear like a benumbed animal. After Gethsemane, with all of his male disciples gone (26:56) and a few female disciples "looking on from a distance" (27:55), Matthew's Jesus dies the death as a lone wolf howling on the cross, "My God, my God, why have you forsaken me?" (27:46).

The death and resurrection of Matthew's sovereign Christ are, therefore, not separable from animality. Referring to Hebrew scriptures, he compares his upcoming death and resurrection to Jonah being eaten and spending three days and three nights in the belly of a "sea monster" (12:39–41; cf. 16:4).[30] Matthew's Christ really does need all kinds of animals to be(come) "Lord," who will in some unknown day and hour move in like a wolf to surprise his followers and all nations with his judgment.

Derrida suggests in *Beast and the Sovereign* that claims and desires to be unique, superior, absolute in knowledge, authority, and judgment is *bêtise*—a French word implying both stupidity and animality that the translator of the seminar has generally left it untranslated, but which the translator of Derrida's *The Animal and Therefore I Am* translates as "asinanity."[31] I think "asinanity" or "asininity" is a good translation in light of the entry into Jerusalem on a donkey and a colt by Matthew's Jesus. The asininity of any assumption of superiority over animals or of sovereignty over others, including the sovereign's claim of having power over life and death, is clearly shown in the reality of death.[32] By repeatedly asking a rhetorical question on the distinction between a "who" or a "what," Derrida points out that every human needs an-other to take care of one's own dead body, and no dead human can really dictate what others do with one's own corpse even if there is a will established before one's death.[33] After all, burial practices generally are strictly regulated by cultural and governmental forces. We see this being played out in the death of Matthew's sovereign Christ (27:57–61). Joseph of Arimathea must ask Pilate's permission for the corpse of Matthew's Jesus, a request that Pilate has the authority to grant or to refuse. Getting the green light from

Pilate, Joseph makes the decision to wrap the corpse of Matthew's Jesus in a clean linen cloth and then bury the wrapped body in the tomb that Joseph has prepared for himself. As Derrida writes, "The other appears to me as the other as such, *qua* he, she, or they who might survive me, survive my decease and then proceed as they wish, sovereignly, and sovereignly have at their disposal the future of my remains, if there any."[34] We don't know if Joseph's actions match the desire of Matthew's sovereign Christ, who does affirm an unnamed woman who anoints him at Bethany as preparing his body for burial (26:6–13). We also know that Matthew's Jesus asks his twelve disciples to take and eat his body at the Passover meal the night of his arrest (27:26), though what he means by that is cryptic. When he claims to have received "all authority in heaven and on earth" to send his disciples to "go [. . .] and make disciples of all nations" (28:18–19), is he not in effect transferring or dividing his sovereignty to multiple parties? Here is yet another case that "the Lord needs them" (21:3), just as a master or a king in those parables still needs his slaves to reap or collect the harvest (13:24–30; 21:33–41), to invite people to or kick people out of his banquet (22:1–14), to run his household (24:45–51), or to invest his property (25:14–30).

We must remember that, as the prayers of Matthew's Jesus in Gethsemane make clear, his death is the result of God's will rather than his own. Matthew's sovereign Christ does not dare oppose God's will. Similarly, the resurrection of his dead body is done by God, who is arguably the ultimate Other. Matthew's sovereign Christ is like a marionette being bobbed down and up by God. Derrida's explanation that the word marionette is a derivative from the name of the Virgin Mary further reminds us that God has been pulling the strings to bring about the birth of Matthew's Jesus.[35] Matthew's God is then the sovereign behind Matthew's sovereign Christ who alone knows when the final judgment will take place. In that sense, the "perfect" Father God (5:48) of Matthew's Jesus is the invisible and imperceptible wolf who devours even his own son, who can, in turn, send those among his followers into "outer darkness" or "furnace of fire, where there will be weeping and gnashing of teeth" (8:12; 13:42, 50; 22:13, 51; 25:30). In Matthew's Gospel, this alpha wolf is one who comes in its son's clothing (cf. 7:15).

Matthew's Gospel does seem to multiply the differences among animals and among humans. Doves and sheep, for instance, are presented more positively than pigs and dogs. One can say that the Gospel recognizes the difference between a donkey and a colt, as well as the diversity of birds with its mention of doves and sparrows. Similarly, as I have repeatedly pointed out, the power differential between household masters and slaves is clearly acknowledged. Matthew's sovereign Christ is ushered onto the stage by animality, talks about and treat others as animals, and embodies animality in himself. While he moves and acts with followers calling him "Lord" and he himself claiming sovereignty, he is also passively controlled by and merely reacting to his Father God. Though called a king at his birth, his birth was orchestrated by God; he was then taken from place to place by his father Joseph (Matt. 2:1–23). At his death and resurrection, his body was again taken care of by Joseph of Arimathea and then raised up by God. The beastly ways of Matthew's sovereign Christ include his becoming a benumbed beast of burden. Sovereignty and animality function in a codependent relationship in Matthew's Jesus, but sovereignty is in an end a phantasm even for this king and Lord. Claiming and clinging to sovereignty to assert control over self, animals, and different others as animals is not only atrocious but also asinine. This realization is important for any public conversation about sovereign and about whose or what lives matter.

NOTES

1. Martin Heidegger, *The Fundamental Concepts of Metaphysics: World, Finitude, Solitude*, trans. William McNeil and Nicholas Walker (Bloomington: Indiana University Press, 1995), 177.

2. Jacques Derrida, *The Beast and the Sovereign*, 2 vols., ed. Michel Lisse, Marie-Louise Mallet, and Ginette Michaud; trans. Geoffrey Bennington (Chicago: University of Chicago Press, 2009–2011), 2.93–118.

3. Jacques Derrida, *The Animal That Therefore I Am*, trans. David Wills (New York: Fordham University Press, 2005), 55. Derrida's long list of targets include Aristotle, Descartes, Kant, Heidegger, Levinas, and Lacan. Derrida does name a few whom he sees as being better able to complicate this rigid separation between humanity and animality, such as Plutarch, Porphyry, Montaigne, Rousseau, Bentham, and Freud, though Derrida does not see any of them as having spent the time to think through the animal question.

4. Derrida, *Beast and Sovereign*, 1.20, 33; 2.xiv. See also Judith Still, *Derrida and Other Animals: The Boundaries of the Human* (Edinburgh: Edinburgh University Press, 2015), 182–357; and Donna Haraway, *Simians, Cyborgs, Women: The Reinvention of Nature* (New York: Routledge, 1991), 11–12, 19.

5. Derrida, *Animal*, 35. Derrida invents the French word *animot* for "animal" to emphasize not only the plurality within what is assumed to be singular (since the invented word sounds like the French plural for animals, *animaux*) but also the artificiality of the (unnatural) distinction that humans make between themselves and non-human animals. Derrida also uses the term "limitrophy," or the growth, multiplication, or pluralization of limits, to describe this emphasis.

6. Derrida, *Animal*, 135.

7. This is not surprising given the long and frequent associations between animals and deities in the Greco-Roman world. See, for example, Emma Aston, "Part-Animal Gods," in *The Oxford Handbook of Animals in Classical Thought and Life*, ed. Gordon Lindsay Campbell (New York: Oxford University Press, 2014), 366–83.

8. Derrida, *Animal*, 14–18.

9. Derrida, *Animal*, 3–12.

10. Derrida, *Beast and Sovereign*, 1.23, 65, 168; 2.216, 227–30.

11. Benjamin W. Bacon, *Studies in Matthew* (New York: Henry Holt, 1930).

12. Gunter Bornkamm, "The Stilling of the Storm in Matthew," in *Tradition and Interpretation in Matthew*, eds. Gunter Bornkamm, Gerhard Barth, and Heinz-Joachim Held (Philadelphia: Westminster, 1963), 52–57.

13. Derrida, *Beast and Sovereign*, 1.217.

14. Derrida, *Beast and Sovereign*, 1.22–23; Still, *Derrida*, 274. See also Stephen Newmyer, *Plutarch's Three Treatises on Animals: A Translation with Introductions and Commentary* (Milton: Taylor and Francis, 2020).

15. Derrida, *Beast and Sovereign*, 1.34–35.

16. Derrida, *Beast and Sovereign*, 1.33.

17. See, for example, Derrida, *Beast and Sovereign*, 1.11, 61, 80–82.

18. Still, *Derrida*, 212.

19. See, for example, Derrida, *Beast and Sovereign*, 1.39–43, 217.

20. Derrida, *Beast and Sovereign*, 1.2.

21. See, for example, Derrida, *Beast and Sovereign*, 1.17–18.

22. See, for example, John P. Meier, *The Vision of Matthew: Christ, Church, and Morality in the First Gospel* (New York: Paulist, 1979), 19–21; W. D. Davies and Dale C. Allison, *Matthew 19–28* (New York: Bloomsbury, 2004), 120–21; Herbert Basser with Marsha B. Cohen, *The Gospel of Matthew and Judaic Traditions: A Relevance-Based Commentary* (Leiden: Brill, 2015), 530; Max Harris, *Christ on a Donkey: Palm Sunday, Triumphal Entries, and Blasphemous Pageants* (Leeds: Arc Humanities, 2019), 106.

23. Derrida, *Beast and Sovereign*, 1.77–92.

24. Derrida, *Beast and Sovereign*, 1.18.

25. See, for example, Derrida, *Beast and Sovereign*, 1.26–28, 39–43, 70.

26. Numerous studies on Matthew have been devoted to the phrase "Son of Man" that Matthew's Jesus tends to use to refer to himself. See, for example, Ulrich Luz, "The Son of Man in Matthew: Heavenly Judge or Human Christ," *Journal for the Study of the New Testament* 48 (1992): 3–21; David C. Sim, *Apocalyptic Eschatology in the Gospel of Matthew* (New York: Cambridge University Press, 1996), 93–109; Leslie W. Walck, *The Son of Man in the Parables of Enoch and in Matthew* (New York: Bloomsbury, 2011).

Many studies point to the potential connection between this phrase in Matthew and in the book of Daniel in the Hebrew scriptures (Dan. 7:13). See, for example, H. Daniel Zacharias, "Old Greek Daniel 7:13–14 and Matthew's Son of Man," *Bulletin for Biblical Research* 21, no. 4 (2011): 453–61; Brendon Robert Witte, "'Who Do You, Matthew, Say the Son of Man Is?' Son of Man and Conflict in the First Gospel" (PhD dissert., University of Edinburgh, 2016), 223–29; and Erin Runions, *The Babylon Complex: Theopolitical Fantasies of War, Sex, and Sovereignty* (New York: Fordham University Press, 2014), 231–35.

While the NRSV does not use this phrase to translate Dan. 7:13, it does make a point to add a note to acknowledge the possibility that "human being" can be alternatively translated as "son of man." Besides depicting four chimera beasts, Daniel 7 affirms that this mysterious figure—who is "like a human being"—will be given "dominion and glory and kingship" (Dan. 7:13–14) over these chimera beasts. As Stephen D. Moore carefully and correctly observes, however, at least two of these chimera beasts also have human-like features: the first beast has a human mind and stands on two feet like a human (Dan. 7:4), and the little horn on the fourth beast has human eyes (Dan. 7:8). See Stephen D. Moore, *Gospel Jesuses and Other Nonhumans: Biblical Criticism, Post-Poststructuralism* (Atlanta: SBL Press, 2017), 67–70.

27. Martin Heidegger, *Being and Time*, trans. John Macquarrie and Edward Robinson (Oxford: Blackwell, 1962), 284–85, 290–92. See also Jacques Derrida, *Aporias*, trans. Thomas Dutoit (Stanford: Stanford University Press, 1993), 35; Stuart Elden, "Heidegger's Animals," *Continental Philosophy Review* 39 (2006): 273–91.

28. David Farrell Krell, *Derrida and Our Animal Others: Derrida's Final Seminar, The Beast and the Sovereign* (Bloomington: Indiana University Press, 2013), 107–109, 118. See also Gerard Kuperus, "Attunement, Deprivation, and Drive: Heidegger and Animality," in *Phenomenology and the Non-Human Animal: At the Limits of Experience*, eds. Corinne Painter and Christian Lotz (Dordrecht: Springer, 2007), 13–28.

29. See, for example, Derrida, *Beast and Sovereign*, 2.1–8.

30. The book of Jonah also ends, as Jione Havea kindly reminded me, with a verse implying that the fate of humans and animals are tied together (Jon. 4:11).

31. Derrida, *Animal*, 18.

32. Derrida, *Animal*, 28.

33. Derrida, *Beast and the Sovereign*, 1.61–62, 137–38, 205–206; 2.119–46. See also Michael Naas, *The End of the World and Other Teachable Moments: Jacques Derrida's Final Seminar* (New York: Fordham University Press, 2015), 64–74.

34. Derrida, *Beast and Sovereign*, 2.127.

35. Derrida, *Beast and Sovereign*, 1.188.

Chapter 4

Resisting the Economic Shitstem

A Postcolonial Filipinx-Korean Reading of Luke 16:1–13 with Mel Chen's Animacies Theory

Dong Hyeon Jeong

My parents are missionaries to the Philippines, thirty-five years and counting. I also served as a missionary for about two years in the Philippines. Growing up in the so-called mission field, I was told that missionary work needs three "Ms": man, method, and money. "Man" is obviously the sexist and patriarchal way of describing the missionaries, who are usually limited to the cis-men, preferably married with children. "Method" refers to the training that missionaries need to have before and during their mission. This training could be but not limited to seminary education or short-term intensive missionary training. Last, "money" means the financial support that missionaries need from their sending church(es) and/or institution(s). For some missionaries, the financial support is extracted from the locals of the mission field.[1] Each of these "Ms" have their own issues, which I cannot cover in detail here. I will focus though on the "money" because the economic *shitstem*,[2] the havoc that have caused so much damage in the mission field (for my part, to the people of the Philippines), is the missionaries' unhealthy relationship with money. The affective relationality or the animacies between the "man" and the "money" produced significant negative consequences to the point that one has to question whether the missionaries were sent by God or by the animacy of mammon/money. As Mel Chen states, animacies consider "how matter that is considered insensate, immobile, deathly, or otherwise 'wrong' animates cultural life in important ways."[3] Perhaps in the adage "you cannot serve God and mammon" (Lk 16:13b), mammon has a stronger animacy, more convincing affective pull, for many missionaries.

I was also told that I should search the Bible for answers to my problems. The problem is my bewilderment on how many (Korean) missionaries are affectively animated by money more than anything else. How should I (and missionaries in general) respond to such animacy to/of mammon/money? More so, how should the locals or the people of the "mission field" respond to the affective overreach, the unhealthy and even viscerally dangerous relationality, between the missionaries/landowners/employers and their unquenchable greed? And so, I found my so-called "solution" in the unconventional ethics/sly civility of Luke 16:1–13 ("The Parable of the Manager of Unjust Wealth").[4] I use the term "solution" not because I am seeking for the ultimate answer/truth/interpretation to either my problem or the aforementioned passage. Rather, the choice of the word with quotation marks encapsulates/ reflects/mimics my critique against missionaries' tendency to justify their cause/reasoning by quoting a biblical passage that works for them. And so, I chose this passage as a way to mirror that aforementioned tendency, ironically concluding with an interpretation that is critical and oppositional to the mammon-reliant missionary enterprise. Hence, I "resonate" with the characters and the plot of the narrative. As a relatively well-to-do Korean who lived in a palatial so-called "mission center" with Filipinx workers catering to our needs felt like a modern-day *latifundium* (Greco-Roman large estate), as espoused in Lk 16:1–13. Our Filipinx workers signify the manager (*oikonómos*). Moreover, the discombobulating interaction that happened between the landowner/employer (*ploúsios*)[5] and the manager of Lk 16:1–13 actually happened and are still happening today. That is why I argue that Lk 16:1–13 is a parable that is based on experiential narratives that the audiences of Luke (and even perhaps Jesus himself) actually encountered in their daily lives. Lk 16:1–13 divulges a haunting narrative on the animacies of the economic *shitstem* happening in the *latifundia*. The parable is also teaching a method of survival and resistance for the workers/managers (in my case, Filipinx workers) and even slaves who had to traverse the difficulties of living in the *latifundia* or modern-day mission centers by tapping into the animacies of money.

ADDRESSING THE DISCOMBOBULATION

Taking a step back, one has to summarize and address the discombobulating interaction found in Lk 16:1–8a. First, the manager (not a slave)[6] or the protagonist of the parable was apparently terminated or at least was about to be terminated for allegedly embezzling the assets of his employer. There was no due process for the manager. He was instead sentenced to begging or digging. I use the verb "sentenced" here because digging (*skáptein*) or begging (*epaiteîn*) are social (and impending physical) death for the manager because he is not accustomed to such intense and unreputable work, let alone being found with other expendables of his time. Rather than accepting his horrible fate, the manager's "solution" or his drastic response to his negative future was to reduce the loans owed by his employer's debtors.[7] The response of the employer is also bewildering. Instead of anger and/or even imprisonment/death, the employer seems to commend the manager's actions of lowering his account receivables, even depicting such arbitrary decision as shrewd act that is worth emulating by others. It didn't end there. Verses 8b–13 seem to act like a commentary for the parable.[8] This commentary doubles down on the unconventional interaction that just happened (v.1–8a) by arguing that managing dishonest wealth is not only inevitable but even necessary in preparing oneself for friendship (v.8b–9a), to be welcomed "into eternal homes" (v.9b), and to manage various forms of wealth (v.10–12). The pericope ends with an adage that baffles and even contradicts the previous listing of teachings: "no servant can serve two masters . . . you cannot serve God and wealth/mammon" (v.13).

The parable baffles because perhaps we, the readers/interpreters, are deeply entrenched and invested in the economic *shitstem* of our context(s): money and emotions are strange bedfellows. What if the parable is an invitation to divest from our economic *shitstem*, as the employer's reaction reflects our own uneasiness and discombobulation, even if such divestment is viscerally uncomfortable? The manager of Lk 16:1–8a does not have the military, political, or financial power over the employer. That is why the manager chose a path of resistance that is unconventional, even discombobulating to the point of unnerving the employer. The manager's resistance is "unconventional" in an economic system that is ruled by law, with a modicum of civility and justice. However, in an economic *shitstem* that is ruled by oppressive structures, with civility and justice defined by the colonizers/oppressors, the manager's resistance manifests clever and evolving survival response. As William R. Herzog II argues, "There is no monolithic moral system to which everyone consents and by which everyone is judged. The entire system of which the steward [manager] is a part is exploitive and predatory."[9] From West African peasant farmers' perspective, Justin Ukpong reinterprets the manager's redistribution of wealth as the assertion for positive economic system: "the manager's action of sharing the debts of his customers is in line with this latter [material wealth is regarded as God's own gift to humanity to be shared equitably] concept of justice."[10] The manager is restitutive and self-critical, like Zacchaeus (Luke 19:1–10). He seeks to counter the colonial economic *shitstem* by going back to the divine mandate in which everyone is treated with dignity and love. Economic justice, as Ukpong asserts, must happen in radical means: the poor does not owe the rich anything; as a matter of fact, the (oppressive) rich owes the poor plus interest.[11]

That is why I follow Herzog's understanding of parables as narratives written within the tense and surreptitiously disruptive agrarian milieu: parables are "not earthly stories with heavenly meanings but earthly stories with heavy meanings, weighted down by an awareness of the workings of exploitation in the world of their hearers."[12] Parables "decode"[13] or problematize the givens, including and especially the so-called conventional ethics imposed by *shistems*, "[. . .] whether the political form of that society was the client kingdom of Herod Antipas, the province of Judaea under the hegemony of the Temple and the Jerusalem elites, or the colonial administration of an imperial province."[14] Norman Perrin sees this parable as a call for immediate action in the face of crisis; however, Perrin "spiritualizes" this crisis by qualifying it within the proclamation of the coming reign of God.[15] I find the crisis of the parable not in the cosmic or spiritual but in the (rural and agrarian) quotidian, the daily struggle of the colonized people. Parables are disruptions or "hidden transcripts," as coined by James C. Scott, that utilize the "weapons of the weak" in fighting back against *shitstems*. The weapons of the weak do not engage or envision large scale violent revolts/revolutions; rather, Scott emphasizes that the weapons of the weak work with decolonial and disruptive powers of the quotidian weaponry such as "foot dragging, dissimulation, false compliance, pilfering, feigned ignorance, slander, arson, [and] sabotage."[16] For this parable, the manager utilizes and exposes the animacy of the money in the equivalence of olive oil and wheat (or "non-organic actants") as a response to his negative future. His response is a glimpse to various expressions of quotidian resistance meant to engage oppressive structures right here and right now.

"MISSION CENTERS" AS MODERN-DAY *LATIFUNDIA*

I am not suggesting that Korean missionaries are exploitative in general. However, we do have some missionaries with colonial mindset who run their mission centers with such oppressive methods especially against their Filipinx managers. The miscommunications and misunderstandings happen quite often due to language and cultural barriers. Since the 1980s, many Korean missionaries stationed themselves all over the Philippines, erecting mansions which they call "mission centers." Please don't get me wrong: these mission centers are not slave-driven, cotton-picking plantations. They provide worship services, cheap motel-like rooms for mission teams, conference rooms for meetings, and even retirement homes for the owners of the mission centers. They are built with good intentions, at least for some.

However, some mission center owners are disrespectful, even patriarchally scornful against their Filipinx workers. They mock the Filipinx workers culturally, politically, and even physically. Their condescending words and actions contradict their vocation as missionaries who came to the Philippines to serve the Filipinx people with the Gospel. In all of these, the interesting dynamic is that the mission center owners become wary of their local Filipinx workers/managers for their savvy dealings. The response of the Filipinx workers echoes the decision of the manager of Lk 16:1–13. Instead of confronting the mission center owner, the Filipinx workers mastered the mission center's operations more than their employers. When mission center owners leave for a few days, even weeks, to visit the mission field or other countries, they ask their Filipinx workers to manage their mission centers. The Filipinx workers manage well in most cases. Sometimes too well to the point that they are able to come up with ways to outsmart their employers. When the mission center owners finally realize what has happened, they tend to fire their employees. However, terminating the employment of their Filipinx manager(s) is not easy because hiring a new person(s) and training them again is a daunting task. Plus, there is no guarantee that the new manager will follow their expectations. So, they usually reprimand their Filipinx managers, and call it a day. And yet, the bitter taste remains.

Such tension echoes the very definition of postcolonial ambivalence in which the mission center owners "hate" their local managers for their sly civility, and yet "love" or desire to be like them for their cunning methods. Unfortunately, my story on the Korean missionary mission center(s) is anecdotal; of course, who would want to write about such economic *shitstem* for the public to read/hear. Hence, explaining this ambivalence with another economic *shitstem* that resonates with the (Korean) mission centers, recorded and academically verified, hopefully would assist in further grounding my arguments here. This economic *shitstem* is the U.S. share-cropping post-bellum southern plantation.[17]

Sharecropping has been the mainstream agrarian arrangement in the South post-bellum until the early 1900s. Serap A. Kayatekin even argues that it could have existed until the Civil Rights Movement in the US.[18] The deal was that the white landowner provide the land, seeds, fertilizers, and other ingredients/tools needed for farming. Meanwhile, the black workers provide labor. The profits/proceeds from the farming are supposed to be equally divided between the two parties. As one would surmise, the white landowners are the descendants of slave owners who inherited the land. The black workers are the descendants of the emancipated who worked the lands of their former slave masters. For decades or even centuries, white landowners were trained to never participate in hard labor because it is supposed to be the role of the black people. In other words, high socio-economic class or financial prestige equals white race; low socio-economic class and/or dirty jobs equals black race.

This hierarchy was apparently translated into father-children relationality as well. According to A. Davis, B. Gardner and M.R. Gardner, the white race is supposed to be the "father" figure who provides, disciplines if one must, and order the "black children" to perform their filial duties.[19] The white father figure felt the burden of caring for their wayward and undisciplined "black children." And yet, Kayatekin narrates that white landowners disdained and at the same time feared their black workers because they were afraid of the black workers' capability to allegedly squander, embezzle, or re-distribute their produce.[20] The white landowners looked down upon the black workers as inferior child-like entities who needed constant care and reprimanding. At the same time, these white landowners are envious of their black workers because of the former's assumption that the latter have carefree attitude and less worry/pressure to thrive.[21] Such feelings of envy and fear metamorphosized into a feeling of desire—the desire to become like their black workers.[22]

Kayatekin argues that this simultaneous feeling of disdain and desire reflects postcolonial ambivalence (Homi Bhabha) in which "[s]uch ambivalence, the production of contradictory feelings at the same time, can go some way in explaining the creation of a hegemonic discourse which interpellates; through and in which subjects exist."[23] The production of contradictory feeling is a weapon of the weak. Interrogating interpellation by muddying ontology unnerves the hegemonic discourse. The white landowners interpellate subjectivity (Althusserian) to/with their black workers. In other words, the white landowners impose identity unto their black workers as a way to subjugate them. And yet, such imposition affectively pulls the white landowners to the subjected/imposed because of their own visceral and ontological involvement in the binary. To interpellate the other is to interpellate oneself in this colonial matrix where the survival of this interpellation depends upon the white landowners' sustained transgression of the binary. By doing so, the white landowners muddy their own ontology, their supposed superior positionality as the "father," because they have to continuously hold on to the iterations of othering—labeling black workers as "children."

By mimicking the subjectivity of the employer, the manager of Lk 16:1–13 utilizes a weapon of the weak (ambivalence) in countering his negative futurity. The manager doubles down on this ambivalence by exposing the animacy of money. Mimicry does not conceal but over-expose. The menace of mimicry, as Bhabha discloses, "is its double vision which in disclosing the ambivalence of colonial discourse also disrupts its authority."[24] The manager over-exposes by engaging his employers' debtors, by "cooking the books" or lowering their debts, and by deciding the futures of everyone involved without the permission of his employer. The manager did not join a resistance movement or destroyed his employer's *latifundium*. He also did not beg for mercy or resorted to digging. Rather, the manager magnified the latent ambivalence "produced within the rules of recognition of dominating discourses as they articulate the signs of cultural difference and reimplicate them within the deferential relations of colonial power—hierarchy, normalization, marginalization, and so forth [. . .]."[25] Instead of running away from the *shitstem*, the manager revealed his deferential relations with(in) the *shitstem* by demonstrating his capacity to produce the machinations of the colonial *shitstem* for oppositional ends. This demonstration manifested through the emergence of the animacy of money.

I see the same pattern of ambivalence in mission centers. The missionaries are the so-called "father figures" who disdain their Filipinx workers for their perceived child-like laziness and ineptitude. At the same time, these missionaries envy their workers for their carefree attitude. Such biased and discriminatory perceptions against the Filipinx workers are obviously unfounded and a product of colonial thinking. One could even wonder if such colonial mindset of some Korean missionaries are byproducts of being colonized themselves by the US and Japan not that long ago—a manifestation of colonial mimicry, neo-colonization, and crab mentality. In any case, such ambivalent feelings between Korean missionaries and their Filipinx workers produce contradictory feelings of want and hate, of desire and repulsion. This feeling of ambivalence is exacerbated by the involvement of money that triggers and disrupts the relationality between the Korean missionaries and their Filipinx workers. Money triggers because the missionaries themselves know that such desire/repulsion for money is contradictory to their calling in the first place. The same goes with the white landowners. They are supposed to be "above" the juvenile relationality with money; they are supposed to have "mastery" over the finances, just like a father. And yet, the white landowners are constantly unnerved, acting like a child, by the animacy of money, especially at the hands of their black workers/managers.

Of course, this ambivalence could also lead to death drive for the manager (Lk 16:1–13)/mission center workers/black workers because one cannot "take the antagonistic edge from relations of exploitation/oppression."[26] The managers (and the slaves) of the *latifundia* were flogged or even killed for re-distributing the produce to their fellow workers. And yet, they still pursue such undertaking because becoming a zealot and trying to kill off the landowners did not turn out well, as history teaches. According to Bruce James, Winfried Blum, and Carmelo Dazzi, wine, wheat, and olive oil are the staple of the Roman Empire. To disrupt the production of these is to disrupt the empire.[27] The Roman Empire transitioned from small farms to *latifundia* because of slavery. *Latifundia* were able to produce crops cheaply because the slaves worked on the fields. The *latifundia* economic system drove small land farmers out of business. This kind of injustice happens frequently for those who are in the Greco-Roman agrarian tenant farming system. The result of this injustice is the rise of absentee landowners (who lived in the city) and the expansive hiring of managers of *latifundia*. The creation of jobs here did not translate to better living conditions. The landowner owns and profits with minimal cost/risk to himself because the managers take the brunt of the danger and hostility that comes with working/living in this economic *shitstem*. Moreover, the Roman Empire demanded more food and tax revenue from the *latifundia*, putting the managers in difficult circumstances.[28] Such difficulty led to insurrections, albeit their revolts failed. In other words, to disrupt the *latifundia* is to disrupt the empire. The three servile wars in southern Italy and Sicily (135–32, 104–100, and 73–71 BCE) is widely known,[29] at least for those who are concerned with the time of Luke. Thus, the manager of Lk 16:1–8a, knowing these circumstances and histories, chose to use surreptitious weapons of the weak (ambivalence and the animacies of money) to resist his way out of his predicament. As Peter Garnsey states, "in [the Greco-Roman] antiquity, food was [is] power."[30] That is why the manager tapped into the animacies of the material.

In this ambivalence one has to note how the manager of Lk 16:1–8a tapped into the animacies of the more-than-human. Interestingly, one does not find an interpretation of Lk 16:1–13 (or however one decides the final verse of the parable should be) that taps into the animacy of olive oil and wheat, or their equivalence to money. And yet, the very idea of losing money drove the narrative into its climactic "resolution." The manager manipulated and the employer was manipulated by the animacies of huge amounts of olive oil (100 jugs or approximately 3,500 liters/930 gallons) and 100 *kors* of wheat (630 bushels),[31] a significant amount of financial loss for the employer. The manager did not beg or dig because he knows the animacies of debt and/or accounts receivables. In other words, the manager lived and worked under the economic *shitstem* of oppressive/unrighteous money long enough to know their animating efficacy. That is why verse 9 teaches that one should "make friends with unrighteous wealth" or use the money brought about by the oppressive system because the animacies of such wealth or money could have enough animating powers to save oneself into the eternal dwellings of one's friends.

ANIMATING THE NON-ORGANIC ACTANTS

I define and heavily rely upon Mel Chen's understanding: animacy(ies) "has the capacity to rewrite conditions of intimacy, engendering different communalisms and revising biopolitical spheres, or, at least, how we might theorize them."[32] Stemming from the posthumanist agenda of questioning human superiority and exclusivity, Chen's animacy interrogates anthropocentrism by acknowledging the animating capacities and the affective entanglements of all entities, particularly the non-organic actants. Coined by Bruno Latour, actant is an expression that helps in eschewing anthropocentric description of the non-organic (and even animals and plants) entities as "object." Latour prefers to call all entities/creations as actants. Latour defines actants as "sources of affects and effects, actions and reactions, something that modifies another entity in a trial [. . . whose] competence is deduced from its performance and not from presumptions."[33] Thus, I chose to describe all entities as actants; moreover, the inanimate actants are preferably described as "non-organic."

Applying Chen's animacies on Lk 16:1–13 seeks to notice and embrace the animacies of money, the influence of mammon, in the lives of the employer, the manager, and even the author and the audience of Luke. This embrace acknowledges that the non-organic actants (olive oil and wheat and their monetary equivalence) determined the outcome of the narrative and divulged one of the struggles (what to do with unrighteous wealth) of the early church/Lukan community (verses 9–13). In other words, the parable admonishes that tapping into the animacies of the non-organic actants is a hidden transcript that teaches sly civility and unconventional ethical response for those who are trapped by the colonial dealings of the *shitstem*. Lk 16:10–12 teaches that one has to be "faithful" (πιστός) to the "little" and "much," even if they/actants are "unrighteous." In other words, I interpret "faithful" here as the call to be cognizant and responsive to the actants in their various expressions (little/much, righteous/unrighteous). "Faithful" (πιστός) is attested four times in Luke: 12:42; 16:10 (x2); 19:17. Just like 16:10, the adjective "faithful" in 12:42 and 19:17 are attested/written within the sphere of finance and in relations with non-organic actants, not as a spiritual/Christian term. These relationalities manifest the affective pull, the animating capacities, of non-organic actants with human survival and relationality. That is why the ultimatum of verse 13 divulges the reality and the necessity of working with the animacy of the non-organic actants. Perhaps, verse 13 is an admission that Luke and his audience are oppressively enmeshed with the *shitstem* of unrighteous mammon. A way to be "faithful" or resist this *shitstem* then is to admit that we are all slaves to and serve the animacy of money (verse 13). Then, like the manager of 16:1–8a, we are invited to find ways to resist *within* the *shitstem* with non-organic actants, a weapon of the weak that is less utilized in our revolutionary hidden transcripts.

CODA: INVERTING THE SYMBOLIC

Although they did not work with the concept of animacy or new materialism per se, Herzog and Kloppenborg's interpretations/resolutions to the conundrum of the parable provide an affective resonance to the sticky entanglements brought about my non-organic animacies. First, Herzog argues that the manager had a long-term plan that benefits his employer, unbeknownst to the debtors. By lowering the debts, the two debtors thought that they have gotten away with free money or a better deal. However, Herzog argues that the so-called reduction of debt is actually a creation of a new contract between his employer and the two debtors. By revising their *grammata* (contracts) with reduced amounts, Herzog argues that "the debtors have also signed a new contract with a different kind of hidden interest, and they will pay for their good fortune."[34] A modern-day example of "they will pay for their good fortune" is the advertisement on mortgage refinancing in which this refinancing promises lower interest rate and reduced payment. At first, this refinancing sounds like a good deal; however, the companies who want to engage in this refinancing are tricking the homeowners, who probably spent a lot of years paying their mortgage off, to restart their fifteen or thirty-year mortgage payment plan with the refinancing companies. By doing so, the homeowners are "locked in" or trapped into another endless payment plan which in the long run means higher expenditure for the homeowners and endless profits for the refinancing companies. For the audience/readers of Luke who know the true financial implications of the reduction of debt by the manager (16:1–8a), one could only imagine the disgust, the jeers and snide remarks thrown here and there, as this parable is narrated. They probably felt it, experienced it themselves, perhaps traumatized by hearing/reading this animacy of money/non-organic actancy once again.

Meanwhile, Kloppenborg discusses the importance of honor and shame culture in reading the parable. The employer's immediate termination of his manager for allegedly embezzling funds is expected in an honor-shame culture because the employer needs to protect/defend his honor or avoid being shamed because he was tricked/shamed by his inferior. And yet, the employer's honor was further jeopardized because the manager was able to lower the debts of his two debtors, a further shaming event for the employer. Hence, Kloppenborg argues that the employer commended the manager or was "laughing"[35] at the debt reduction incident (and of himself) because this was his knee-jerk reaction to save his face, declaring to the public that he is above this incident. His reaction is his way of manifesting his hyper-masculinity in which he declares that he is above the honor-shame culture: nothing can faze him. Kloppenborg supports this reading of the parable by corroborating it with other parables with somewhat similar ethos of challenging the conventional norms: "The Parable of the Great Dinner" (14:15–24), "The Prodigal Son" (15:11–32), and "The Good Samaritan" (10:25–37). These parables, as Kloppenborg states, "challenges by inversion or burlesque, elements of the auditor's *symbolic universe*."[36]

For my reading, the *symbolic universe* that needs to be inverted and challenged is the *shitstem* of anthropocentricity and unhealthy relationality of missionaries with money. My reading of the parable echoes Kloppenborg's reading in which the parable challenges the social codes of its time. Where we part ways is that for Kloppenborg the challenge/inversion was instigated primarily by the employer. I argue that the manager disrupts the social codes, which led to the employer's subsequent onboarding of this challenge. Moreover, my reading adds a layer to this inversion by arguing that the non-organic actants are actually the ones who affectively caused the reactions (both manager and employer): the renegotiations and the "laughing." To read as such takes a certain philosophical acceptance that humans are not the prime or sole mover of events. Rather, in many cases, the non-organic actants are actually the instigators of events, the contract-makers and breakers. Lk 12:16–21 ("The Parable of the Rich Fool") speaks of the folly of storing riches in this material world but not with God. And yet, this parable's precursor (v.15) warns of the folly of trying to control one's happiness and future by controlling material goods or non-organic actants. Humans try to extract some form of positive emotions from non-organic actants/money: "And I will say to my soul, soul, you have ample goods laid up for many years; relax, eat, drink, be merry" (v.19). However, the parable teaches that such extraction does not always happen as one expects. We, humans, need to question our anthropocentric assumption that we have a stranglehold on the non-organic or even of all entities. The animacy of the olive oil and wheat (and their monetary equivalence) moved the humans to act otherwise.

We question because money moves. Lk 16:1–8a's manager and his employer, the Korean missionaries and their Filipinx workers, and the US post-bellum southern plantation landowners and their black workers felt the affective animacy of money. The ambivalent emotions and relationality are brought about by the animacies of non-organic actants who were able to tap into the emotions of humans, moving and controlling them in ways that are unknown to human logic. Money moves and determines who should be regarded as "worthy of being animated." This is the so-called "lesson" of the parable: to acknowledge the precarity of anthropocentricity, and to recognize the animacy of the non-organic actants, perhaps even stronger in their affective animacy than the divine. Stronger to the point that Luke expresses his frustration, his ambivalence, in the form of coerced bifurcation: "You cannot serve God and wealth/mammon" (16:13).

NOTES

1. I am grateful to Jione Havea for the reminder that missionaries extract funds as well from the people they are supposed to serve.
2. *Shitstem* is rasta-speak for the oppressive system (*Discernment and Radical Engagement* (DARE) Global Forum 2021).
3. Mel Chen, *Animacies: Biopolitics, Racial Mattering, and Queer Affect* (Durham: Duke University Press, 2012), 2.
4. I translate "τὸν οἰκονόμον τῆς ἀδικίας" (v.8a) as "the manager of unjust (wealth)" because I prefer to translate the genitival modifier (τῆς ἀδικίας) in the possessive form rather than the descriptive ("the unjust manager"). David DeSilva also translates the phrase in the possessive (he uses subjective/descriptive versus objective/possessive genitive) by providing textual evidence in which the same Greek phrasing is translated with objective/possessive genitive form. For example: Lk 16:8b's "sons of this age . . . sons of light" (οἱ υἱοὶ τοῦ αἰῶνος τούτου . . . τοὺς υἱοὺς τοῦ φωτός) are not translated as "worldly sons or radiant sons" even if their grammar is similar with "τὸν οἰκονόμον τῆς ἀδικίας." See David A. DeSilva, "The Parable of the Prudent Steward and Its Lucan Context." *Criswell Theological Review* 6.2 (1993): 264–6.
5. I use "employer" as the catch-all translation for *ploúsios*. Such utilization is due to expediency even though ploúsios could be translated in other ways. Moreover, I do not think that ploúsios represents God or Jesus. Rather, ploúsios is any rich person who owns a *latifundium*. As Bernard Brandon Scott points out, ploúsios in Luke (6:24; 12:16; 14:12; 16:19, 21, 22; 18:23, 25; 21:1 but contrast these with Zacchaeus [19:1–10] who has a more redeeming narrative) has negative connotations. Thus, representing the divine/messianic in such sustained negativity does not bode well to the message of the Gospel. See Scott, "A Master's Praise: Luke 16,1–8a." *Biblica* 64:2 (1983): 179–80.
6. Jennifer Glancy does not see the οἰκονόμος (manager) as a slave because slaves would be severely punished or even killed for such alleged wrongdoing. See Jennifer A. Glancy, *Slavery in Early Christianity* (Oxford, UK: Oxford University Press, 2002), 108–10. Herzog considers the manager as a "retainer" (not a slave). Retainers usually handle the business of their employers because their employers/landowners are frequently absent from the land/compound. William R. Herzog II, *Jesus as Pedagogue of the Oppressed* (Louisville: Westminster/John Knox, 1994), 241. On the other hand, King, Beavis, and Hopkins argue that slaves are sometimes released not because of kindness but due to financial expediency. So, one cannot simply preclude the manager from being a slave. Fergus J. King, "A Funny Thing Happened on The Way to the Parable: The Steward, Tricksters and (Non)Sense in Luke 16:1–8." *Biblical Theology Bulletin* 48.1 (2018): 20; Mary Ann Beavis, "Ancient Slavery as an

Interpretive Context for the New Testament Servant Parables with Special Reference to the Unjust Steward (Luke 16:1–8)." *Journal of Biblical Literature* 111.1 (1992): 49; Keith Hopkins, *Conquerors and Slaves* (Cambridge, UK: Cambridge University Press, 1978), 117–20.

7. Was the reason for this reduction a cancellation of usury or lowering of high interest rate? The parable does not elaborate. And yet, scholars find the Jewish (Ex 22:25–27; Deut 23:19–20) and/or Palestinian economic milieu a fertile ground in explaining the conundrum even if usury/ high interest rate/ promissory notes are common in the Greco-Roman world. See J.D.M. Derrett, "Fresh Light on St. Luke XVI. I. The Parable of the Unjust Servant." *New Testament Studies* 7 (1960–61): 198–219; Joseph A. Fitzmyer, "The Parable of the Dishonest Manager (Lk 16:1–8a)," in *The Gospel According to Luke X-XXIV* (New York: Doubleday, 1985), 1097. In any case, Ireland marshaled various scholarly arguments on the reasons why the manager resorted to reducing the debts. His comprehensive work summarizes various interpretations of this passage beyond the issue of the reduction of debt. Dennis Ireland, *Stewardship and the Kingdom of God: An Historical, Exegetical, and Contextual Study of the Parable of the Unjust Steward in Luke 16:1–13* (Netherlands, Brill, 1992).

8. There is no scholarly consensus on the ending of the parable. The possible endings for this parable are verse 7 (Jeremiah Jeremias, *The Parables of Jesus* [London: SCM, 1963], 46–48); verse 8a (Kenneth E. Bailey, *Poet and Peasant: A Literary and Cultural Approach to the Parables of Luke* [Grand Rapids: Eerdmans, 1976]; Joseph A. Fitzmyer, "The Story of the Dishonest Manager," *TS* 25 [1964]: 23–42; John R. Donahue, *The Gospel in Parable: Metaphor, Narrative, and Theology in the Synoptic Gospels* [New York: Fortress, 1988], 162–179); verse 8b (W.O.E. Oesterley, *The Gospel Parables in the Light of the Jewish Background* [New York: MacMillan, 1936], 198); verse 9 (A.H. Baverstock, "The Parable of the Unjust Steward: An Interpretation," *Theology* 35, 206 [1937]: 81). These are just a few references compared to King's latest count of at least 107 books/articles/book chapters on this parable as of 2017. See King, "A Funny Thing Happened on The Way to the Parable," 18.

9. Herzog, *Jesus as Pedagogue of the Oppressed*, 253.

10. Justin S. Ukpong, "The Parable of the Shrewd Manager (Luke 16:1–13): An Essay in Inculturation Biblical Hermeneutic." *Semeia* 73 (1996): 206.

11. Ukpong, "The Parable of the Shrewd Manager (Luke 16:1–13)," 207.

12. Herzog, *Jesus as Pedagogue of the Oppressed*, 3.

13. Herzog, *Jesus as Pedagogue of the Oppressed*, 21.

14. Herzog, *Jesus as Pedagogue of the Oppressed*, 53–73.

15. Norman Perrin, *Rediscovering the Teaching of Jesus* (New York: Harper & Row, 1967), 109–15.

16. James C. Scott, *Weapons of the Weak: Everyday Forms of Peasant Resistance* (New Haven: Yale University Press, 1985), 29. King's reading of the manager as a slave (*servus fallax/callidus*) trickster could be an addition to this list of weaponry. See "A Funny Thing Happened on The Way to the Parable," 22–24.

17. Another possibility is the *hacienda* system found in many Spanish colonized nations, such as the Philippines. See Ada María Isasi-Diaz, "A Mujerista Hermeneutics of Justice and Human Flourishing," in *The Bible and The Hermeneutics of*

Liberation, ed. Alejandro F. Botta and Pablo R. Andiñach (Atlanta: SBL, 2009), 181–195.

18. Serap A. Kayatekin, "Sharecropping and Feudal Class Process in the Postbellum Mississippi Delta," in *Re/Presenting Class: Essays in Postmodern Marxism,* ed. J.K. Gibson-Graham, S. Resnick, and R. Wolff (Durham, NC: Duke University Press, 2001).

19. A. Davis, B. Gardner, and M.R. Gardner, *Deep South: A Social Anthropological Study of Caste and Class* (Chicago: University of Chicago Press, 1941), 19.

20. Serap A. Kayatekin, "Hegemony, Ambivalence, and Class Subjectivity: Southern Planters in Sharecropping Relations in the Post-Bellum United States," in *Postcolonialism Meets Economics*, ed. Eiman O. Zein-Elabdin and S. Charusheela (London; New York: Routledge, 2004), 242–4.

21. Davis, Gardner and Gardner, *Deep South*, 19.

22. Davis, Gardner and Gardner, *Deep South*, 19.

23. Kayatekin, "Hegemony, Ambivalence, and Class Subjectivity," 248. Homi Bhabha, *The Location of Culture* (London and New York: Routledge, 1994), 122.

24. Bhabha, *The Location of Culture*, 126.

25. Bhabha, *The Location of Culture*, 157–158.

26. Kayatekin, "Hegemony, Ambivalence, and Class Subjectivity," 250.

27. Bruce James, Winfried Blum, and Carmelo Dazzi, "Bread and Soil in Ancient Rome: A Vision of Abundance and an Ideal of Order Based on Wheat, Grapes, and Olives," in *The Soil Underfoot: Infinite Possibilities for a Finite Resource, eds.* J. Churchman and E. Landa (CRC Press: Boca Raton, FL, 2013), 155.

28. N. Morley, "The Transformation of Italy, 225–28 B.C." *Journal of Roman Studies* 91 (2001): 50–62.

29. Bruce, Blum, and Dazzi, "Bread and Soil in Ancient Rome," 161.

30. Peter Garnsey, *Food and Society in Classical Antiquity* (Cambridge: Cambridge University Press, 1999).

31. Manson argues that 100 *cors* of wheat equals 1,083 bushels or 2,500 to 3,000 denarii. This is based on his take on *Baba Metzia* 5:1, which sets the price of a *cor* to twenty-five to thirty denarii. See T.W. Manson, *The Sayings of Jesus* (London: SCM, 1949), 292.

32. Chen, *Animacies*, 3.

33. See *Politics of Nature: How to Bring the Sciences into Democracy* (trans. Catherine Porter; Cambridge, MA: Harvard University Press. 2004), 236; and, *Reassembling the Social: An Introduction to Actor-Network-Theory* (Oxford: Oxford University Press, 2005), 10–1.

34. Herzog, *Jesus as Pedagogue of the Oppressed*, 257.

35. John Kloppenborg, "The Dishonoured Master (Luke 16:1–8a)." *Biblica* vol.70, no.4 (1989): 492–3.

36. Kloppenborg elaborates on the inversion or the challenge to the *symbolic universe* as challenge (based on the aforementioned parables) to the "security of the social and ethnic boundaries between Jews and Samaritans, or the legitimate expectations of the commensurability of achievement and compensation, or the self-evident appropriateness of insisting upon one's honour." Kloppenborg, "The Dishonoured Master (Luke 16:1–8a)," 494.

Chapter 5

Interrogating the Silence

Jesus' Response to a Mother's Cry, for a Daughter's Disability (Matthew 15:21–28)

Wendy Elson

The Canaanite woman—marginalised through gender, class, ethnicity, and her daughter's disability (presented as "demon possession" in the story)—approaches Jesus and pleads, "Have mercy on me, Lord, Son of David; my daughter is tormented by a demon" (v.22, NRSV). Jesus "did not answer her at all" (v.23). Jesus' silence, this pause, can be heard in different ways and may hold profound meaning for those who experience marginalisation, particularly because of disability. Might Jesus' silence be interpreted as analogous to contemporary institutional silence?

As the mother of a son born with a disability, I identify with the woman in the story. I am like Justa (the name tradition gives the Canaanite woman),[1] and as I reflect on my own story alongside this narrative, further questions emerge regarding Jesus' response to Justa and her daughter who has been named Berenice. Silence itself communicates, and the experiences of women who have encountered institutional silence allow us to hear Jesus' silence in this story differently.

While my identification with Justa allows me to engage deeply, there are limits to this. Her levels of marginalisation are profound, and her daughter is even more marginalised. I witness her suffering in the aching experience of powerlessness and frustration with the silence of the Divine. I hear her bond with her child amidst the struggle to fully embrace wholeness in their relationship. I acknowledge, however, my bias as a Christian woman from the dominant culture who holds white, feminist theological views and who is privileged through education and status. I am able-bodied. I am appropriating the story of Justa—who did not tell her own story—for my own purposes.

Various theories around the meaning of "demon possession" have been put forward. I adopt the view that Berenice's suffering results in some form of disability (physically, mentally). I use the term "disability" cautiously, as all alternatives have limitations. There is a continuum of ability in all people and sometimes it is the label that places limitations.

FEMINIST, INTERSECTIONAL, IMAGINATIVE

Traditional interpretations of the text are "discordant" and inadequate to fully encompass a range of perspectives, demonstrating a relatively narrow focus.[2] At worst, when this story has been reduced to reinforcement of doctrinal arguments, it has settled into "certain grooves" which have served to boost "power and prejudice" and exclusion losing the "transformative power" and texture of the story.[3] Attempts to fathom its "harsh" and "dismissive" tone,[4] particularly in exploring it through diverse means and perspectives, open it to renewed scrutiny.

My approach to the text is influenced by the creative, imaginative approaches used by feminist scholars. I broaden Sarah Coakley's definition of feminism, as an approach which is "committed to overcoming economic, cultural, societal, or psychological disadvantages,"[5] particularly as it pertains to women, to encompass all those oppressed by patriarchal systems. Feminism functions best intersectionally, paying attention to the impact of "multiple interacting systems of oppression and privilege."[6] Examining inequalities and power relations through gender, race, indigeneity, sexual orientation, and ability enables the silenced and the subjugated to be heard. This approach gives space for the recontextualising of the Biblical narrative and opens up a "critical spiraling dance of interpretation," rather than a closed circle which confines interpretation to a traditionalist agenda.[7] Schüssler Fiorenza advocates a "feminist reconstructive approach" that uses images, role-plays, storytelling and "inhabiting" characters,[8] in exploring reactions and emotions.[9]

THE PLOT

I revisit Matt 15:21–28 from the position of the marginalised and silenced, breaking the confines imposed on Justa's story through traditional exegesis to allow the text's rich texture and vitality to emerge. This narrative, the embodiment of a lament psalm, is one of fourteen healing miracles in Matthew.[10] The story's placement signals a "turning point" in the chiastic structure of

Matthew's gospel, situated between two "feeding stories," and their link to the healing stories.[11] Justa is at the "axis point" of the story and the story is the "axis point" in the Gospel, a chiastic structure within a chiastic structure, placing her at its heart.[12]

The story loses its shape through appropriation in doctrines and debates of worthiness, beginning and ending with the Jewish-Gentile debate.[13] The narrative circles around the relationships and the characters and then back again as it builds its tensions toward its word of conclusive blessing. The story spirals on, functioning as a signpost and touchstone in the path climbing toward Matthew's culmination in its universal missional agenda.

Matthew's Alterations

The racial tensions are heightened through Matthew's term "Canaanite," compared to Mark's "Syro-Phoenician" (Mark 7:24–30), indicating his intention to intensify the harshness of the narrative and the sullen demeanour of Jesus.[14] This alteration categorises the woman and exacerbates the cultural divide. Donaldson links it to "charam" (a "devotion to destruction") referring to the edict by Yahweh to annihilate the Canaanite people who originally inhabited the land.[15] The genocidal overtones in the label "Canaanite"[16] invoke erasure of whole peoples,[17] a potent alteration full of meanings. It suggests that Matthew's "Canaanite" sets up the colonising and subjugation of unequal subjects implied in the Great Commission.[18] Engaging with the term intertextually positions this woman as one who can be "invaded, conquered, annihilated."[19] Gullotta suggests that the inclusion of Rahab the Canaanite prostitute in Matthew's genealogy lifts "dramatic tension" by making Justa both "'other' and 'kin,' both 'enemy' and 'family.'"[20] Alexander goes further in imagining Jesus already present in the womb of the Canaanite prostitute before the conquest of Canaan even occurred.[21] In heightening hostility toward Justa, the author demonises her and makes her representative of total "otherness," yet she also belongs in this place and could be said to represent Jesus' own kin.

Mission to the Gentiles

Noting Jesus' Gentile (even "Canaanite")[22] heritage through Rahab in the opening verses of Matthew and concluding with the demand to take the gospel into all the nations, Matthew redefines mission to include the Gentiles—they are permitted to eat the crumbs under the table.[23] Dube is convincing that Matthew's author had an agenda in alignment with empire tactically hidden throughout the gospel in his nuancing of Mark's material.[24] I note here that Guardiola-Sáenz describes the "oppressive" "ideology of chosenness," which diminishes Matthew's concept of the *basileia,* the Reign of God.[25] Justa re-defines the concept, however, in asserting her belief that the *basileia* includes her and dispossessed others like her.

Dogs and Bread

Two images stand out: dogs, and bread. The language is harsh, distressing, and offensive. Jesus' bad manners in using the term 'dog' are inexcusable, though they may serve as a plot device.[26] The imagery is stark with Justa kneeling like a submissive dog before Jesus. Most, though not all, interpreters of this passage consider the term 'dog' insulting, its function supporting Jewish superiority while demeaning Justa by reducing her to animal status.[27] First, Justa must acknowledge her place beneath the table to access the crumbs. While her "witty reply" may be the punchline of the narrative, the question remains whether she accepts this insult to her ethnicity and status.[28] It appears that when Justa accepts this "social category" her request is granted, though some argue against her acceptance of this insult. Nonetheless, Justa refuses to "be coerced by the politics of submission," and it is in her marginality and vulnerability that she takes a stand against injustice.[29]

The story of Justa sits between Matt 14:13–21 and 15:29–39, feeding narratives where bread is shared so generously that there are many crumbs left over, an image of abundance and health, a sharing around the table as equals. Justa uses liturgical language, this Gentile 'other' acknowledging Jesus as Messiah, and links "Lord" with Sophia and Wisdom imageries for Christ and the bread "of understanding."[30] While there appears to be food in abundance surrounding the story it is used as justification for Justa's rejection. To mix metaphors, why can the host not get a bigger table so that the crumbs can be used by all God's children? Why must Justa remain hungry amid abundant bread?

Justa's heart is broken, longing for wholeness for her child. Jesus uses the language of the satisfaction and flourishing of the deserving children as a reason to deny Justa the relief from suffering of her own child. He reserves bread for children who are already healthy and whole, the children of privilege, while withholding it from the one in need of its sustenance and restoration. On the surface, this is cruel and callous in the extreme, an insensitivity which has been largely overlooked.

The Other

Matthew's heightening and intensifying of the drama of the text increases the total otherness of Justa and Berenice. The women together represent those on the margins. While Justa is 'other,' she is also a challenge to the usual dichotomies because she defines her own place.[31] While Justa is "out of place" and displaced, she is also in her place as an indigenous woman. Holding up the vision of the inclusive kingdom, Justa (re)imparts it to Jesus becoming "the Christ herself."[32] Justa stands in for all on the edges who resist and protest, embodying "intersections of identity" in this "interpretive encounter."[33] In faith, which is unbound and uncontained, she refuses to accept the limits which attempt to confine the gospel.

While Justa is marginalised on many levels, she is "strong and determined," and she displays some considerable knowledge.[34] Her anger rises up from the "submissive whisper of the alienated."[35] She is acquainted with the language of faith and how best to flatter Jesus. As a model of faith, Justa is a reminder that God operates outside the "bounds of cultural norms" which function to create limitations around worth, value, and identity.[36] She reminds the church that it too can be "surprised" by the gospel from outside, by those who do not normally fit its "parameters."[37]

Justa, as the presence of the "resistant oppressed" brings healing and transformation to Jesus and those complicit in the oppression of the marginalised.[38] With "cleverness and wit," Justa stands before Jesus as prophet. Risking rejection, she asserts her dignity, teaching Jesus about mission and liberation.[39] Justa's tale is told by others, used against her while appropriating her story and her pain.[40] It is in the shift from a stubborn place of privilege that Jesus is open to hearing her reality and can recognise his place in her oppression, and in her healing. It is here at the margins that Jesus sees his own teaching on the *basileia*. It is here at the "borderlands," where places of transformation are discovered through a new experience of reality, through marginality and vulnerability, and through the struggle for justice.[41] In the "unsettled and unsettling" energy of the space in between boundaries, Jesus' vision of the Kingdom mission is expanded.[42]

BERENICE, DISABILITY, AND HEALING

Berenice is present in the encounter through her mother's advocacy. In Matthew's text, Berenice was "tormented by a demon." Perhaps the manifestation of the demonic in Berenice is the gesticulation of sign language,[43] or epileptic seizures. Whatever choices we make in interpreting this "devil," Berenice is suffering some form of disability. In encounters between Jesus and voiceless, nameless, disabled figures, healing and disability are incidental, and here Berenice functions as a plot device enlisted to spotlight Jesus and convey shifts in missional teaching.[44] This functions to dehumanise her and restrict her presence, and like many others suffering with disability, she has no voice in her own story.

The dignity and status of the disabled, and those of other "diverse communities" is diminished by continual depiction of them as sites where the divine is active.[45] Donaldson asks why these narratives "manifest such anxiety" about those exhibiting disability, putting forward the notion that disabled bodies remind us of our own self out of control and "running rampant."[46] She refers to this as confirming the "cultural other" which lies "dormant" in us.[47]

Linking terms such as "unclean spirits" with mental illness, highlights the "dis-ease" around the "unacceptable" and "out of order" nature of such phenomena and the discomfort this causes society.[48] The tendency to treat "anomalies" by either ignoring their existence or acknowledging but condemning them, remains common in today's society.[49] Metzger, writing from the "perspective of the disabled," laments the perpetuation of a "causal link" between sin and disability/illness/demon possession,[50] where healing becomes the addendum to repentance and forgiveness. Instead of models based on encounters which appear to offer full and immediate healing and the "fantasy of cure" (tied to faith), disabled people need to be accommodated through "access and justice."[51]

Matthew's Jesus appears to regard disability as "impairment," a "dysfunction" and "deficit to be remediated."[52] Seen through what functions as a medical model, disability is constructed and located in an individual body to be "rehabilitate[d]," rather than a social model which addresses disability as a societal responsibility and acknowledges an "array" of different dis/abilities.[53] Transformation in this sense becomes about support, acceptance, and accessibility. However, in this text, the seekers of transformation and healing must plead for mercy, using "insider" language to flatter and "ingratiate" themselves, to declare their own "unworthiness."[54] Healing presents as an "afterthought," a "commodity" rather than gift, and is "contingent" on faith, with Berenice totally dependent on her mother's faith.[55]

Concerned about "facile appropriations" of those who are oppressed by "radicals" with good intentions, Donaldson describes interpretations of disability as inferiority and "deviance" in her study of links between "colonial oppression and forms of mental illness" and labels of demon possession.[56] An anti-colonial and postcolonial lens highlights those who serve as "plot-devices" and "throwaway" characters and allows the struggles of this "extraordinary daughter" to cause alteration and displacement.[57] Bringing Berenice to the foreground allows the full presence of this currently invisible daughter, allowing healing through the questioning and de-construction of the labels. Berenice is a "passive site," and her "indigenous power" has been "robbed" from her through the colonising effects of past interpretations.[58] Her healing may be seen as an anti-colonial act on Jesus' part.[59]

People who experience disability call for inclusion through new "symbols, practices, and beliefs."[60] Concepts such as impurity and disability are social constructions and as such can be changed and "deconstructed" by the inclusive retelling of the story.[61] Perhaps a way to achieve this is it to tell the story with Berenice in the centre.[62] Just as Jesus is taught by Justa, so we can learn from Berenice. The challenge for churches and societies is to find healing and transformation by lifting the silence, to allow themselves to be ministered to by hearing those with disability.[63] When barriers to thriving through societal attitudes bend to accommodate people to be themselves, the environment supports them to flourish.

Justa stands with mothers who have pleaded and called, who have spoken the "right" language and "played the game." She gives witness to those who choked while uttering placating words to the powerful who offer nothing in return and withhold resources. She is a reminder of mothers who beseech the authorities for crumbs. I hear the cry of mothers whose children are ill, whose children cannot flourish or find decent social connection and the affirmation of the community. When the children of the powerful and the privileged are given precedence over the children of the marginalised, silence is more than dismissal. When those with the power to change, heal and transform by saying a word or flourishing a pen, remain silent and hoard the breadcrumbs for themselves, the response of silence speaks volumes.

Justa and My Story

We stood in a circle surrounding the chairs, one chair for each of the characters in Matt 15:21–28. Participants were invited to sit in any chair as the drama unfolded and witness the encounter by being present as characters within it. My friend "Kate"[64] sat in Justa's place and began to plead and wail for her child. In real life, Kate struggled for services to support her own child. As I witnessed this moment, I became aware of my own place in Justa's story. Sharing the profound moment, I recognised Berenice as truly invisible in the text.

Accepting Justa's invitation to enter the narrative from my own context, I offer my story. Since the birth of my son Tim in 1982 with a significant disability,[65] there have been many times when I pleaded and wailed to those who had the power to assist me. Many times, my pleas were met with silence. I hear myself in Justa's story and because I believe theology is done and lived through encounter with the hermeneutics of real life, I relate some of our experience here. Like Justa, I have been told to accept the "breadcrumbs," causing me to wonder how the sharing of resources can be considered stealing from the "children."[66] I remember a woman complaining that her own children (who were doing well as "mainstream" students at school) were deprived because the "special needs" children were entitled to extra funding resources. I am reminded of the saying: "When you are accustomed to privilege, equality feels like oppression" (source unknown).

The withholding of resources, lest there be a cost to others, was particularly notable when our family moved from New South Wales to Victoria in 1992. We had been granted a few extra hours of support in the classroom and when we moved to the regional town where we would be based, I visited five schools. Each one of them admitted that they technically had to agree to take Tim but made it clear that he would not be truly welcomed due to the extra effort they would need to make. Finally, the regional officer responsible for inclusion of those with special needs said we could choose whichever school we wanted, and she would see to the change of attitude. Our reliance on the few special funding "crumbs" simply provided a slightly more level playing field, but the sting of being unwelcome remained.

When I pleaded for assistance in housing Tim because his behaviour in his adolescent years was beyond our ability to manage and was putting our other two sons at risk, "the system" suggested that I keep silent or face the other two being rehoused which would be an easier solution for "the system."

After a whistle-blower complaint from a public servant in a government housing facility forced the revelation of serious abuse on Tim, I begged to no avail to receive the official reports that were generated but kept confidential. When Tim set himself on fire, we were at least granted a consultation with bureaucrats who agreed that they had not truly listened to Tim's needs. When Tim made significant allegations of abuse by a predator at a day placement, the police told us they accepted the voracity of the allegation. They declined to pursue the case as intellectually disabled people are rarely successful in court due to concerns around their capacity as credible witnesses.

I have regularly called out for one thing and been given another. Our family sought behavioural assistance and we were seen by a team of psychologists who clearly did not understand the dysfunction in Tim's brain and just kept giving us strategies and bar graphs while our family sank further into extreme distress. We have been well supported by church communities, but there have been times when we have sought care and prayer and were offered prayers for cure and healing (through repentance and forgiveness). Every cell in Tim's body is affected and I have come to see Tim's healing as being achieved by those who will allow him to be himself and who celebrate Tim's ministry to others.

I have cried, wailed, and lamented before (what appeared to be) a mute and deaf Divine Presence. The change that I encountered has been my own transformation in learning to advocate for my child, in regrouping as I find the steadiness in myself, in challenging society's limits and responses, its definitions and labels. I have come to see that Tim's greatest disability is the limit to his flourishing through the attitudes of others.

Like Justa, I remained unheard in my pleas and suffered silence from the institutional system set up to deliver care and support. I have at times known the experience of the silence of God. Jesus' lingering silence in his encounter with Justa is profound in its echoes. When a mother wails her pain in deep lament, if the one who holds the key to healing speaks not a word in answer, it feels like a petty withholding of presence and of transformational space. Justa forsakes convention and calls again, proclaiming to the world her daughter's affliction. Without deviating from her purpose Justa focuses on her daughter. Gathering her wits and her voice, she prepares her argument, rising up to insist on the rights and entitlement of Berenice to access structures and resources to support her dignity and empowerment.

BREAKING THE SILENCE

Jesus' silence speaks loudly. Exploring textual features, such as who speaks and acts and who is silent, can reveal significant pointers in interpretation. Jesus holds that moment of silence. Berenice is entirely silent. The disciples want Justa to be silent (by granting or dismissing). The silence becomes a roar as Justa considers, in that moment of Jesus' silence, and then uses the pause to declare her desire. Justa uses the silence to find deeper communion with Jesus, to meet him in his place.

Justa's boldness is a form of "agency," a "truth telling" to authority which, through corruption and bias, would deny life and healing.[67] Such strength is a legitimate form of resistance in confronting exploitative and oppressive treatment, and Justa and Berenice deserve to have their stories told and celebrated.[68]

Guardiola-Sáenz argues that the "strident silence of indifference" is the typical response of oppressors to the pain of those whom they oppress.[69] When the "Other" responds through "dialectic presence," such oppressive silence reflects "speechless" astonishment.[70] Jesus' silence is "rebuff," and attempts to justify it add "insult to injury," and the church is often complicit in this same pattern of response.[71] When disciples use Jesus as a model for discipleship, such dismissive behaviour must be acknowledged and challenged, the faith of the struggling affirmed, and mission redefined and "transformed."[72]

In Jesus' silent, enigmatic response, we hear echoes of our own experience of suffering God's deafness. Within this silence, which could have felt like "game over," the end of the story, and an "escalation" deserving of "indignant anger," Justa shows a remarkable capacity to find equilibrium, to hold steady.[73] Justa, electing not to take it personally, regroups. Not distracted from her purpose, tenacious in her compassion for her child, she de-centres herself and chooses a different entry point to engage again.

The Silencing of Women

When women call out systems of patriarchy, the response is often silence. Like the disciples attempting to silence Justa, silence is often imposed on women to deny and dismiss their pain. Positions of privilege and dominance provide platforms from which silence can be imposed on the marginalised, eclipsing them through their silence. When the church follows this example, it is complicit in perpetuating the silence.[74]

The "meaning of silence" must be "re-thought" due to its part in the "web" of domination and subordination of women.[75] "Control and regulation" around women's communicative practices is a patriarchal tool of domination and power.[76] Silence has also been described as the discovery site of patience, courage and determination.[77] Silent characters are often seen as resistant rather than passive, and Berenice's silence calls out the reader to challenge their own "ideologies" of health.[78] Her silence is witness in itself to the wordiness and emphasis on hearing in the narrative. Hegde finds that when marginal voices are appropriated the agency, determination, and expression of those who are oppressed is threatened.[79] Matters of agency must be considered in communication studies and resistance is the "locus from which action can be initiated."[80] Meaning can be "constructed," rather than simply found and experienced, enabling empowerment and agency.[81]

Silence may offer a sheltering place for restoration and recovery from which to regather resources, and to regroup. However, when silence denies justice, the church must stand for the abused and vulnerable and give voice to the silenced. When silence is used as "the weaponised tool of preference" by Christian communities in the face of sexism, racism, and classism, it is in support of the abusers[82] and thus, we either stand with the "victim or the executioner."[83] The church must stand beside women when, like Justa, they wail and scream out their pain.

Justa's overwhelming need to access what Jesus offered others, drives her to respond to his silence by establishing a new resistant relationship with the dominant power. If women are to be able to truly embrace God as equal and mutual relationship, they need to believe that God hears them and stands with them against oppression and abuse.

The silence ends and Justa finds her answer, but questions remain about whether the silence was response or the absence of response, whether the Divine is hidden within it or absent from it.

Lament

Justa began the encounter with deep lament. The shared prayer of lament emerges as a tool of recovery. Sighs and groans, tears and silence, a cry for help, space to grieve, to vent anger and fear and pain, lament offers a valuable space of waiting and hope.[84] It is in the prayer of lament that a space opens where women of dominant classes can stand with all those who are marginalised.[85] Justa the despised Canaanite, finds her voice and speaks out tenaciously in her desperation for something to change and her daughter to be made whole.

I hear the stories of other women, and of myself, in Justa's story. Women who remain unheard after speaking truth to power (e.g., following the reporting of abuse in the places of power and privilege), will hear Jesus' silence. What texture does the silence weave when we wail our pain to God in the night and feel a palpable awareness that heaven is silent? Yet, I have heard the whisper of the solidarity of other women. Perhaps there is in the silence, a transformative quality. Perhaps it is here where the voice of God is found.

If speaking always says something of "power, authority and love,"[86] silence can speak of lack of worth, disregard and dismissal. However, it may also be the space of empowerment and respite, a place to gather resources and summon power. Something happens in the silence in the text that deepens the encounter and leads to a space of liminality. Justa's lament leads to transformative outcomes, as she finds that the silence gives her shelter to regroup, to steady herself, as she discovers within her the resources for empowerment which enable her to advocate for Berenice.

Advocacy

Berenice finds voice through Justa but is powerless to tell her own story and seek her own healing. She is wholly dependent on Justa's voice and her healing hinges on Jesus' response to Justa's pleas. The relationship between the women as peripheral characters is important, but little is said of it in the literature.[87] Justa finds her own voice in the activism of giving voice to Berenice. Berenice deserves to be more than just a "prop," an absent character whose healing is peripheral to the plot. Her silence and suffering, and ultimately her transformation, deeply affect the implications of the story. The marginalisation of Justa and Berenice is multi-layered. While the story speaks of the marginalising of the disabled in already marginalised cultures, little comment has been made about this. I wonder what happens for daughters who have no Justa to speak for them. The disabled among colonised and marginalised cultures are seriously under-resourced, disempowered, and rarely given full presence or personhood.[88]

Protest and activism enable the finding of voice and the reclaiming of power which are key in recovery for sexual abuse victims.[89] The process of moving from silence and shaming to freedom and empowerment through finding voice, naming the abuse, and calling out the perpetrator, can foster a growing depth of understanding. Validation, support, and activism, crucial for recovery, can provide the solidarity of good connections, the ability to assist others in their healing, and the freedom and courage to stand up and speak out.

CONCLUSION

While opinions differ regarding the motivations behind Jesus' offering of no words in response to Justa's pain, the rudeness (punctuated by further insults) must be neither overlooked nor justified. Matthew uses it as a plot device to heighten the tension and increase the otherness of Justa, ultimately accentuating her inclusion. It is Justa's bold use of the silence as gift and invitation to transformation which emerges as key. However, the impacts of silence as a response continue to marginalise women and deepen their pain and suffering. When the silence is heard through the eyes of those who suffer and remain unheard, the story offers new meaning. Justa's ongoing invitation to Jesus' disciples is to hear and respond to her, and to Berenice, compassionately and inclusively. The link between the silence of Jesus and the intended silencing of Justa may be heard by contemporary women who have also met silence and been silenced. Justa offers a model of courage, compassion, and "sass" as she uses her voice in the desperate desire for wholeness for her child.

NOTES

1. Elaine M. Wainwright, *Towards a Feminist Critical Reading of the Gospel According to Matthew* (New York: De Gruyter, 1991), 46. The names are traced back to Pseudo-Clementine Epistles and tell of further aspects of their lives following this narrative; Laura E. Donaldson, "Gospel Hauntings: The Postcolonial Demons of New Testament Criticism," in *Postcolonial Biblical Criticism: Interdisciplinary Intersections*, eds. Fernando F. Segovia and Stephen D. Moore (London: Bloomsbury, 2007), 100; Also Louise J. Lawrence, "Crumb trails and puppy-dog tales: Reading afterlives of a Canaanite woman," in *From the Margins: Women of the New Testament and their afterlives*, eds. Peter S. Hawkins, Lesleigh Cushing Stahlberg (Sheffield: Sheffield Phoenix, 2009), 270.

2. Lawrence, "Crumb trails," 262, 269.

3. Lawrence, "Crumb trails," 262, 269.

4. Daniel Gullotta, "Among Dogs and Disciples: An Examination of the Story of the Canaanite Woman (Matthew 15:21–28) and the Question of the Gentile Mission within the Matthean Community," *Neotestamentica* 48 (2014): 325.

5. Sarah Coakley, *God, Sexuality, and the Self: An Eessay "On the Trinity"* (Cambridge: Cambridge University Press, 2013), 347.

6. Gale A. Yee, "Thinking Intersectionally: Gender, Race, Class, and the Etceteras of Our Discipline." *JBL* 139.1 (2020): 7–26. doi:10.15699/jbl.1391.2020.1b.

7. Elizabeth Schüssler Fiorenza, *Wisdom Ways: Introducing Feminist Biblical Interpretation* (Maryknoll: Orbis, 2001), 166.

8. Donaldson refers to being "haunted" by them ("Gospel Hauntings," 111).

9. Schüssler Fiorenza, *Wisdom Ways,* 145, 148.

10. Melanie S. Baffes, "Jesus and the Canaanite woman: A story of reversal," *Journal of Theta Alpha Kappa* 35.2 (Fall 2011): 16, 13.

11. Elaine M. Wainwright, "Of Dogs and Women: Ethology and Gender in Ancient Healing," in *Miracles Revisited: New Testament Miracle Stories and Their Concepts of Reality,* eds., Stefan Alkier, and Annette Weissenrieder (Berlin/Boston: De Gruyter, 2013), 56.

12. Elaine M. Wainwright, "Of Dogs and Women," 56.

13. L. J. Lawrence, "Reading Matthew's Gospel with Deaf Culture" in Nicole Wilkinson Duran, and James F. Grimshaw, eds. *Matthew: Texts @ Contexts Series* (Minneapolis: Fortress, 2013), 268.

14. J. Martin C. Scott, "Matthew 15:21–28: A Test-Case for Jesus' Manners." *JSNT* 19.63 (Jan 1997): 27.

15. Donaldson, "Gospel Hauntings," 104.

16. Alan H. Cadwallader, "Surprised by faith: A centurion and a Canaanite query the limits of Jesus and the disciples," In Alan Cadwallader, *Pieces of Ease and Grace: Biblical Essays on Sexuality and Welcome* (Adelaide: ATF, 2013), 86.

17. Lawrence, "Crumb trails," 268.

18. Musa W. Shomanah Dube, *Postcolonial Feminist Interpretation of the Bible* (St. Louis: Chalice, 2000), 148.

19. Dube, *Postcolonial Feminist Interpretation,* 147.

20. Gullotta, "Among Dogs and Disciples," 330, 331. While others have also seen links with Rahab, I reference these only in direct relation to my own argument.

21. Paul Alexander, "Raced, gendered, faithed, and sexed," *Pneuma* 35.3 (2013): 330, https://doi.org/10.1163/15700747-12341364.

22. Anita Monro argues that Justa has been considered dangerous through being "sexually aggressive" ("Alterity and the Canaanite Woman: A Postmodern Feminist Theological Reflection on Political Action." *Colloquium* 26.1 [May 1994]: 37). Cadwallader explores associations between "Canaanite" and the term "harlot" because of Justa's public call ("Surprised by faith," 91, 92).

23. Lawrence, "Crumb trails," 268, 270.

24. Dube, *Postcolonial Feminist Interpretation,* 147, 148.

25. Leticia A. Guardiola-Sáenz, "Borderless Women and Borderless Texts: A Cultural Reading of Matthew 15:21–28." *Semeia* 78 (1997): 73, fn 2.

26. Scott, "Matthew," 27.

27. Gullotta, "Among Dogs and Disciples," 334.
28. Gullotta, "Among Dogs and Disciples," 334.
29. Elaine Wainwright, "A Voice from the Margin: Reading Matthew 15:21–28 in an Australian Feminist Key," in *Reading from this Place, Vol. 2: Social Location and Biblical Interpretation in Global Perspective.* Edited by Fernando F. Segovia & Mary Ann Tolbert (Minneapolis: Fortress, 1995), 143.
30. Monro, "Alterity," 37.
31. Monro, "Alterity," 39.
32. Monro, "Alterity," 41.
33. Kara J. Lyons-Pardue, "A Syrophoenician Becomes a Canaanite: Jesus Exegetes the Canaanite Woman in Matthew." *Journal of Theological Interpretation* 13.2 (2019): 246, 247.
34. Guardiola-Sáenz, "Borderless Women," 76.
35. Guardiola-Sáenz, "Borderless Women," 76.
36. Baffes, "Jesus and the Canaanite woman," 20, 21.
37. Cadwallader, "Surprised by faith," 100.
38. Alexander, "Raced," 330, 332.
39. Alexander, "Raced," 333.
40. Dube, *Postcolonial Feminist Interpretation*, 177.
41. Daniel S. Schipani, "Transformation in the Borderlands: A Study of Matthew 15:21–28," *Vision* 2.2 (Fall 2001): 21.
42. Musa W. Dube, "Boundaries and Bridges: Journeys of a Postcolonial Feminist in Biblical Studies," in *Journal of the European Society of Women in Theological Research* 22 (2014): 155.
43. Lawrence, "Reading Matthew's Gospel," 160.
44. James A. Metzger and James P. Grimshaw. "Reading Matthew's Healing Narratives from the Perspectives of the Caregiver and the Disabled," in *Matthew: Texts @ Contexts*, Eds. Nicole Wilkinson Duran and James P. Grimshaw (Minneapolis: Fortress, 2013): 136.
45. Donaldson, "Gospel Hauntings," 101.
46. Donaldson, "Gospel Hauntings," 101.
47. Donaldson, "Gospel Hauntings," 101.
48. Mitzi Smith, "Race, Gender, and the Politics of 'Sass': Reading Mark 7: 24–30 through a Womanist Lens of Intersectionality and Inter(con)textuality," in *Womanist Interpretations of the Bible: Expanding the Discourse,* edited by Gay L. Byron, and Vanessa Lovelace, Semeia Studies 85 (Atlanta: SBL, 2016), 103.
49. Smith, "Race, Gender, and the Politics of 'Sass,'" 102.
50. Metzger and Grimshaw, "Reading Matthew's Healing Narratives," 133.
51. Metzger and Grimshaw, "Reading Matthew's Healing Narratives," 133.
52. Metzger and Grimshaw, "Reading Matthew's Healing Narratives," 3.
53. Metzger and Grimshaw, "Reading Matthew's Healing Narratives," 135.
54. Metzger and Grimshaw, "Reading Matthew's Healing Narratives," 137, 138.
55. Metzger and Grimshaw, "Reading Matthew's Healing Narratives," 138.
56. Donaldson, "Gospel Hauntings," 98, 99, 102.
57. Donaldson, "Gospel Hauntings," 101.

58. Lawrence, "Reading Matthew's Gospel," 272, 273.
59. Donaldson, "Gospel Hauntings," 102, 103.
60. Nancy L. Eiesland, *The disabled God: Toward a Liberatory Theology of Disability* (Nashville: Abingdon, 1994), 25.
61. Smith, "Race, Gender, and the Politics of 'Sass,'" 102.
62. Donaldson, "Gospel Hauntings," 100.
63. Lawrence, "Crumb trails," 270, 272.
64. Her name is altered to protect privacy.
65. Tim was diagnosed with Prader-Willi Syndrome in 1988. I have Tim's explicit permission to talk about our story, but I recognise that only Tim can truly tell his own story.
66. Lyons-Pardue, "A Syrophoenician Woman," 242.
67. Smith, "Race, Gender, and the Politics of 'Sass,'" 110.
68. Smith, "Race, Gender, and the Politics of 'Sass,'" 110.
69. Guardiola-Sáenz, "Borderless Women," 77.
70. Guardiola-Sáenz, "Borderless Women," 77.
71. Daniel Patte, "The Canaanite woman and Jesus: Surprising models of discipleship (Matt. 15:21–28)." In Ingrid R. Kitzberger, ed. *Transformative encounters: Jesus and women re-viewed* (Leiden: Brill, 2000), 35, 41.
72. Patte, "The Canaanite woman," 35.
73. Craig Anthony Rubano, "Where Do the Mermaids Stand? Toward a 'Gender-Creative' Pastoral Sensibility." *Pastoral Psychology* 65.6 (Dec 2016): 829.
74. I note Dorothee Soelle's view that theologians have an "intolerable passion" for finding explanation and reasoning when silence would be the appropriate response (*Suffering* (Philadelphia: Fortress, 1975), 19, 20).
75. Radha S. Hegde, "Narratives of silence: Rethinking gender, agency, and power from the communication experiences of battered women in South India," *Communication Studies* 47:4 (1996) 309.
76. Hegde, "Narratives of Silence," 312.
77. Hegde, "Narratives of Silence," 307.
78. Lawrence, "Reading Matthew's Gospel," 160.
79. Hegde, "Narratives of Silence," 313.
80. Hegde, "Narratives of Silence," 310.
81. Hegde, "Narratives of Silence," 311.
82. Valerie Ranee Landfair, "Complicity and silence: How Lament Could Lead us to a Better Place," in "*Womanist Theology: Unravelling the Double Bind of Racism and Sexism," Mutuality Magazine* (September 05, 2020): 25.
83. Soelle, *Suffering*, 32.
84. Soelle, *Suffering*, 12, 16.
85. Landfair, "Complicity and silence," 27.
86. Kerrie Handasyde, Rebekah Pryor, and Cathryn McKinney, eds. *Contemporary Feminist Theologies: Power, Authority, Love* (New York: Routledge, 2021), 11/193 eBook.
87. Cadwallader alludes to this as same gender relationship ("Surprised by faith," 91, 92).

88. Royal commission into Violence, Abuse, Neglect, and Exploitation of Peoples with a Disability. https://disability.royalcommission.gov.au/system/files/exhibit/EXP.0020.0001.0001.pdf.

89. Charlotte Strauss Swanson, & Dawn Szymanski, "From pain to power: An exploration of activism, the #Metoo movement, and healing from sexual assault trauma," *Journal of Counselling Psychology* 67 (2020): 653–657.

Chapter 6

Translating Leviathan, Talking Back to God, Doing Public Theology from Below

Gerald O. West

"The crisis" that drives the poetry of the book of Job "is not about God's power," argues Bruce Birch. "It is about God's justice."[1] Yet, when God finally does enter the protracted debate between Job and his friends, "[i]t is as though God has no interest in Job—no interest in justice."[2] The justice question that drives the theological debate between Job and his three (or four) friends seems to disappear, replaced instead by an assertion of God's power. When Job responds to God's response to him, in the enigmatic 42:1–6, "the pivotal point of the entire drama," Job's response "may be yielding to power without conceding the point of justice," argues Birch. "Or it may be an ironic statement, wherein God misses the irony that the listener is intended to perceive."[3] Or, as I will argue, this response to God's show of power may reflect a Job, in alliance with Leviathan, continuing to talk back to God about injustice, summoning forth a different God. God must answer the justice question; simply asserting power does not answer the justice question. Is God's power just power?

FROM ABOVE: DODGING JUSTICE

John Calvin too, the Genevan Reformer, is among interpreters of the book of Job who locate justice as the central concept of the book of Job. Calvin devoted considerable time to grappling with God's justice in a series of sermons in 1554 on the book of Job. "In his search for justice," Susan Schreiner argues, "Calvin's Job came face to face with the darker side of God."[4] To describe this "disquieting realization," Schreiner continues, Calvin develops a theory of "double justice," which includes both "created or ordinary justice, which is revealed in the Law (*ordinaire, iustice manifeste*)" and "'secret justice' (*iustice cachee, secrette*), which surpasses the Law and is incomprehensible to human reason."[5] In Calvin's own words: "But there is another kind of justice which is most strange to us, namely, if God willed to treat us not according to the Law but as he justly wills to act."[6] God's justice may be a form of justice that neither Job nor we recognise as justice. But, I will ask, what kind of justice is it if we do not recognise it as justice?

Similarly, the Peruvian liberation theologian, Gustavo Gutiérrez, asserts: "The justice of God has been the main subject of the debate."[7] What is it then, Gutiérrez concludes, "that Job has understood" when he speaks in 42:1–6?[8] Is it, "That justice does not reign in the world God has created? No. The truth that he has grasped and that has lifted him to the level of contemplation is that justice alone does not have the final say about how we are to speak of God."[9] God's love and God's grace have the final say: "Only when we have come to realize that God's love is freely bestowed do we enter fully and definitively into the presence of the God of faith. Grace is not opposed to the quest for justice nor does it play it down; on the contrary, it gives it its full meaning."[10] Gutiérrez, we note here, brings the book of Job into dialogue with the New Testament. "As always in the Bible," he says, "the new and unparalleled fact of Christ brings a rupture but at the same time establishes a continuity. The poet's [Job's] insight continues to be valid for us: the gratuitousness of God's love is the framework within which the requirement of practicing justice is to be located."[11] What if, as I will argue, we refuse to follow this canonical shift, remaining with Job and Leviathan?

This essay lingers a little longer with the book of Job, especially with Leviathan (and its companion, Behemoth), wondering not what Christ may have to offer by way of our understanding of Job and justice 'from above,' but what Job and justice, via Leviathan, may have to offer to our understanding of Christ 'from below.' What if we give up defending God? What if we defend justice instead? Put differently, what if we return to the core Third World theology question: "The question about God in the world of the oppressed is not knowing whether God exists or not, but knowing on which side God is."[12] This is the justice question in another guise, as is Neil Thorogood's powerful postcolonial image, "There Must be a God Somewhere" (2021, see Figure 1.2 on page 8).

In his first response speech to Job, his friend Eliphaz chides Job: "Remember now, who perished being innocent? Or where were the just destroyed?" (Job 4:7).[13] If we can remember just one such person then God must respond to the justice question.

FROM BELOW: JOB'S TURNING TO THE ANIMALS AND THE MONSTERS

"The poetic dialogue of the Book of Job (Job 3–31) may be read, in part," argues Paul Cho, "as Job's halting, sometimes inspired, attempt to give expression to his traumatic experience and to his evolving understanding of himself within that experience."[14] In the poetic dialogues, Cho continues, "we see traditional language fail to provide Job with adequate resources to describe his turmoil. Job consequently turns to the animal world and, time and again, compares himself to animals under duress from entrapment and mortal danger."[15] Cho recognises, with other scholars, that while Job draws on analogies from the human and vegetation worlds to express his experience and sense of injustice, "it is only among animals that he ultimately finds metaphorical kinship."[16] Cho insists that "the animal imagery is more than expressive. Job is devolving into an animal,"[17] "a brother of jackals/ And a friend of ostriches" (30:29).[18]

The prevailing picture Job invokes is "the brutal reality" of animal life, "marked by struggle and conflict: prey caught in traps (13:27; 19:6), the hunted unable to flee the hunter (6:4; 7:12; 16:9–17), and the hungry in pursuit of prey (9:26; 10:16; 29:17)."[19] "In fact," Cho summarises, "by the end of his wide-ranging search for a language adequate to the task of describing himself in the terrifying world, Job comes to understand the world as a zoological dystopia and himself as a helpless animal trapped in that world of horrifying predators and trembling prey."[20] Job's own experience of injustice, I would argue, enables him to see the animal world differently, recognising it no longer as a monovocal testimony to the just order of creation and the coherent source of Wisdom theology.

Furthermore, Job's experience has revealed to him that the reality experienced by animals is a reality shared by humans. In the midst of Job 16:7–17, the poetic stanza that Cho refers to as "[t]he most graphic depiction of Job's sense of being a hunted, captured, and gutted animal,"[21] we hear "God hands me over to the unjust; /And he throws me into the hands of the wicked."[22] This passage, Cho comments, "reads like a lament against enemies, against whom psalmists usually call God to act." "The problem for Job, however," Cho continues, "is that God is in league with his enemies. In fact, God is their ringleader."[23] Reflecting on lived experience,[24] as Wisdom theology summons us to do, reveals, Job now understands, God's world riven with injustice.

Cho focuses on Job's desire for death within this world of dystopian injustice.[25] My focus is different. While recognising Job's desire for death (in a world raked with injustice), evident in his very first speech, a soliloquy (Job 3), Job has a related desire: a desire to speak out against injustice and those who defend the unjust order of things. This includes his friends and God. We listen in on this dimension of Job's desire in his second speech (6–7), the first of his speeches provoked by his friend Eliphaz's response (Job 4–5) to his clearly articulated desire for death in an unjust world (Job 3). Job responds, in turn, beginning the poetic cycles of debate between Job and his friends (and God), provoked by Eliphaz's defence of an unjust system. "Remember now," argues Eliphaz, "who ever perished being innocent? Or where were the righteous destroyed?" (Job 4:7). The reader knows, of course, that the story of Job is a story of the innocent perishing and the righteous being destroyed. The book of Job does not dispute this reality, but seeks to understand it. Job, at least, refuses to give up on seeking to understand this reality. His friends do not even try, simply restating a theological understanding that no longer reflects reality. They deny reality rather than question their theology. But Job does question the theology he grew up with and once propounded (Job 4:3): "I desire to argue with God" (Job 13:3), Job insists, "I will argue my ways before God" (Job 13:15). "I will say to God, 'Do not condemn me; let me know why you contend with me. Is it right for you indeed to oppress, to reject the labour of your hands, and to look favourably on the schemes of the wicked?'" (Job 10:2–3).

In Job's first extended contestation with this friends (Job 6–7), Job exegetes unjust reality and the response it evokes in him. Job's own experience of unjust reality enables him to identify with the injustice of others: "Is not humankind forced to labour on earth, and are not their days like the days of a hired worker? As a slave who pants for the shade, and as a hired worker who eagerly waits for his wages, so am I allotted months of vanity, and nights of trouble are appointed me" (Job 7:1–3). Though previously economically prosperous, Job now recognises a shared reality with those who are economically exploited. Overwhelmed by this recognition of reality as unjust, Job veers between despair (7:6), the desire for death (7:9, 15), and resistant protest (7:12–21). Turning the direction of his discourse away from Eliphaz, he addresses God directly. Significantly, in talking back to God, Job turns once again to the animals, or rather to the monsters: "Am I the sea, or the sea monster, that you set a guard over me?" (7:12). As Cho eloquently argues, Job's "shocking self-comparison to cosmic monsters" in this rhetorical question, "Am I Sea or Dragon / that you set a guard over me?" (7:12),[26]

> hints at the potential cosmic significance of Job—that is, of Job as a new datum in the cosmos that questions and challenges God and the world of God's creation, just as Sea, within the theological landscape of the Hebrew Bible, continually threatens cosmic order so as to necessitate that God "set a boundary that they may not pass, / that they may not again cover the earth" (Ps. 104:9, NRSV; cf. Job 38:8–11). Job as Sea/ Dragon represents at once the shattered viability of

traditional answers to the question of anthropology and the search for a radical redefinition of what it means to be human after trauma.[27]

For a moment here, Job recognises a kinship with cosmic forces (Sea) and mythical creatures (Dragon) who resist God. Heeding his wife's theological insight and summons (2:9), Job is now prepared to "curse God and die," to call God out, if indeed God sustains injustice. She 'dares' Job to declare publicly how they experience—their story[28] of—God's injustice.

FROM BELOW: GOD'S TURNING TO THE ANIMALS AND THE MONSTERS

As Cho and the attentive reader note, God too turns to the animals and the monsters, concluding the God speeches with the summoning of Leviathan, an embodiment of Sea-and-Dragon. Though Job may question his likeness to Leviathan, God does not. Though Cho emphasises God's embrace of Leviathan,[29] I discern a more apprehensive and tensive relationship. God knows that Leviathan bites back.

Imagining, and so translating לִוְיָתָן (Leviathan), requires readers of Job to make a decision concerning the relationship between God and Leviathan as well as between Job and Leviathan. Translations of Job which choose to leave the term untranslated invite us as readers to imagine. But translators often cannot resist the temptation to intervene with a semantic choice, limiting and perhaps even misleading readers. When God turns to לִוְיָתָן (41:1/Hebrew 40:25), most English translations used in South Africa retain the Hebrew transliteration, 'Leviathan,' as do the 1893 and 1959 isiZulu translations, but the Afrikaans translations, both the 1953 and 1983 translations, use 'krokodil' (crocodile), as do the 1975 and 1996 isiXhosa translations (ingwenya). The imaginary becomes ordinary in such translations. Monsters are domesticated. Prophetic theology becomes church theology.[30]

Fortunately, artists have released לִוְיָתָן from captured translation. As I have analysed more fully in my contribution to the The Visual Commentary on Scripture (VCS) project,[31] artists as diverse as William Blake (1825–26), Trevor Makhoba (2001), and Anish Kapoor (2011), have grappled with 'Leviathan.' Blake's engravings imagine Leviathan circumscribed and constrained by God's power; Makhoba's linoleum cut imagines Leviathan about to consume those with HIV and AIDS, perhaps as God's agent but hopefully about to be restrained by God; and Kapoor's massive PVC installation draws us into the very body of Leviathan, devouring us, but inviting us to view the world and God from 'Leviathan's' perspective. Both Makhoba and Kapoor recognise the autonomy and power of Leviathan. Leviathan is not quite in God's control.

The poetry of the book of Job too, both as Job reflects on 'Leviathan' in the guise of Sea-and-Dragon (7:12) and as God represents 'Leviathan' (41:1–34; Hebrew 40:25–41:26) alongside its companion monster 'Behemoth' (40:15–24), creates space for the reader to imagine 'Leviathan.'

As I have said, when God responds to Job, God too turns to the animal world. "After offering a tour of the edges of the cosmos," Scott Jones argues, "YHWH turns to the animal kingdom for instruction, as Job and his friends have done throughout the book."[32] In the first God speech (38:39–39:30), "YYHW's world is filled with powerful creatures that he [sic] has domesticated and now cares for," with an emphasis on animals "found at the borders of civilization."[33] While Job's reflections on Leviathan-and/as-Sea-and-Dragon are fleeting, in the second God speech (40:15–41:34; Hebrew 40:15–41:26), God engages extensively with these most magnificent and most full of power creatures, summoning them forth before Job in pride and love,[34] but also, I would argue, with some anxiety.

Behemoth, "the first of the ways/ works of God," requires that "his maker bring near his sword" (Job 40:19); the Hebrew invites a variety of translations, but most imply apprehension on the part of God and only partial control. "Can anyone capture him when he is on watch, with barbs can anyone pierce his nose?" (Job 40:24), invites the question of whether this 'anyone' includes God. Similarly, though once again the Hebrew is unclear (and uncomfortable), Leviathan too inhabits power over which even God has only partial control: "No one is so fierce that he dares to arouse him; who then is he that can stand before me /him?" (Job 41:10; Hebrew 41:2).

Remarkably, just as Job briefly imagined himself as Leviathan, "the Sea, or the Sea Monster" (7:12), it is God now who identifies Job with Behemoth: "Behold now, Behemoth, which I made with /as you" (Job 40:15). "These creatures," both Behemoth and Leviathan, argues Jones, "have didactic significance, and Job is to view them as a mirror of himself."[35] There is even a hint in Job's first response to Eliphaz (discussed above) where he briefly imagines but then rejects a likeness with Behemoth: "What is my strength, that I should wait? And what is my end, that I should endure? Is my strength the strength of stones, or is my flesh bronze?" (Job 6:11–12). God picks up on this image when boasting about Behemoth: "Behold now, his strength in his loins and his power in the muscles of his belly. He moves his tail like a cedar; the sinews of his thighs are bound together. His bones are tubes of bronze; his limbs are like bars of iron. He is the first of the ways /works of God; let his maker bring near his sword" (Job 40:16–19). "It is no coincidence," Jones argues, "that immediately after Job confesses his smallness and insignificance (קלתי) [40:4], YHWH instructs Job with the two most corpulent, powerful, and exalted creatures in existence."[36] Jones' focus is on Job's body and virility, an important contribution to our reflections, but not my emphasis here. In resisting protest against injustice Job has moments when he imagines himself as an irruptive presence, like Leviathan and like Behemoth, disrupting the order of an unjust world defended by his friends and sustained by God. God's reply, however, offers Job another perspective, a summons by God for Job to embrace (and embody) the irruptive and disruptive power of Behemoth and Leviathan.

FROM BELOW: GOD AND JOB COLLABORATE

But what of Job 42:1–6?[37] Most translations and most biblical scholarship has Job 'retracting' and 'repenting.' My argument thus far in this essay offers a rather different reading. While Job certainly reconsiders, I do not think that Job repents, recants, or retracts in his concluding speech (42:1–6).[38] Notwithstanding the syntactic, semantic, translation, and composition complexities of these verses,[39] I cannot see the lamenting, protesting, and resisting Job we have come to know in the poetry reacting in these ways to God's responses (38–41).[40] Job has never been in any doubt that God is controlling and powerful; he has experienced in his family, community, and body the effects of God's control and power. What Job does not understand is the logic of God's control (as just) or God's exercise of power (as just).[41]

Leo Perdue also wonders whether a contrite and repentant Job fits with a character who is, so far, full of integrity.[42] Though, Perdue admits, the orientation of verses 2–6 is one of praise,[43] "what is not rejected is the process of engaging in lament, indictment, and assault which have led him and the implied audience to this point."[44] Similarly, Carol Newsom maintains that Job refuses "not to see the rent at the heart of world."[45] David Clines concurs, arguing that in Job's first speech within the divine speeches (40:3–5), Job "does not withdraw a word he has said, he does not admit that God is in the right or that he is in the wrong, he does not confess to any sins or apologize for what he has said."[46] Clines recognises too that the nodal verse of Job's second speech within the divine speeches (42:1–6) is verse 6, in which Job "faces two ways: in respect to the past, he has had no satisfaction, but he will draw a line beneath it; in respect of the future, he intends to live as a social being surrounded by his support group, no longer as an outcast on the ash heap."[47] Crucially, for Clines, it is only in the legal sense that Job "submits." He formally withdraws the formal lawsuit he lodged against Yahweh. Since, Clines continues, "he has done no wrong, he cannot 'repent,' but having been in mourning he now brings the period of mourning to an end by 'accepting consolation,' for his lost children as well as for the loss of his honor, a consolation that is being offered to him both from the friends and (in his own way) from Yahweh."[48]

According to Clines, Job "acknowledges the omnipotence of Yahweh (v2)," "he accepts that he has intruded into the area of 'marvels,' in which he has no competence (v3b)," and "now that he has heard the utterances Yahweh has addressed personally to him (v5), he abandons his suit against God (v6a) together with his mourning and he intends to resume his normal life (v6b)."[49] While I concur with the second and third points, I wonder about the first. In my reading of the God speeches, I have wondered whether God-self is not only exploring the limits of Job's (and so humanity's) power, but also the limits of God's power. Perhaps the God speeches, particularly the discourses on Behemoth (40:15–24) and Leviathan (41:1–34), probe the limits of God's power.

This more reflective God, as I have argued in this essay, summons Job to embrace the irruptive and disruptive power of Behemoth and Leviathan, creatures who constantly remind God of the limits of God's power and of the need to continue to work for a more just order. This God summons Job to collaborate with God in the unfinished business of bringing about a just order.[50] The God speeches become, in this reading, a call to Job to join God in the ongoing and incomplete work of redemption. Given that Job quotes, in an adapted form (42:2b), from Genesis 11:6, and that this text rejects the hubris of human power,[51] perhaps these same words in Job's mouth question God's power. So I would translate 42:6 as follows:

> Consequently, [given what you, God, have said, particularly about Behemoth and Leviathan] I reconsider [my view that you are fully powerful and fully in control], and I turn from [lamenting in] dust and ashes [in order to join you in your ongoing work of redemption and in order to participate in a more just community and a community that now has a different theological understanding of your power and control].

FROM BELOW: DOING PUBLIC THEOLOGY

My translation not only acknowledges the integrity of the poetic Job, but it also aligns the Job of the poetry with the Job of the prose, especially the concluding prose 'epilogue.' In the prose prologue Job's wife provokes Job to find his voice (2:9); in the poetry Job finds his resisting voice; in the poetry God affirms Job's irruptive likeness with Behemoth and Leviathan; in the poetry Job accepts God's limitations and God's summons; in the prose God and Job (and the narrator) collaborate in disrupting the bankrupt retributive theology of the three friends and in reconstituting an inclusive and just community.

My reading of 42:6, though revisionary, enacts the kind of connection Cho is looking for in his reading. "That is," he argues, "we should expect 42:6 to enact a transition from the poetry to the prose, as opposed to marking a disjunction between them."[52] However, it is Cho's alternative account of the compositional history of Job which enables him to conclude that Job both does not repent and does repent: "Job does not repent of what he said in conversation with his friends. In fact, God affirms Job in relation to his friends and restores him to honor in human society (42:7–10). But Job does repent of what he said in conversation with his God."[53] Cho does not discern in the book of Job a God who betrays God-self. I do. Cho is correct in stating: "If we maintain that Job does not repent in 42:6, then we would have a God who, after rebuking Job, affirms a still defiant Job. That is, the cost of holding on to a Job who does not repent—because for Job to repent would be tantamount to self-betrayal—is a God who betrays himself [sic]."[54]

In his reading of an earlier draft of this essay Jione Havea asks at this point, "Does it matter if God is (un)just?" My argument is that God must answer this question. If God does not care about justice then we will have to work around God;[55] if God does care about justice then we must collaborate with God. Avoiding the question of justice by asserting God's power is not sufficient. Job, I, and others need a clearer answer than God seems willing to give. Yet I discern, via Leviathan, a glimpse of a God who does care about justice but who has been ensnared so thoroughly in Job's friends' church theology-type dogmatics that God finds it difficult to speak clearly. Yet speak about justice God must.

Here are theological resources for doing public theology, from below. My reading of Job 42:7–11, discussed more fully in other publications,[56] recognises that the restoration of a more just community, rejecting theologies of retribution (42:7–10) and affirming inclusion and economic equality (42:11), requires a public recognition that God's power and control is constrained and that God has summoned us to collaborate with God's ongoing and as yet incomplete project for a just creation. Job's family and community include and restore Job (socially and economically) *because* they now understand God's limitations and so complicity with an unjust world:

> Then all his brothers and all his sisters and all who had known him before came to him, and they ate bread with him in his house; and they consoled him and comforted him for all the adversities that Yahweh had brought on him. And each one gave him one piece of money, and each a ring of gold (Job 42:11).

Crucial to this recognition is the public nature of God's confession in 42:7, the public performance of repentance by the friends who have claimed a different theological identity for God in 42:8, and the public collaboration of Job with God and God with Job in 42:9. These public discourses and rites unsettle Job's community, having revealed a God their church-type theology had not prepared them for, though which their lived realities may have incipiently recognised.[57] A clearer sense of where God stands with respect to justice overcomes their earlier reluctance to include and collaborate with a dis-eased Job:

> Then all his brothers and all his sisters and all who had known him before came to him, and they ate bread with him in his house; and they consoled him and comforted him for all the injustice that Yahweh had brought on him. And each one gave him one piece of money, and each a ring of gold (Job 42:11).

God may join their collaborative reconstruction of local community, but while they wait to hear more fully and see more clearly God's response to the justice question, they are empowered by the public realm contestation to embrace Job and through him each other.

The theological impulses for this public theology, a public theology that confronts injustice and an as yet unjust God, arise from below, from Behemoth and Leviathan (and from Emmanuel Garibay's image, "Teolohiya (Theology)" (2021; see Figure 1.1 on page 5), and continue their theological trajectory into the public cry of Jesus on the cross: "My God, my God, why have you forsaken me?" (Mark 15:34). My God, my God, (why) have you deserted justice?

NOTES

1. Bruce C. Birch et al., *A theological introduction to the Old Testament* (Nashville: Abingdon, 1999), 404.
2. Birch et al., *A theological introduction to the Old Testament*, 404.
3. Birch et al., *A theological introduction to the Old Testament*, 404.
4. Susan E Schreiner, "Exegesis and double justice in Calvin's sermons on Job," *Church history* 58.3 (1989): 327.
5. Schreiner, "Exegesis and double justice in Calvin's sermons on Job," 327–28.
6. Cited in Schreiner, "Exegesis and double justice in Calvin's sermons on Job," 332.
7. Gustavo Gutiérrez, *On Job: God-talk and the suffering of the innocent* (Maryknoll: Orbis, 1991), 72.
8. Gutiérrez, *On Job: God-talk and the suffering of the innocent*, 87.
9. Gutiérrez, *On Job: God-talk and the suffering of the innocent*, 87.
10. Gutiérrez, *On Job: God-talk and the suffering of the innocent*, 87.

11. Gutiérrez, *On Job: God-talk and the suffering of the innocent*, 89.

12. See the "Final Statement" of The Ecumenical Association of Third World Theologians (EATWOT) in Virginia Fabella and Sergio Torres, eds., *Doing theology in a divided world* (Maryknoll: Orbis, 1985), 190.

13. All translations are my own or those of cited scholars, unless otherwise specified.

14. Paul K-K Cho, "'I have become a brother of jackals': Evolutionary psychology and suicide in the book of Job," *Biblical Interpretation* 27.2 (2019): 209.

15. Cho, "Evolutionary psychology and suicide in the book of Job," 209.

16. Cho, "Evolutionary psychology and suicide in the book of Job," 209–10.

17. Cho, "Evolutionary psychology and suicide in the book of Job," 210–11.

18. Cited in Cho, "Evolutionary psychology and suicide in the book of Job," 211.

19. Cho, "Evolutionary psychology and suicide in the book of Job," 214.

20. Cho, "Evolutionary psychology and suicide in the book of Job," 213.

21. Cho, "Evolutionary psychology and suicide in the book of Job," 220.

22. As translated by Cho, "Evolutionary psychology and suicide in the book of Job," 220.

23. Cho, "Evolutionary psychology and suicide in the book of Job," 221.

24. Birch et al., *A theological introduction to the Old Testament*, 374–77.

25. Cho, "Evolutionary psychology and suicide in the book of Job," 212.

26. This is Cho's translation.

27. Cho, "Evolutionary psychology and suicide in the book of Job," 216–17.

28. She tells a fuller story in the Septuagint version of the text; see Job 2:9 a-d.

29. Cho, "Evolutionary psychology and suicide in the book of Job," 217.

30. Gerald O. West, "Kairos 2000: moving beyond Church Theology," *Journal of Theology for Southern Africa* 108 (2000); Gerald O. West, "The co-optation of the Bible by 'Church Theology' in post-liberation South Africa: Returning to the Bible as a 'site of struggle,'" *Journal of Theology for Southern Africa* 157 (2017); Gerald O. West, "Reopening the churches and/as reopening the economy: Covid's uncovering of the contours of 'church theology,'" in *Doing Theology in the New Normal*, ed. Jione Havea (London: SCM, 2021).

31. https://thevcs.org/behemoth-and-leviathan.

32. Scott C. Jones, "Corporeal discourse in the book of Job," *Journal of Biblical Literature* (2013): 856.

33. Jones, "Corporeal discourse in the book of Job," 857, 58.

34. Cho, "Evolutionary psychology and suicide in the book of Job," 230–32.

35. Jones, "Corporeal discourse in the book of Job," 861. In correspondence, Paul Cho made a similar point, drawing my attention to this verse.

36. Jones, "Corporeal discourse in the book of Job," 862.

37. I return here to reflections published in Gerald O. West, "Senzeni na? Speaking of God 'what is right' and the 're-turn' of the stigmatising community in the context of HIV," *Scriptura* 116.2 (2017).

38. David J. A. Clines, *Word Biblical Commentary: Job 38–42* (Nashville: Thomas Nelson, 2011), 1218–24. This, however, is the minority analysis. The majority see a more penitent Job; see for example Kenneth Numfor Ngwa, *The hermeneutics of the*

'*happy ending*' *in Job 42:7–17* (Berlin and New York: Walter de Gruyter, 2005), 55, 128; Gutiérrez, *On Job: God-talk and the suffering of the innocent*, 86–87. Cho provides a useful overview, as well as his own nuanced analysis, in Paul K-K Cho, "Job the penitent: Whether and why Job repents (Job 42:6)," in *Landscapes of Korean and Korean American biblical interpretation*, ed. John Ahn (Atlanta: SBL, 2019).

39. Ellen van Wolde, "Job 42,1–6: the reversal of Job," in *The book of Job*, ed. W.A.M. Beuken (Leuven: Leuven University Press, 1994); Cho, "Job the penitent."

40. David Clines encourages the reader not to read the difficult parts of the poetry in ways that are not 'in character' for Job; see David J.A. Clines, *Word Biblical Commentary: Job 1–20* (Dallas: Word, 1989). From an alternative compositional perspective on the book of Job see also Cho, "Job the penitent," 161–62.

41. Birch et al., *A theological introduction to the Old Testament*, 404–06.

42. Leo G. Perdue, *Wisdom in revolt:* M*etaphorical theology in the book of Job* (Sheffield: Almond, 1991), 233.

43. Perdue, *Wisdom in revolt*, 234.

44. Perdue, *Wisdom in revolt*, 236.

45. Carol A. Newsom, *The book of Job:* A *contest of moral imaginations* (Oxford: Oxford University Press, 2003), 257.

46. Clines, *Word Biblical Commentary: Job 38–42*, 1212.

47. Clines, *Word Biblical Commentary: Job 38–42*, 1212.

48. Clines, *Word Biblical Commentary: Job 38–42*, 1218.

49. Clines, *Word Biblical Commentary: Job 38–42*, 1212.

50. There are hints of this in Perdue, *Wisdom in revolt*, 226, 32.

51. Perdue, *Wisdom in revolt*, 234.

52. Cho, "Job the penitent," 162.

53. Cho, "Job the penitent," 174.

54. Cho, "Job the penitent," 163, where Cho's use of 'himself' is acknowledging the grammar of this ancient text.

55. See Robert Heinlein's evocation of such a God in his novel, *Job, a comedy of justice* (New York: Ballantine, 1984).

56. See also Gerald O. West, "Between text and trauma: Reading Job with people living with HIV," in *Bible through the lens of trauma*, ed. Elizabeth C. Boase and Frechette Christopher G. (Atlanta: SBL, 2016); West, "Senzeni na? Speaking of God 'what is right' and the 're-turn' of the stigmatising community in the context of HIV."

57. I draw here on the sense of 'incipient' analysed so carefully by James R. Cochrane, *Circles of dignity: Community wisdom and theological reflection* (Minneapolis: Fortress, 1999).

Chapter 7

Sitting and Weeping by the Rivers of Babylon

Miguel A. De La Torre

> *Beside the rivers of Miami we sat and wept when we remembered la Habana. There on the palm trees we hung our conga drums and maracas. Our oppressors asked us for songs, our tormentors demanded songs of joy. "Sing," they said, "Sing us one of the songs of Cuba, sing us some mambo." How can we sing our rumba in a pagan land? If I forget you, mi Habana, may my right-hand wither. May my tongue cling to the roof of my mouth if I do not remember you, if I do not consider la Habana my greatest joy. Remember, Lord, what the yanquis did . . . O daughter of Babylon, doomed to destruction, happy is the one who repays you according to what you have done to us. Happy is the one who seizes your infants and dashes them against the rocks.*[1]

Both the poet of the 137th psalm in the Hebrew Bible and myself suffer from a post-traumatic stress caused by being ripped from our homes. Although some 2,600 years separate us, we share a similar experience and can thus relate to each other's pain of being cast out of the land which witnessed our birth. Forever foreigners, sojourners who will never belong *aquí* (here) or *allá* (there). How can the psalmist, or me, ever find fulfillment *aquí*, when *allá* continuously beckons for our return? How can either of us ever die in peace when our hearts were left behind, buried in the land of our parents? Since going into exile, I left behind the bright blue skies of my island which never again will hang above my head, or her ocean waters which provided its warm loving embrace. How can either the psalmist or I forge an identity in exile? What if my love for la Habana remains stronger than my allegiance to the Babylon in where I find myself? How can I call myself a Cuban without a Cuba? Never again will I be able to lay on her hot tropical beaches, my bones destined to be interned in a cold foreign land which never accepted me, despising my very presence. Perhaps there can never be a return to one's native land, only fractured memories upon which it is recreated—a new way of (re)membering which conveniently forgets reality.

WEPT WHEN WE REMEMBERED LA HABANA

José was not very educated; but he was a hard worker with callous hands. He took pride in building things, making a living as a carpenter. Times were hard, liberties curtailed, and taxes high. Even though his homeland suffered the indignity of a foreign military presence, he kept his focus on providing for his growing family. He had little time, and less energy to become involved with those revolutionary groups doing maneuvers in the hills surrounding his town. A newlywed for just a few months, his wife María already gave birth to a child, a healthy boy who was rumored not to be his. José didn't care, he loved the child as his own. One night, José sprinted through the sleeping town terrified, hoping he wasn't too late. He needed to reach his makeshift home and save his new family from certain death! Bursting into the hut which he called home, he approached his wife sleeping on the dirt floor on a straw mat. "*Despierta María*," José silently whispered as he gently shook her. "A messenger warned me that *la milicia*, the militia, is coming for us. We are in grave danger of disappearing like so many others! *Apúrate*, hurry up, we must leave this very moment, we must go into exile away from the reaches of this brutal dictatorship." José wasn't political, but that didn't matter. His family was wanted. There was no time to pack belongings nor personal mementoes. No time to bid farewell to friends and family. Just moments before the National Guard arrived at his home, José took his small family into *el exilio*. Wearing only the clothes on their backs, they would illegally cross borders to enter a foreign country. Even though they could not speak the language, nor understand the cultural idiosyncrasies, they, at least, would be physically safe. For this poor family, their salvation laid *south* of the border.[2]

Over two millenniums ago this family, comprised of José, María, and baby Jesús arrived as political refugees in Egypt, fleeing Herod's tyrannical regime. Over sixty years ago my own father came home to his wife, my mother, with similar news. His involvement with the former political regime marked him for death by new government. He would face a firing squad if apprehended. They gathered me, their eighteen-month-old child, and headed north, arriving in the United States literally with only the clothes on their backs. I, like Jesús, was a child political refugee.

The importance of José's story seeking refuge in Egypt is lost to those privileged with citizenship. Those of us who have been undocumented in Babylon, read in this story a God actively present in the hopelessness of being uprooted. To be an alien is so important that God incarnated God's self as an alien fleeing the oppressive consequences of the empire of the time. The petit dictator Herod was tasked with ensuring profits—in the form of taxes—flowed to the Roman center. Like many Global South elites today, Herod financially benefited by signing trade agreements detrimental to his compatriots. To ask why Jesús, a colonized man, was in Egypt is to understand why Latinxs are today in the United States.

Jesús is not the only migrant found in Holy Writ. The biblical story is a story of aliens, foreigners, and sojourners. The first political refugees were Adam and Eve, forced to leave the land from which they were formed. Only those who have been torn from their homeland understand the gut-wrenching pain of being ousted from all one knows. It matters not who is at fault for expatriation and the resulting despair, distress, dispossession and disenfranchisement which follows. The tales of Abraham, Isaac, Jacob, and Joseph are the stories of aliens attempting to survive on the margins of a people who are not their own in a land which they cannot claim. If they were living today, we would probably pejoratively call them "illegals." The people who came to be called Jews are a people formed while suffering under slavery in the foreign land of Egypt. They became a nation while traversing the desert, having no land to claim as their own. They experienced exile in a far-off place called Babylon as well as disenfranchisement on their own terrain due to colonial military occupation by the foreign empire of Rome.

Many who today are refugees, like the Jews taken in captivity to Babylon (587 BCE), are forced to deal with the incomprehensible pain of being torn from one's own Eden. While sitting by the rivers of Babylon, the Jews, from the midst of their pain questioned the sovereignty of a God who would tear God's people from their homes and plant them in an alien land which despises them. A major concern for those in exile—from Adam and Eve to the patriarchs to the Jews in Babylon to Jesús to me—is what does our status as deportees mean. Does our removal from our homeland, by which our very identity is constructed, signify divine rejection, voiding any future participation in God's plan? Does resettlement in a foreign land mean assimilation to a culture perceived to be inferior to our own?

The Hebrew word for forced removal, *galut*, means more than simply the results of international forces. For those cast into the diaspora, *galut* becomes a religious condition, a condition which forces the displaced person to ask the basic theodicy question: How can a loving and powerful God allow such unbearable pain to befall God's people? The hopelessness of never returning to what was left behind makes the deeply political 137 Psalm also a deeply religious proclamation. For all the biblical wanderers, and me sitting by the rivers of Miami, faith is a means of coping with the existential situation of dislodgment, hopelessly trying to give meaning to the shame and humiliation of displacement; of still remembering as a small boy white teenagers spit on my father while calling him a spic. For here is the irony: while North Americans claim to love Jesus and welcome him into their hearts, they hate Jesús and casts him in cages located on their southern borders. To this day, refugees like me carry the emotional, spiritual, and physical stigmata caused by growing up as a spic in a culture and society that loathes my presence, consistently defining me—to this day—as less-than. I am left to wonder, did Jesús, like me, cry himself to sleep? Was he ever beaten up for speaking with a funny accent? Did he ever internalized feelings of inferiority imposed by the dominant culture? If so, then Jesús knows the anxieties and frustrations of the undocumented. And with me, Jesús wept.

SING US ONE OF THE SONGS OF CUBA

Sitting by the rivers of Babylon, refugees sing about their inability to sing. Sitting by the rivers of Miami, I join my compatriots in singing the song taught to us by Cuban exile salsa queen Celia Cruz. The song "*Cuando salí de Cuba* (When I left Cuba)" best captures and articulates the pain of our displacement. This popular Cuban ballad, written by a Chilean, rejects the reality of living on foreign soil. "Never can I die; my heart is not *aquí. Allá* it is waiting for me; it is waiting for me to return there. When I left Cuba, I left my life, I left my love. When I left Cuba, I left my heart buried there." Lourdes Casal best captures this pain when she wrote: "Exile is living where no house holds the memories of our childhood and where we cannot visit our grandmother's grave."[3] To live in *el exilio*, is to live where what was familiar to one's parents is now foreign. Even if it would be possible to return to the country of one's birth, it will never compare to the mythical imaginary land which my parents painted deep in the recesses of my brain, where I learned to cherish and love the illusion as if it was real.

To read our pain within the verses of Psalm 137 is to be stirred to the very being of our soul. We fully understand the tragic pain of sitting by the rivers of an alien land singing about our inability to sing to a God we secretly hold responsible for our pain of displacement. There is no hope of ever returning as each passing year witnesses the increase of headstones engraved with Cuban surnames in the cemeteries of Miami. Like Jews who once proclaimed, "next year in Jerusalem," we tell each other "next year in *la Habana*." Stuck in a foreign land we are tempted by the advice Jeremiah gives. In a letter to the expatriated Jews living in Babylon, he advises them to forget about their hope of returning. He instructs them: "to build houses, settle down, plant gardens and eat what they produce; [. . . they are to] work for the good of the country to which [they have been] exiled [. . .] praying on its behalf, since on its welfare [they] depend" (29:5–9).

Like some Jews in Babylon, some Cubans in the heart of the empire found opportunities which were unavailable in their homeland. Some, because of their light skin pigmentation, avoided the rabid racism of the U.S. These Cubans were able to grow rich through trade. Some, like Nehemiah, ascended political structures to hold profound power over those who did not go into Exile. What happens when one assimilates to the Babylonian cultural ethos? Many Cuban refugees placed their hope in the U.S. Babylon. Does this make them complicit with the empire's hunger for global strength made possible by the subordination of cultures and peoples they deem inferior? How does one live in Babylon without becoming a Babylonian? The prophet Jeremiah provides a contradictory clue. As Jerusalem was on the verge of falling, Jeremiah bought a plot of land (32:9–11). For him, salvation will never lay in Babylon even when he advises them to prosper there. Liberation is rooted in the homeland, on the margins of empire. Jeremiah's message is as relevant today as it was to the Babylonian Jews.

WE HUNG OUR CONGA DRUMS

Refugees, whether they be Jews or Cubans in where Babylon exists, were forced to deal with the incompressible pain of displacement. Judaism came into being in Babylon through the pain of questioning a God who would tear God's people from their homes and cast them into hostile land. Cubans also were forced to reimagine their identity, internalizing and naturalizing a false sense of belonging to overcome displacement and serve as protection from the pain of initial economic and psychological difficulties caused by uprootedness. How do I, and other refugees sitting and weeping by the rivers flowing through foreign lands make a home for ourselves? How do we construct identity out of our parent's false memories? Maybe by looking into Lacan's mirror.

In *la sagüesera* (Southwest Miami), on the fame *Calle Ocho* (Eighth Street), is a restaurant called Versailles, dubbed *el palacio de los espejos* (the mirrored palace)—an attempt to reproduce in exile a nostalgic nightspot from the homeland. What makes this restaurant unique is its mirrored walls. But Versailles is more than just a restaurant; it is the epicenter of Miami's politics. Since its opening, Cubans have gathered there to discuss politics. No politician can ever expect to win a Miami election without first visiting this sacred space for a *cafecito* with future constituents.

Growing up in Miami, my family, on most Sunday evenings, would get all dressed up, put on all the jewelry we possessed, get all perfumed, and go have dinner at Versailles. Sitting at the table in the crowded salon, I constantly saw our reflection on one of many heavily gilded mirrors. This experience of seeing myself in the mirror vividly illustrates Lacan's theory concerning the Mirror Stage. While I sit there eating my *arroz con pollo*, I see myself reflected—a secondary reflection faithful (more or less) to the likeness of the existing original self. But Lacan would propose the opposite. He would argue that the image in the mirror is truly what construct the self. My encounter with the mirror literally reverses the direction, and serves the function of forming my "I," my "I" in the diaspora. Lacan's theory describes the fact that the delusive reflection of the Cuban in the mirror constructs an Exilic Cuban 'self' captivated by the belief in the projected 'imaginary,' where both future and past is grounded within an illusion. In short, the ideal formed in the mirror situates the agency of the 'ego' in fiction, while projecting the formation of the 'self' into history.[4] This projected 'self' is one that achieved the American Dream which Jeremiah suggested to those in Babylon while looking back to the purchased plot of land left behind in a romanticized country.

My Cuban eyes see in the mirror the anticipated maturation of the power I desire to possess in Babylon and read into my history the illusion of a Cuba which never existed. Therefore, I wear my best outfit and all my jewelry, not so much to be seen by others but so that I can see what I plan to become. Striving for power in the belly of the empire creates a history where we remind ourselves that we come from an Eden; an ethereal place where every conceivable item *es mejor* (is better): where the mangos taste sweeter, the skies are bluer, the pests less bothersome. Everything *aquí* when contrasted with *allá* is found lacking. Unlike the predominate stereotypes of other immigrant groups (mainly white Europeans) leaving behind painful memories of the old country and joyfully anticipating a new country where the streets were paved with gold, Cubans, as refugees, never wanted to leave paradise for what they perceived to be an inferior culture. Like the Babylonian Jews, we rejoiced every time someone said, "Let us go to our house" (Ps 122). But as Lacan would ask, which is the illusion, the self or the reflection? Does a home exist within reality to go back to?

IF I FORGET YOU, MI HABANA

Aquí I am a spic, *allá* I am a *gusano*—a maggot. Living in the shadows of my parent's (dis)membered remembrance, I try to forget the fantasy island of my origins. Those of a certain age, who were cast into exile as children, live with a particular trauma caused by the hardships of being a refugee. Homesickness for a place that was never home, mixed with a mythological nostalgia, romanticization and an unnaturally taught hatred toward various actors blamed for our Babylonian captivity contribute to the pain of not having *any place*, of not ever being able to enjoy the island's gentle sea breezes as the brutally scorching sun finally sets at the end of the day. I live in the in-between space where both sides—the capitalists to the north and the communists to the south—rejected me. I would never be accepted *aquí* because I would always be a spic and if I was to return *allá*, I would always be a *gusano*, someone who betrayed his homeland in favor of the *yanqui* imperialists, a betrayal for which I am still held responsible, even though I could barely walk or talk when it occurred.

Not belonging *aquí* or *allá* became clear the day I returned to the island for my first visit, over half a century since I first left. One night I strolled with pride and elation down *el Paseo del Prado* of *la Habana*, a beautiful avenue containing a middle pedestrian walkway, guarded on either side by bronze lions. As I amble down the picturesque boulevard toward the bay to watch the sunset and hear *el cañonazo de las nueve*; a young, gaunt *jinetero* (hustler) suddenly appeared out of the shadows, trying to get my attention. The young man began to first hawk cigars, then rum, and finally the services of a woman or a boy. After a few minutes, it became obvious to him that I was not going to buy anything. As the *jinetero* walked away, over his left shoulder he asked, "*¿de donde eres?*—Where are you from?" Boastfully, sticking out my chest as it nearly burst with pride, I replied "I'm from *aquí, la Habana*, I'm Cuban!" The young man immediately stopped, turned around, and sneered with indignation, "you might be from here, but you are no Cuban." He leaned in so close that when he spewed these venomous words, I felt a few drops of his spittle land on my cheek.

This encounter was the first of many which would continuously happen every time I have visited the island—and not just by *jineteros*. Held in contempt and suspicion on both sides of the Florida Straits, when *aquí* I remain too Cuban to ever be American, and when *allá*, too American to ever be a Cuban. The truth is that I am both and I am neither. To construct one's identity upon ambiguities reinforces the trauma of never belonging; a constant reminder that belonging nowhere prevents the healing to my festering scar, an open wound kept fresh every time I am asked "where are you from," both on the streets of la Habana or on the avenues of the United States.

REMEMBER, LORD, WHAT THE YANQUIS DID

On the eve of José Martí's death, killed on the battlefield early during the War for Independence, he composed a letter to his friend Mercado. Martí, known throughout all Latin America, was a late nineteenth century poet, philosopher, diplomat, and revolutionary. He too was a refugee who found himself living for fifteen years in what he called the new Rome. "I have lived in the monster whose entrails I know, with my only weapon being the slingshot of David."[5] Part of the dilemma of "living in the belly of the beast," a phrase first written by Martí, is that those who end up living in Babylon are there because Babylon is responsible for their expulsion in the first place.

Contrary to popular mythology surrounding the quest for the "American Dream," we who find ourselves living in Babylon did not arrive to these shores seeking liberty or pursuing economic opportunities. We are in this alien land as a direct result of U.S. foreign policies designed to deprive our countries of origins of political and economic sovereignty. Rome's *pax romana* and the U.S. *pax americana* each pursued its own "Manifest Destiny." Roman colonization during Jesús' time pushed his family, in response to fearing for their lives, toward Egypt; just as U.S. neocolonialism pushed my own family northward. U.S. foreign policies—in the form of Gunboat Diplomacy—caused this push factor from my homeland, as my people fled in fear to the country responsible for our exodus. Crossing the border, a festering scar caused when the First World rub against the Third, is life threatening. The Babylon of North America has an immigration problem because for the past two centuries, its wealth was based on stealing the cheap labor and natural resources from neighboring countries to the south. Why then should we be surprised when immigrants take the same roads built by the empire to extract our cheap labor and natural resources, following all that was stolen?

The reason I—and many of my fellow Latinxs—are here, forced to leave our homelands for the insecurity of border crossing, is because the U.S. empire—like all colonizers—created political and economic insecurities and uncertainty in our countries of origins due to a foreign policy designed to secure the avarice of multinational corporations. We live in Babylon because the U.S. foreign policy justified regime change among every country on the Caribbean Basin to protect U.S. foreign interest and to insure resources and cheap labor flowed toward the center of empire. During the twentieth century, every country along the Caribbean Basin (except Venezuela) experienced a regime change at least once, either by military invasion (21 times) or CIA covert operation (26 times). That's forty-seven regime changes, or almost one every two years. My own country Cuba experienced four U.S. military invasions and at least two covert CIA operations. Should we therefore be surprised that we find ourselves sitting and weeping by the rivers of Babylon?

When Cubans declared independence from Spain in 1895, the Babylon to the north would have none of that. If Spain was not going to physically rule Cuba, then the U.S. would by means of controlling their economy and thus launching on the world stage their first entrance into colonialism. The Cuban

War for Independence had its name changed when the U.S. first sought colonial possessions. Hence, to indicate a struggle between two empires, the localize war came to be globally known as the Spanish-American War. Against the will of Cubans who were winning the war for independence, the U.S. entered the fray, and within a month when victory was claimed, the Spanish flag was replaced with the "Bars-N-Stripes." Within a decade, the U.S. controlled Cuba's economy, a template for the invasion of and the economic absorption of other Caribbean nation economies. This economic control of Cuba can be clearly noted when we consider 80 percent of her imports and 60 percent of her exports went to U.S. markets; 95 percent of her main crop—sugar—was U.S. bound; 40 percent of all raw sugar production was owned by North Americans; two-thirds of the entire output of sugar was processed in United States-owned mills (mostly located in Baltimore), and the product left the island through the Havana Dock Company, also in U.S. hands. Additionally, 23 percent of non-sugar industry, 50 percent of public service railways, and 90 percent of telephone and electric services were also U.S. owned. Nickel deposits were mined and processed by Nicaro, a U.S. built plant; of the four oil refineries, two were U.S. owned and the rest owned by Europeans. All banks were in U.S. and British hands, with one-quarter of all deposits located in foreign branches. Approximately 90 percent of the export trade of Havana cigars went through North America which controlled half of the entire manufactory process.[6] Yes, Lord, remember what the *yanquis* did. They stole our independence, our economic resources, our sovereignty. These are the actions which led to our Babylonian captivity.

DOOM TO DESTRUCTION

Separation from my parent's fantasy island has now lasted five times longer than that of Odysseus to his. But unlike Odysseus who was returning to a place with which he was familiar, I failed in piecing together some type of rootedness upon the shifting sands of my parents' false memories. Even when I have returned for a visit, it is always as a stranger in a familiar land which remains so foreign. During a recent return to the island, I attempted to gaze upon the consequences of living on an island so close to Babylon and so far from God. As I strolled down *el malecón* where pretty *cubanitas* offered their young bodies for the price of a meal, as I ambled along *calle Obispo* smoking a *Cohiba*, as I drank a daiquiri at *el Floridita*—Ernest Hemmingway's old haunt—I simply observed, jotting down notes of randomly scrutinized surroundings, reflecting upon what is hidden, attempting to understand what was occurring beneath the surface—all with the hope of understanding my troubled soul.

I walked by many drunken *yuma* (American) lechers who constantly bump into me, spilling their drinks on my shoes, and offering apologies in broken Spanish. These old white men with young beautiful *mulatas* hanging from their arms are hoping to do to them what the embargo has done to the island. In the heat of the night where the odor of sweat intermingled with aroma of rum, the pulsating sound of 1950s musical hits fill the streets as the white tourists salsa dance down the middle of well-preserved avenues, stumbling and lurching, and unable to find the rhythmic beat even if their lives depended on it. But one block over from the merriment are dilapidated buildings on the verge of collapse, crumbling tall scraps of painted stone threatening to crush the people who have no other place to live but within the ruins, hoping to make a living out of the disposable coins discarded by those perceived as mortal enemies for over half a century.

Some of the tourists visiting the island are idealistic leftists rushing to see Cuba before it changes, before it is spoiled by the imagined ending of the embargo, voyeurs fetishizing the misery and poverty of others, ignoring how much the local people want change because they are hungry and because they hunger for something better. These perfumed and bath-soap-smelling vacationers apotheosize *el Ché*, dismissing the murderous rampage in which he partook after the triumph of the revolution. They marvel at a society which declared it has conquered racism, oblivious to *la buena presente*—the good presentation—where the faces of tourism's representatives have a light hue like mine, thus denying their darker compatriots lucrative tourist tips. From the safety of first-world middle-class privilege, they paint Cuba as some socialist paradise, ignoring how sexism and racism continue to thrive, along with a very sophisticated and not-so-well-hidden classism which is connected to political power as demonstrated by Fidel's grandson Tony, whose jet-setting ways on fancy yachts have been a tabloid embarrassment to the regime.

Other American tourists who are more conservative can also be found walking around with a noticeable air of superiority, politically painting Cuba with broad brush strokes, imposing hues of oppression in order to color a portrait of repression. They ignore the survival mentality of a people fluent in a doublespeak which hurl words masking sharp barbs of criticism. These political moralists insist on removing the human rights violation mote out of Cuba's eye while ignoring the beam of children in cages, the beam of black lives not mattering, the beam of human rights violations against people of color, all firmly lodged in the eyes of Euroamericans. They salsa with the swagger of neocons who are quick to dictate the conditions under which someone else's sovereignty and humanity would be recognized, holding on to the self-conceived hegemonic birthright of Babylonian empire. These bar stool pundits, sipping their *mojitos*, argue in false dichotomies, relenting to end their genocidal embargo only once greater political participation among the people takes place as if such solutions were simple.

For centuries my island and her people suffered because it is only ninety miles south of Babylon. Our riches stolen, our sovereignty undermined, our people prostituted. I can understand the psalmist's claim of happiness for the one who repays. I can understand the call to dash the infants of one's enemies against the rocks. As difficult as these verses are to comprehend, refugees in Babylon facing centuries of humiliating foreign policies and lifelong experiences of domestic ethnic discrimination can relate to the unquenching thirst for revenge. But revenge is not the answer. Babylon, along with all empires since, have fallen, mainly due to the celebration of their own hubris and the expansion of their ignorance. As state governors from conservative states legislatively prohibit schoolchildren from wearing face masks during a pandemic, we are left to wonder if the Babylonians are themselves the ones dashing their own children against the rocks?

DASHES THEM AGAINST THE ROCKS

The book of Revelation provides a warning against the "whore of Babylon [. . .] a woman [. . .] drunk with the blood of God's holy people" (Rev. 17:1–6). Obviously, this text is highly problematic because it feminizes idolatry by signifying religious unfaithfulness with female sexuality; even though scholars have argued that the term "whore" has less to do with supposed sexual transgression and more to do with the act of idolatry. The warning is of the churches "whoring" themselves to obtain power, profit, and privilege from secular rulers by attending to their economic and political interests at the cost of their moral proclamations. But who is this Babylon? Early Christian scholars believed Babylon was a reference to the then Roman Empire who until 313 CE persecuted Christians. If the empire was Babylon, then who was the one playing the whore? During medieval times, Protestant reformers (i.e., Luther, Zwingli, Calvin, Knox, Wesley), with anti-Catholic fervor, equated the Pope with the whore of Babylon.

Recognizing who the "whore" is, especially as it is used by men, remains a problem; still, a valid critique exists for churches which place themselves at the service of empire, exchanging the radical gospel message of liberation and justice for the loose change falling from the table of politicians. Within different societies, different faith leaders have sold their bodies and souls to oppressive political ideologies by tailoring their religious message to be ravished by the highest bidder. But who are these religious leaders who lead the people into spiritual infidelity? White Christians are today's "whore" of Babylon. White Christians in service to Babylon voted in record numbers (81% white Evangelical and 60% white Catholic)[7] for a candidate who ran a sham university, engaged in tax-fraud through his charitable foundation, refused to pay contractors forcing some into bankruptcy, engaged in housing discrimination, had ties with organized crime, paid hush money to a porn star to keep quiet about trysts during his wife's pregnancy, made lascivious comments about his daughter, and has been accused by seventeen women—and counting—of sexual misconduct. These white Christian supporters of one who is the antithesis of Jesús are the ones playing the "whore."

Today's nationalist Christians are the spiritual descendants of white Christians who actively supported the extermination of Indians, promoted slavery, invaded countries to the south to steal their cheap labor and natural resources. Like their ancestors, they prostitute the Gospel. To be a God-fearing American Christian, a patriot, is best demonstrated by storming the Capitol to protect and secure liberty for true Americans, to secure that their power, privilege, and profit are not now, nor ever will be threatened. White nationalist Christianity is a political movement disguised in religious garb to serve Babylon. The God it worships led Europeans to conquer a new Promised Land occupied by a different people with a different spirituality. And like the chosen, these Godfearing men and women of Jamestown and Puritans of Plymouth had a moral calling to genocide everyone who drew breath and stood between them and the land promised to them by God. This is the God of Manifest Destiny, the God of Jim and Jane Crow, the God of immigrant exclusion acts, the tribal God who justifies feeling of exceptionalism. Over the centuries, Eurocentric Christianity has fostered a culture of cruelty, a culture of death which bows its knees before the cult of firearms. Every Latin American child thrown into a cage, every Black life which did not matter and met its end because of a broken taillight, every Asian beaten up for supposedly bringing the virus, and very Indian living in Third World conditions on their own land continues unabated by those who worship this white God of Babylon and follow this white nationalist Christianity.

To follow the white God of Babylon leads to death. Salvation for those of us negatively impacted by Babylon, especially those of us sitting and crying by its rivers, is to reject this white God with its white Jesus peddling a white theology within white churches. To follow the God of Babylon is to worship a satanic angel of darkness masquerading as an angel of light. And because liberation is also meant for the oppressor, Babylonians can only find their salvation and liberation the day they drop to their knees and worship the Black God, the Asian God, the Latinx God, the Feminine God, the Queer God—in short, the God of the oppressed.

NOTES

1. A reinterpretation of Psalm 137.
2. Miguel A. De La Torre, *Reading the Bible from the Margins* (Maryknoll: Orbis Books, 2002), 112–13.
3. As cited by Teishan A. Latner in *Cuban Revolution in America: Havana and the Making of a United States Left, 1968–1992* (Chapel Hill: University of North Carolina, 2018), 159.
4. Jacques Lacan, *Écrits* (Paris: Seuil, 1966), 94–95.
5. José Martí letter to Manuel Mercado from the Dos Rio military camp (May 18, 1895) in *Obras Completas* Vol 4, page 168.
6. Leo Huberman and Paul M. Sweezy, "The Revolutionary Heritage," in *The Cuba Reader: The Making of a Revolutionary Society*, ed. by Philip Brenner et al. (New York: Grove, 1989), 5–7, 45; Franklin W. Knight, *The Caribbean: The Genesis of a Fragmented Nationalism, 2nd edition* (New York: Oxford University Press, 1990), 237; Philip C. Newman, *Cuba Before Castro: An Economic Appraisal* (New Delhi: Prentice Hall, 1965); and Hugh Thomas, *Cuba: The Pursuit of Freedom* (New York: Harper & Row, 1971), 466.
7. Jessica Martínez and Gregory A. Smith, "How the Faithful Voted: A Preliminary 2016 Analysis," *Pew Research Center* (November 9, 2016).

Chapter 8

Lamentations as a Healing Response to Necropower at the Texas-Mexico Border

Gregory L. Cuéllar

To encounter the agony of colonized people through the representations of another, a range of ethical dilemmas are bound to emerge, from voyeurism to consumerism to narcissism to outright denial of the veracity of such realities. But are our ethics of representation only to be determined by this cynical array of human responses? To pose the question Susie Linfield asks about photographs of suffering people, "since such images are cesspools of manipulation and exploitation: why look?"[1] Indeed, if witnessing from afar the traumatization of the Other does little to change what Edward Said calls "the grotesqueries and pathologies of power,"[2] why then read texts, hear lyrical music, or see images that depict their suffering?

Without question, global media outlets in general and the entertainment industry in particular has inundated our line of sight with around-the-clock images of people fleeing from wars, famine, and natural disasters, or mass shootings and black and brown people dying from unjust police violence. To render these revolving images of wounded people consumable, their producers concede to a re-victimizing dynamic in which the sufferer is confined to a single mode of expression—terror. As Sayak Valencia describes in her book *Gore Capitalism*, "this denial of discourse and agency has a derealizing effect on these subjects, depicting them as silent, inarticulate, and ineffectual."[3] And yet does this information overload mean that the only ethical way to understand the lives of terrorized people is to censor them from public view? I am not at all convinced that silencing them is a viable ethical mode of representation, let alone feasible in the current age of digital image overload. Here, I am reminded of Linfield's sobering assessment of postmodern social critics when she declares: "It has become all too easy to avert one's eyes; indeed, to do so is considered a virtue."[4]

But as the video of George Floyd struggling to breathe while handcuffed and pinned to the ground by a Minneapolis police officer has shown us, how can we not look at the proliferation of unjust police violence against black and brown people? Ironically, has not our surplus access to digital images made it impossible for us not to see the unjust killing of black and brown people by agents (police officers, border patrol, immigration judges, prison guards, etc.) of the nation-state? Have we become as Karen Georgia A. Thompson describes in her poem "testify" (see Chap. 2)?

> we are silent onlookers
> surveying the carnage of centuries
> eyewitnesses to the bruising of hope
> our lips mouthing words
> inadequate to describe the breaches we see.

How is the inhumane carnage ever redressed in our world if professional interpreters of social reality, both past and present, avert their eyes from the people in power who sanction and perform deadly violence? For just as representing suffering people can be ethically fraught, remaining in a postmodern ethic that privileges the spectator's discomfort over what the injured subject has lived and witnessed is equally prone to expert malpractice. If public awareness of the governmental dealings is integral to the democratic process, how can we not listen to the wounded people bearing witness to their victimization by state sponsored violence?

Consider, for instance, the expert interpreters who mitigate the terror inflicted on colonized people as a way to avert their eyes. A consequence of this censoring tactic is to underestimate the extent of the suffering that colonized people endure. Within the European tradition of empire-building, there is ample precedence of discrediting or dismissing altogether the personal injury assessments of those deemed the colonized Other. Its agents of empire were thoroughly convinced of their superior civilizational position and the righteousness of their imperial cause. Through various sublimating and reconfiguring schemes, the violence of empires and nation-states is casted as part of a civilizing enterprise—which is a retelling of the story that would undoubtably be unrecognizable to the colonized victims themselves. People ravaged by empire-building wars, economies, policies, etc., recur not only by virtue of physical acts of violence but also because of what Said calls "a discourse of occultation and legitimation."[5] By attenuating the material violence, Western critics of social and historical processes allow empire to remain an elusive and abstract force, so much so that attempts to interrogate it become overwhelmed by its perceived intangibility. For to contextualize critically imperializing power—especially the kind that begins with the testimonies of colonized people—is to jeopardize the very economy of privilege that ascribes prestige and authority to agents of empire. But rather than adopt an attenuating discourse and risk becoming accomplices to the violence of empire-building, are there discourses, images, or narratives we could engage that come directly from the colonized victims themselves? Are there victim-produced portraits of suffering and violence that beckon us to listen? In answering these questions, let us for a moment consider these poignant words by Susan Sontag in her decisive book *Regarding the Pain of Others*:

> It is not a defect that we are not seared, that we do not suffer enough, when we see these images. Neither is the photograph supposed to repair our ignorance about the history and causes of the suffering it picks out and frames. Such images cannot be more than an invitation to pay attention, to reflect, to learn, to examine the rationalizations for mass suffering offered by established powers. Who caused what the picture shows? Who is responsible? Is it excusable? Was it inevitable? Is there some state of affairs which we have accepted up to now that ought to be challenged?[6]

Although not modern photographs, the poetic images of postcolonial trauma in the book of Lamentations invites or, rather, summons us to pay attention, to reflect, to learn, to examine how imperializing violence operates in the mass production of human suffering. Here, lamenting in the aftermath of inhuman carnage also serves as a way of critically knowing about the pathologies of empire. Through lament, the colonized poet of Lamentations registered the melancholic depths of the imperial wound while at the same time mapping an imperial praxis of violence as a form of social critique. The colonized poet risked investing in an ethic of knowing how empire and its agents operate rather than succumbing to a posture of not knowing, not seeing, not listening, and hence not testifying. In this way, the poetry of Lamentations attests to a resilient mode of mourning in which the gore of colonization deserves full creative expression, without acquiescing to the debilitating effects of postcolonial melancholia. In presenting us with the gory details of imperial conquest, the colonized poet is not glorifying violence—as is typical in the current entertainment industry—but rather provides a trustworthy guide or blueprint of what exactly agents of empire are capable of doing to those they have deemed their enemies. This approach to lament and mourning takes seriously a resonating proposition that Ashis Nandy, a founding figure of postcolonial studies, made in response to the tragic aftermath of Western colonialism in Asia, "that we have forgotten the language of mourning."[7] For the book of Lamentations, its postcolonial language of mourning does not merely recognize what the Judeans had tragically lost in the sixth century BCE. For the surplus production of exilic literature alone in the Hebrew Bible attests to how severe the sting of the empire's violence was for many Judean witnesses. It reveals in its own postcolonial way how they lost their city, people, and livelihoods to a violently expanding empire.

Rather than deny their veracity—an epistemic move typical of agents of empire—this essay aims to distill the poetics of mourning in the book of Lamentations into an ethical discourse for engaging contemporary people victimized by colonizing and empire-building forms of elite power. Such a discourse would also include an ethic of representation—that is, a way to testify to others—the suffering we have been summoned to see. The particular context that I aim to apply this ethical poetics of mourning to is the Texas-Mexico borderlands and the perennial wounding that migrants, asylum-seekers, and refugees receive at the hands of agents of the nation-state. Although we are flooded with images of their precarity on cable news and social media, this way of seeing has yielded more a language of statistics for data's sake than a language of mourning for actual living people.

MOURNING THE DEATH WORLDS AT THE TEXAS-MEXICO BORDER

As an expert interpreter of biblical texts who is also from the Texas-Mexico borderlands, I have witnessed firsthand how colonizing power not only gave rise to the construction of the U.S. southern border, but also how it has morphed into what Achille Mbembe terms "necropower"—a term that aims "to account for the various ways in which, in our contemporary world, weapons are deployed in the interest of maximally destroying persons and creating *death-worlds*."[8] At the Texas-Mexico border, black- and brown-bodied migrants, asylum-seekers, and refugees have come to define its death worlds. Classified by those in power as the people who do not matter and are hence disposable, U.S. border security operations and anti-black and -brown immigration policies have been weaponized to drive migrants to their deaths, whether by drowning in the Rio Grande, by dehydration in the desert, by cartel-kidnappers, or by suicide in immigration detention, to name a few. Rather than adopt the Western postmodern virtue of not looking (which is a spectator-centric mindset), how might we ethically heed their cries for freedom? What sorts of genres, images, narratives, lyrical poetry, or cultural productions should we consider when testifying about their traumatizing push to the end of life by agents of the nation-state? How do their own representations of their victimization both beckon us to pay attention as well as indict us as accomplices to the very nefarious power structures that strive to shorten their lifespans? In an attempt to respond to these probing ethical questions, I turn to the poetics of mourning in the book of Lamentations in an effort to learn a mode of mourning that doesn't simply trouble our souls over their tragic deaths but also quickens our political awareness of the pathologies of necropower at the Texas-Mexico border.

Mourning in the book of Lamentations is a language born of death. This language admits to investments not in make-believe death, but rather the actual death of living beings (Lam. 1:19–20). Dependent on the lived experience of imperial violence, this language of mourning anticipates a sincere readership—those with a willingness to accept that empires subjugate (Lam. 1:1) and kill actual people (Lam. 1:16, 19–20). Yet for agents of empire, the mourning language of colonized people represents an affront to empire-building systems and thereby triggers an elaborate ideological counter-response to discredit or silence their witness. To accept the testimony that Lamentations' mourning language puts forth about imperial violence means adopting a way of seeing the world that trusts the pain of colonized people to be genuinely felt. (Even more so when the colonized individuals expressing the pain of conquest give no indication whatsoever that their testimony should be mistrusted.) Hence, to mourn that "my priests and elders perished in the city while seeking food to revive their strength" (Lam. 1:19) or that "infants and babes faint in the streets of the city" (Lam. 2:11), the aim is not to prove the veracity of the underlining pain but instead to orient our gaze to the catastrophic outcomes of empire-building systems. Regardless of the era, what empire-building systems hold in common is their desire to conquer, dominate, accumulate, totalize, and ultimately master everything and everyone. And yet knowing that this imperializing desire for ultimate power exists requires a scrutinizing gaze, the kind that empires and their agents work hard to discourage through a multiplicity of ideological campaigns, carceral operations, and acts of physical violence.

It seems that a viable source for such a counter-gaze to empire would be from the colonized people themselves. For as Frantz Fanon describes, the native town of the colonized people "is a hungry town, starved of bread, of meat, of shoes, of coal, of light. The native town is a crouching village, a town on its knees, a town wallowing in the mire [cf. Lam. 4:3]."[9] For the victims of empire, their expressions of pain possess an indelible awareness of how imperial violence destroys human bodies, as lamented here: "Our skin is black as an oven from the scorching heat of famine. Women are raped in Zion, virgins in the towns of Judah. Princes are hung up by their hands; no respect is shown to the elders" (Lam. 5:10–12), while at the same time also knowing the pathology of empire-building violence at the macro-level, with the destruction of physical landscapes (Lam. 1:4), sacred spaces (Lam. 1:10), and ancestral dwellings (Lam. 2:2, 5). In this sense, the mourning language of Lamentations maps the imperial violence on both bodies and buildings, showing us a high threshold of suffering for its victims: "What can I say for you, to what compare you, O daughter Jerusalem? To what can I liken you, that I may comfort you, O virgin daughter Zion? For vast as the sea is your ruin; who can heal you?" (Lam. 2:13).

Though Deuteronomistic theology of divine retribution in Lamentations would have us conflate the empire with God—"the Lord has become like an enemy" (Lam. 2:5)—it is clearly understood to constitute a human-made system with agents, machinery, and institutions, all of which work to accumulate power by destroying other humans. And sometimes, the colonized poet even pivots from this provisional theology of God as empire to a new ontological awareness where the empire acts autonomously as a destructive human-made system—a notion more in line with reality. This theological slippage in turn leaves God open to act on behalf of the colonized people: "Pay them back for their deeds, O LORD, according to the work of their hands! Give them anguish of heart; your curse be on them! Pursue them in anger and destroy them under the LORD's heavens" (Lam. 3: 64–66). On the other hand, as morally difficult as it may seem for modern readers to accept the colonized poet's theological formula of the empire as God's chosen instrument of punishment, it does show an element of subversiveness in that it displaces the legitimating religious ideology of the empire. Here, for instance, the colonized poet has the God of Israel as the primary actor of imperializing violence, "The Lord determined to lay ruins the wall of daughter Zion; he stretched the line; he did not withhold his hand from destroying; he caused rampart and wall to lament, they languish together" (Lam 4:8). In other words, for the Neo-Babylonian empire, the conquest of Jerusalem had nothing to do with the God of Israel—for in its eyes Israel's God had been conquered.

When applied to the death-worlds at the Texas-Mexico border—or for that matter, any Western nation-state border (the Belarusian-Polish, British-French, etc.)—the mourning language of Lamentations attunes our awareness toward the painful wounds of migrants, asylum seekers, and refugees, while also opening our activist gaze to the empire-building systems that inflict them. To trust the mourning language of a mother who is grieving the loss of a daughter or son who died by suicide while in immigration detention or the cry of children as they witnessed the early-morning arrest of their parents by U.S. Immigration and Customs Enforcement and then deported to their deaths is to gain a pain-based awareness that should reorient our moral compass toward the work of dismantling empire-building systems. Their mourning is also expressed on their lifeless bodies—dried up, drowned, dangling, decomposed, and yet sacred bodies. As mourned by the colonized poet, "Now their visage is blacker than soot; they are not recognized in the streets. Their skin has shriveled on their bones; it has become as dry as wood" (Lam. 4:8). To rely solely on the statistical grids and percentage graphs of dispassionate social critics for inspiring social transformation, the pain of victimized border-crossers is susceptible to losing its moral urgency in exchange for their scientification. Whereas when their language of mourning stands as our primary source of knowing about human need and the nature of empire-building systems, their cries of pain are then able to serve as the moral foundation of our activist passions. This, at least, ensures that their vision for what they would like the world to look like, specifically in terms of citizenship and nation-state borders, plays an important conceptual role in the policy-making process.

THE THERAPEUTIC POWER OF A SACRED POETICS OF MOURNING

The poetics of mourning in Lamentations also leads us to affirm the therapeutic power of the sacred, which in a postcolonial state of being demonstrates what Mbembe calls "the poetic productivity of the sacred."[10] Here, the process of poetry-making (poetics) itself is consecrated; not because it yields a consumable product for our enjoyment, but because it attends in liberating and subversive ways to the lived traumas of people conquered and displaced by empire. As such, the sacred in Lamentations is linked to a capacitating process in which the colonized self finds a reprieve from the mental and physical torments of everyday imperial violence. Again, these words by Mbembe are worth reproducing:

> the struggle to escape from an inhuman order of things cannot do without what may be called the poetic productivity of the sacred. Here the sacred represents the imaginative *par excellence*. The sacred is to be understood not only in relation to the divine, but also as the "power of therapy" and of hope in a historical context in which violence has touched not only material infrastructures but psychological infrastructures too, through the denigration of the Other, through the assertion of the latter's worthlessness.[11]

By extending care to the wounded self through poetry-making, the colonized poet foreclosed the empire's devaluation standards for conquered people. Through the poetics of mourning, in other words, the colonized poet fashioned a new domain for defining reality outside of the empire's legitimating religious metanarratives. What emerges here are two constitutive features of what Mbembe calls "the poetic productivity of the sacred." The first is the self-care moments that poetry-making afforded the colonized poet. In other words, translating the wounds of imperial violence into an intricate poetic discourse points to a life-giving valuation of the colonized poet's self-worth. Secondly, poetry opened the colonized poet to a creative life—one where the empire was no longer in control of defining the meaning of life. The sacred, however, in Lamentations is not limited to the poetry-making process, which entails a creative praxis for validating self-worth and agential empowerment in the context of imperial domination. For the message of its poetry is also sacred.

In a post-9/11 context, the US war on drugs and terror has designated the US-Mexico borderlands as what Nicholas De Genova calls "the premier site for staging the perpetual demand for more securitization" against migrant invasion.[12] Although this demonizing strategy is not new to the US political imagination, what has intensified in the name of homeland security is the construction of intermittent border fencing that stretches nearly 1,500 miles from the Gulf of Mexico to the Pacific Ocean (cf. Secure Fence Act 2006; Consolidation Appropriations Act 2008). The southern border walls separating the US from Mexico is, indeed, the reification of a conventional belief that black- and brown-bodied migrants, refugees, and asylum seekers are socially inferior and hence more prone to criminality. This racist nationalist thinking can be retraced to the mid-nineteenth century and the empire-building ideology of Anglo-American Manifest Destiny. Armed with a legitimating theology of conquest, European white settlers expanded across the North American continent as part of a purifying (Puritan) mission, excluding and subjugating along the way—often with brutal force—non-white-bodied people. The spirit of this colonizing mission still resounds in the militarization and fortification of the US-Mexico border. Hence, rather than deny the death-worlds that have come about as a result of this border zone, particularly in the Texas-Mexico region,[13] how might the poetics of the sacred in Lamentations offer us some therapeutic power and hope in the face of state-sponsored necropower?

As proposed in my previous discussion, the language of mourning in Lamentations constitutes a moral state of awareness that urgently trusts the painful witness of colonized people and the imperial violence that caused it. Yet the authority of this language does not lie solely in its moral sting, but also in how mourning represents a form of sacred poetics—for it is a unique communicative response to the loss of life in that it channels creative desire not through dispassionate reasoning but, rather, through passionate/activist forms of grief. Consider this visceral expression from the colonized poet of Lamentations: "My eyes are spent with weeping; my stomach churns; my bile is poured out on the ground because of the destruction of my people, because infants and babes faint in the streets of the city" (Lam. 2:11). Channeled through the sacred poetics of mourning was the colonized poet's creative desire for what needs to change—a conquered people and city. Here, the situational cue of fainting infants and babies in the city streets triggered a poetic form of mourning that draws less from pragmatic thinking than from a morally driven impulse of care for human life. In conjunction with its dense God-language, the poetics of mourning in Lamentations also receives its sacredness from its exclusive use during times of human loss (a kind of funerary genre), its moral-based valuation of human life, and its channeling of a creative desire for a better world. For the colonized poet, making the world a better place for children was a particularly potent moral stimulus: "Arise, cry out in the night, at the beginning of the watches! Pour out your heart like water before the presence of the Lord! Lift your hands to him for the lives of your children, who faint for hunger at the head of every street" (Lam. 2:19). This moral valuation of children's lives comes into poetic form both through the felt pain of their victimization and the creative desire to change their impoverished condition. The effects of imperial violence on society's most vulnerable population—in this case children—reveals again the high threshold of suffering that the empire had set for its conquered victims. And yet in Lamentations, mourning for infants, babies, and children functions as a passionate critique of the empire's world—a world that has the capacity to leave children starving, abandoned, and devoured. Again, the colonized poet's words of mourning paint this grim picture of life under empire: "The tongue of the infant sticks to the roof of its mouth for thirst; the children beg for food, but no one gives them anything" (Lam. 4:4). Here, the colonized poet reveals the utter moral depravity that comes with empire-building systems. While offering a few the luxury of totalizing power, this comes at the cost of children's lives. While in mourning the plight of children under empire, the colonized poet infers a different world where infants, babies, and children are physically nourished and treasured in all facets of life.

At the Texas-Mexico border, we encounter a world forged by U.S. empire-building systems. Within the United States' version of empire, the transnational capitalist economy has served as a key weapon in dominating smaller countries that are south of its southern border. Hyper-consumption by its citizens, high outputs of CO_2 emissions (second to China),[14] and growing demand for low-wage manual labor are among the salient features of the U.S. empire-building machine. When mourning this version of empire, we encounter its flipside where migrant children, infants, and babies have followed the legalized movements of cheaply made merchandise to its southern ports of entry. Unlike the merchandise, however, these wounded migrant children find themselves barred from entry, which leaves them vulnerable to desperate people forced into violence, in part because of the rampant scarcity that the U.S. empire-building system has created. Here I am eerily reminded of these words by the colonized poet, "The hands of compassionate women have boiled their own children; they became their food in the destruction of my people" (Lam 4:10). Similar to the colonized poet's lament, the construction of the death worlds at the Texas-Mexico border has forced many of us to mourn year after year for starving, encaged, abandoned, exploited, and disposed migrant children, infants, and babies. Here, I hope that our mourning for these victimized children leads us all to what the colonized poet desired: a world in which the brutal destruction of children never exists—which is a world without empires.

CONCLUSION

The colonized poet of Lamentations mourned for both a world that existed—under empire—and was yet to exist—without empire. Despite what we may perceive as theological flaws, the colonized poet's scared poetics of mourning represented a critical move in a traumatic context of widespread imperial violence. This move points to a desire for healing that summons us to open our critical gaze to witness the pain of colonized people in our midst and to discern the empire-building systems causing their pain.

NOTES

1. Susie Linfield, *The Cruel Radiance: Photography and Political Violence* (Chicago, IL: The University of Chicago Press, 2010), 12.
2. Edward W. Said, "The Politics of Knowledge," *Raritan: A Quarterly Review* 11, no. 1 (Summer 1991): 17–31.
3. Sayak Valencia, *Gore Capitalism* (South Pasadena, CA: Semiotext, 2018), 249.
4. Linfield, *The Cruel Radiance*, 12.
5. Edward W. Said, "Opponents, Audiences, Constituencies, and Community," *Critical Inquiry* 9, no. 1, *The Politics of Interpretation* (September 1982): 2.
6. Susan Sontag, *Regarding the Pain of Others* (New York, NY: Farrar, Straus and Giroux, 2003), 116–17.
7. Ashis Nandy, "Open Pasts, Open Futures," *Monsoon* 4 (2009): 2, https://almostisland.com/monsoon_2009/essay/china.html.
8. Achille Mbembe, *Necropolitics* (Durham, NC: Duke University Press, 2019), 92.
9. Frantz Fanon, *The Wretched of the Earth*, trans. Constance Farrington (New York, NY: Grove, 1963), 39.
10. Achille Mbembe, "What is Postcolonial Thinking? An Interview with Achille Mbembe," *Eurozine*, September 1, 2008, http://www.eurozine.com/articles/2008-01-09-mbembe-en.html.
11. Mbembe, "What is Postcolonial Thinking?"
12. Nicholas De Genova, "'We are of the connections': migration, methodological nationalism, and 'militant research,'" *Postcolonial Studies* 16, no. 3 (2013): 254.

13. Jasmine Aguilera, "More Migrants Die Crossing the Border in South Texas Than Anywhere Else in the U.S. This Documentary Depicts the Human Toll," *Time*, August 20, 2021, https://time.com/6091742/migrant-deaths-texas-documentary/.

14. "CO2 Emissions by Country," World Population Review, https://worldpopulationreview.com/country-rankings/co2-emissions-by-country.

Chapter 9

Tūturu Whiti Whakamaua, Kia Tina, Tina! Haumi e, Hui e! Taiki e!

Defiance, Determination and Decolonisation!

Te Aroha Rountree
(Ngai Tuteāuru, Ngā Puhi)

The title of this essay is a call of defiance and a call to *haka* (ceremonial Māori dance). The *whakataukī* (proverbial saying) *Tūturu whiti whakamaua, Kia tina, tina! Haumi e, Hui e! Taiki e!* calls our people to gather, to unite for a common purpose or cause. It is most often associated with the defiant nature of haka, the domain of *Tane Rore* (ancestor of dance). The tradition of haka is reflected in the oral narratives of *Tinirau* and *Kae*, most specifically the haka of *Hineteiwaiwa*[1] and has been globalised by Te Rauparaha of Ngāti Toa Rangatira and his haka *Ka mate, ka mate, ka ora, ka ora* (see below). Haka are synonymous with strategies of intimidation, persuasion, and challenge. However, haka in large part are enacted to signal an issue or conflict and to seek restoration of an imbalance created by that conflict.

The phrase, common to many composed haka, *Tūturu whiti whakamaua* announces a dedication and devotion to the purpose or cause. The second phrase *Kia tina, tina! Haumi e, Hui e! Taiki e!* proclaims the alliance of the people, gathered and united ready to proceed or progress their common cause. The popular phrase is as much a rallying cry to battle then, as it is a call to action today. Echoing the call in this saying for people to engage in a dance of defiance, this essay is a declaration of *Defiance, Determination and Decolonisation*. It is a pertinent challenge against the imperialism and colonialism that exist in our context and continually impose themselves on our life, faith and theology as *tangata whenua* (people of the land).

TŪTURU WHITI WHAKAMAUA

First, tangata whenua engage in *Defiance*. As native peoples we are defiant, we haka, we battle, we resist, we deconstruct, we reStory, and we un-tell lies that they tell about us, about empire, and about invasions and intrusions into our lives and into our faith. As native peoples who were colonised by the British, we are constantly and inevitably engaged in *Defiance*. In modern day Aotearoa (New Zealand) we often express our defiance through oral tradition, performance art and dance, music, activism, radical resistance and truth-telling. The whitewashed and whitewashing history of colonisation and the romanticising of missionary impact in our context serves to further assimilationist policies of dominant western *Pākehā*[2] society.

We are defiant and we exercise our capacity to resist, to push back against the expectations to conform and to compromise. Our theologies are no different, they are mechanisms for freedom and cultural expressions of faith that demand change, in church and society. The *marae-ātea* is the public place/space where we are able to put into practice our lived theologies and to affect change with and for our people. The deconstructing of imposed theologies from our colonial history and experience seek to give voice and volume to our native theologies derived from our native language and wisdoms. The reStorying requires a defiant revisiting of our missionary and Māori encounters that have often sought to minimise the impacts of imperialism and eurocentrism. The truth-telling requires an honest *kōrerorero* (dialogue) about systemic racism that continues to manifest itself within structures of church governance, and in the policies and practices of church systems.

Second, tangata whenua demand self-*Determination*. As native peoples we fight for what all peoples desire, the right to determine our own ways of knowing and being in the world. There exists persistent and pervasive systemic and institutional racism founded on colonial pre-conceptions of white supremacy. These systems are perpetuated by those within church institutions who benefit from white dominance and power. Church governance most often provides for policies and processes that continue to privilege Pākehā and give preference to Pākehā ideology and theology. We seek to dismantle oppressive structures, processes and ideologies that exclude Māori from self-determining power.

Even within those liberal church entities that purport to be bicultural in structure and decision-making, there are still practices that clearly and definitively disadvantage Māori peoples and congregations. Even those church communities that seek to uphold Te Tiriti o Waitangi[3] and claim to be just, equitable and life-affirming faith communities continue to struggle with power-sharing. Our theologies of the *marae*[4] and the *papa kainga*[5] reflect our capacity to determine the *tikanga*[6] and *kawa*[7] of our places/spaces, and where our wisdoms and kōrero take precedence.

We seek to both extend beyond these spaces and to draw others into our *marae-ātea*.[8] Just as the public square serves as a space for radical affirmation and theology, so too is the potential of the marae-ātea. In our marae traditions the ātea is the domain of *Tūmatauenga*[9] where debate and discussion often take place. The marae-ātea is therefore a place/space/system/process for reimagining and reclaiming Māori theologies.

Tangata whenua seek the "Road to *Decolonisation*." As native peoples we evoke story-telling and truth-telling for justice, for *whenua*, for *moana*, for *iwi*, and all creation. In our defiant quest for liberation for ourselves, our vision also extends beyond ourselves to *Papatuanuku me Ranginui* (earth and sky personified) and to the realms of *Tane me Tangaroa* (forest and sea manifest). The liberation of creation is part of our own liberation, each is reliant and dependent on the other, we as humanity cannot attain true wellbeing without the environment that sustains us. The road to decolonisation is a cumbersome and cobbled path that requires us to be steadfast and persistent.

Rev. Maori Marsden, in his writings described colonisation of Māori as a "highly predictable form" that followed a successful "pattern of domination and socio-political control" including pacification, appropriation of lands and resources, cultural genocide and assimilation.[10] Decolonisation may require the reverse approach, a recognition of *tino rangatiratanga* (autonomy, self-determination), a cultural renaissance, returning of lands and resources, and reconstituting of affirmative legislation. We are starting to see the beginnings of this decolonising process within the socio-political arena of education and healthcare in Aotearoa. This essay begins to explore the decolonising process in an Aotearoa theological context and the implications for tangata whenua.

There are significant and life-affirming implications for decolonising ourselves and our theologies as tangata whenua. Many Māori theologians have looked to the prophetic voices of the past like Rev. Rua Rakena who suggested that we needed the freedoms to meet Christ as Māori, and not to have our view filtered through a Pākehā lens. Rakena was in fact suggesting a decolonising of western Christological models which he considered paternalistic and created Māori dependency. He suggests that for authentic Māori theology to come to light, we must undertake a decolonising of our theological lens, that has often been blurred by a historically Pākehā Missionary one. If as tangata whenua we are to decolonise ourselves and our theologies this could potentially require an approach imbedded in our *tikanga* (customary values, beliefs) and expressed through our own oral traditions. Essentially if we are to meet Christ as Māori, true, authentic, and decolonised, we need to see and experience Christ through *te ao* Māori (Māori world) and using our own *mātauranga* Māori (Māori knowledge).

DANCE OF DEFIANCE

In contemporary Māori society, the tradition of haka has been adapted as a way to retain the practice as a genre of Māori performance art. Haka has become the war cry of sports teams across Aotearoa, giving both the haka and Māori culture global status. However, this has also opened up the capacity for exploitation and appropriation of haka for commercial purposes. The national Matatini Festival is an exemplar of the innovation of haka, that often responds to the issues of the day and continues to be a call of defiance. The *whakatauki* (proverbial saying in the title of this essay) calls our people to unite for a common cause. The saying is common in haka and is a proclamation of the alliance of the people, gathered and united in our purpose.

Haka

Haka is a demonstration of prowess, an act of defiance and intimidation, a challenge, a show of resistance and a manifestation of protest. The inter-active nature of haka reflects a fluidity between the performer and the audience, a reciprocity of reaction and response.

> Ka mate, ka mate, ka ora, ka ora!
> tēnei te tangata, pūhuruhuru
> nāna i tiki mai whakawhiti te rā
> upane, ka upane!
> upane ka upane, whiti te rā, hi!

> Will I die, will I die, or will I live, will I live
> for it was the wonderous power of a woman
> that captured the sun and caused it to shine again
> rally in rows!
> rally in rows, the sun is shining!

(my translation)

This haka originated from the tribal group of *Ngati Toa Rangatira*, descendants of *Hoturoa* of the *Tainui Waka* (tribal groups affiliated to the Tainui canoe). *Ka Mate* was composed by the *Ngāti Toa* chief Te Rauparaha (born 1760s at

Kawhia, died 1849 at Ōtaki). The story of the composition of *Ka Mate* is well known within the oral histories of *Ngāti Toa* and *Ngāti Tūwharetoa*, the two *iwi* (tribes) most associated with the origins of the *haka*.[11] Haka is used here as a metaphor for defiance and disobedience.

The history of Māori defiance engaged to bring about radical social change has most often been encapsulated in the activist movements of the 1970s and 80s in Aotearoa. While Māori social activism was heightened during that period it was not the beginning of a collective Māori consciousness for radical change. This essay suggests that Māori defiance and activism can also find its roots in the nineteenth and twentieth century Māori responses to Christianity. The early Māori Prophet movements were a form of defiance against Pākehā missionary intrusion and imposition upon Māori life, and belief systems. When describing the development of mystical religious sects and cults in the South Pacific, Binney suggested that "Their appearance is, in itself, a definite rejection of Christian teachings."[12]

Savages

Early Pākehā missionary accounts of Māori were often demeaning and derogatory, serving to portray a savage people in desperate need of civilising and Christianising. Reverend Richard Taylor's summation of Māori prior to the arrival of the Gospel was damning, and cast Māori among the most savage that had ever been encountered stating,

> In taking a view of the past state of the New Zealand Church, it will be necessary first to give a short description of the state of the Maori race before the Gospel was introduced amongst them. We cannot well picture to ourselves a race of men more savage and debased, more strongly bound with an age-rivetted chain, than they were. Killing was literally no murder, and man regarded his fellow-man as his proper food, which he was justified in using whenever it could be procured.[13]

The Wesleyan Methodist Missionary Society accounts of Māori were often denigrating and exaggerated. The WMMS Annual Report of 1830 gave a critical account of Māori, "the perverse levity and awful depravity of these savages appear to be unequalled in the history of man."[14] The monthly publication of the *Missionary Notices*[15] as well as the journal entries of Samuel Leigh were most condemning of Māori. Ward argued when discussing the missionary views of the Māori prophetic movement Papahurihia that "the comments that the Protestant evangelicals made about Papahurihia were shaped by theology and biblical prophecy and that their textual evidence on him should be reinterpreted from within the Protestant evangelical paradigm."[16] What Ward was suggesting is that the missionaries' theology and biblical interpretation contributed to their views of Papahurihia, and therefore must be reinterpreted through the same missionary paradigm of theology. If so, how might understanding the missionary theological imperative change the interpretation of comments such as "perverse levity and awful depravity of these savages"? We are now left to deconstruct and un-tell such lies and untruths, to challenge and change the Eurocentric lens of Pākehā missionaries that often determined the narrative of our history and culture.

By the mid-1830s missionary society reports declared large scale conversions of Māori particularly at Rangihoua in the Bay of Islands and in Mangungu, Hokianga. Binney asserted, "1833 also saw the beginning of a large scale baptism of Maori converts. At Waimate North the centre of the expanding Anglican missionary movement, 90 converts were recorded in that year and within seven years the Anglicans claimed 2000 baptisms and 30,000 attending instruction."[17] However, Māori had many issues of discontent including what were seen as the inadequacies of the "old Gods" and the practicing tohunga to cure new foreign diseases and to appease the new Pakeha God. As Binney described it, "The omnipotent God of the white-faces apparently kept his people alive while the Maoris died. The obvious conclusion was drawn that the *Pakeha* God, *Atua,* had sent *ngarara*, the lizard of death, to devour the entrails of his opponents."[18]

Papahurihia

The nineteenth century saw the rise of one of the earliest recorded Māori Prophet movements in Aotearoa, Papahurihia. The 1830s was thought to be the time of significant conversion of Māori to Christianity. Papahurihia, of Te Hikutu in Rangihoua, was the first of many Māori Prophets to combine his existing mātauranga and tikanga Māori with Christian understandings of God. Papahurihia was defiant in his determination of the Pākehā missionaries and was particularly critical of the CMS mission at Rangihoua. Papahurihia was not simply a passive recipient of the Gospel and missionary teachings, he was critical of both the early Pākehā missionary theology and their inconsistent ways of life that at times were contrary to their teachings.

Papahurihia provided a prophetic voice for his people by undertaking his own interpretations of the biblical text and not relying solely on the Eurocentric interpretations of the early missionaries. Papahurihia challenged the authority of the early Pākehā missionaries in his willingness to defy their teachings and present to his people an alternative rendering of the biblical text. Papahurihia found affinity with the biblical plight of the Israelites and made reference to his followers as Hūrai (Jews). These simple acts of resistance against Pākehā missionaries and their teachings illustrated his capacity for defiance.

There have been several key commentators on Papahurihia, including Ormond Wilson and the author and historian, Judith Binney—who wrote of Papahurihia: "By 1833, he was teaching that the holy day was Saturday not Sunday. And the missionaries, he said, had got it wrong: God's messages came directly to him by means of the serpent, Nākahi. Nākahi was the emblem on the rod of Moses and, as such, the image of the covenanted relationship between the Israelites of old and God."[19] However Binney's argument is contested by Judith Ward in her doctoral thesis entitled, *The Invention of Papahurihia*. Ward wrote that "Papahurihia responded to the advent of Christianity in a way that was consistent with the behaviour of tohunga at the time, rather than as the founder of a syncretistic religion."[20] Ward suggests that Papahurihia's reaction or response to the Gospel was more about his practice as a tohunga and less about consciously forming a syncretic faith or movement.

This same propensity to resist against missionary imposition was seen time and again with other prophetic leaders such as Te Ua Haumene and the Pai Marire faith, Te Kooti Arikirangi Te Turuki and his Ringatu movement, and the leadership of Te Whiti o Rongomai and Tohu Kākahi at Parihaka. This defiance continued into the twentieth century with Rua Kēnana with his Hiruharama Hou (New Jerusalem) in Maungapohatu and later with Tahupotiki Wiremu Ratana and his movement that eventually became an established church and political giant of the late 1970s and into early 1980s.

The Māori Prophet movements of the nineteenth and twentieth centuries are examples of resistance and defiance against Pākehā impositions of faith and theology. These ancestral voices of political and prophetic resistance continue to be an inspiration of defiance to new generations of Māori. Mike Ross when describing the impacts of colonisation wrote, "The brutality of Pākehā dominance was evident in the ways resistance groups of Māori people were killed, imprisoned, made destitute, separated from their families and lands, discredited, demonised and ridiculed. This behaviour toward Māori was normalised and became the basis of a system built to benefit Pākehā by endowing them with wealth and privilege."[21]

Theology like history is narrated by the powerful. Missionary theology was a colonised theology of imperialist origins. It was a theology of superiority that sought to occupy, to take over and to lay claim to existing native wisdoms and spirituality—toward replacing them with Christianity. The Māori prophetic movements were a response to a colonised theology that sought to undermine and disregard any form of Māori spirituality and theology. History has largely deemed Māori prophetic movements as cults, sects and syncretic faiths, with little value placed on doctrinal or theological foundations. We must dismantle the theologies of oppressive colonialism and build anew the theologies of hope and justice. We must seek tangata whenua theologies of *tino rangatiratanga* (self-determination, autonomy) and *kaitiakitanga* (guardianship, duty of care), that dare to defy the Pākehā normalisation of white, colonial theology.

SELF-DETERMINATION, A MIRAGE

Self-*Determination* is a mirage, not an illusion but it is at times invisible and unattainable. I use "mirage" here as a naturally occurring optical phenomenon of bending light. It is derived from the Latin *mirari*, meaning "to look at in wonder." Self-Determination occurs naturally and is a phenomenon not as a result of bending light, but rather the consequence of enlightenment and knowledge, or a sense of knowing. Rev Māori Marsden described the difference between knowledge and knowing well: "When the illumination of the spirit arrives in the mind of a person that is when understanding occurs—for knowledge belongs to the head and knowing belongs to the heart."[22] It is important to know and understand with the head and the heart, what it is for our people and our theologies to be self-determining.

Church Systems

The capacity to determine one's own worldview and to live in accordance with it, is a privilege that the colonised are often denied. The exercising of privilege in the context of church is inherited from the same colonial theologies of superiority that the nineteenth-century missionaries imposed upon Māori. The nature of systemic racism within church in Aotearoa today is the result of colonialism and ideologies of dominance and power. The idea that racism exists within an institution that purports to be a beacon of God's truth and love can often be confronting and easily denied. The insidious nature of church systems that preserve and enable racism in practice and theology can be subtle and are often explained away.

The governance of church institutions is one of the structures and processes where systemic or institutional racism exists and thrives. In most mainline churches, elements of bicultural partnership have been established. For the Methodist Church of New Zealand, a bicultural journey (1983) determines Te Taha Māori and Tauiwi as power-sharing partners in the governance of the church. For the Mihinare (Anglicans)—their church governance is undertaken through the three-tikanga model of Māori, Pākehā and Pasefika.

While church institutions work at being inclusive and sharing power, many fall short as policies and processes continue to privilege Pākehā ways of knowing and being. We often see this in the boards and committees of the church (in a broad context) that are corrupted by complacency and the normalisation of all things Pākehā. The selection process for members of those boards and committees is often ad hoc or privileges those known to existing members (who are largely old, Pākehā men, who nominate and appoint other old, Pākehā men). The membership is not often required to have knowledge and experience of Te Tiriti o Waitangi 1840, to have undertaken bicultural training or to know church history of any kind. Although we are often assured by our Pākehā friends that selection is skills based, it often appears that Māori and Pasefika do not possess the skills required. The make-up of boards and how they are governed often disadvantage anyone who is not Pākehā. What this points to are colonial systems that maintain the status quo, and allow Pākehā to remain in power. Something as simple as access to decision-making bodies or voting processes within an organisation is varied amongst ethnic or cultural minorities within church structures. In spite of the systemic racism, we as Māori are determined to carve out our own path by revealing the structures and processes that exclude and disregard our valuable contributions to church and theology.

Marae-ātea

Self-Determination of Māori theology draws us to the marae and the papa kainga, to safe spaces where our tikanga is self-determining. The marae-ātea is the key to our self-determination and is where our theologies (whether we call them theologies or not) are lived out and where our faith comes to life in song, prayer, worship and even *tautohetohe* (debate), theological or otherwise. The wisdoms of our *tupuna* (ancestors) and the theological reflections of the day come to bare on the marae-ātea, a space that welcomes all who gather at the *waharoa* (gateway, entrance) seeking to engage.

The marae-ātea as metaphor suggests that a Māori environment is necessary for the revitalisation of Māori theologies and biblical interpretations that are reflective of te ao Māori (Māori world) and our Māori brand of *Karaitiana* (Christianity). To be self-determining is to exercise certain freedoms . . . to live, to think, to be and to theologise as Māori/tangata whenua; to determine theologies that serve our people and to bring hope and healing; to determine theologies rooted in our whenua and determined by our relationship to and with God.

THE ROAD TO DECOLONISATION

Colonisation is like a *ngāngara* (insect, reptile), it is stealthy, crafty and covert. Colonisation was and is about power, dominance and superiority derived from a colonial paradigm smuggled here to Aotearoa. There were no border restrictions for this ngāngara, colonisation needed no passport or customs checks. Colonisation was an inevitability after the exposure of Aotearoa by Abel Tasman (Dutch) and James Cook (British). The empire-building British were relentless in their pursuit of new lands and resources to conquer and the violence of colonisation has had significant consequences for indigenous peoples everywhere. The impacts of colonisation in our Aotearoa context are profound and far-reaching. Ross stated that, "The process of colonisation has consistently and continuously attacked and destroyed many of the foundations of Māori society, seeking to replace one house with another. Māori resistance has also been consistent and continuous, although battling from an impoverished and fragmented position."[23] Acknowledging the adverse effects of colonisation are important to the beginnings of hope, of reconciliation and the road to decolonisation. Understanding the part that colonial theology played in the denial of Māori faith is also a step towards restoring Māori theology.

Decolonisation is in many ways a stripping back of the colonial facade that has been imposed on Māori, or in some instances that has been intentionally taken on by Māori for survival. Decolonisation as a concept and a construct may yet be reframed, fit for our purpose as Moana Jackson described it, "'Decolonisation' may not be the most appropriate word [. . .]. Perhaps it could be replaced with the ethic of restoration."[24] Therefore, we look to *tikanga* to guide our response to the widespread implications of colonisation.

Ocean Ripeka Mercier, when describing decolonisation as a DIY project wrote, "Decolonisation involves critical self-reflection and outward observation; it seeks to embody pre-colonial, Indigenous and non-colonial paradigms; it unearths and addresses embedded colonial thinking. Decolonisation, then, takes individual and collaborative action to root out the weeds of colonisation and provide space for Indigenous ways of knowing and being—and more besides."[25] Decolonisation requires our Pākehā friends, colleagues and allies to do some of the heavy lifting when it comes to critical self-reflection and rooting out weeds of colonisation. We are a DIY nation and it makes sense that Māori should lead the way in the decolonising of our people, places, minds, bodies and souls. However, should we as Māori be content with the "provision of space" for us to know and be, or should we simply take our rightful place/space to know (in hearts) and to be Māori?

If we seek to be just and to reconcile our colonial past, the decolonising of theology is never more important, particularly to the progress of theological study and education in Aotearoa. For Māori theology to thrive it needs to be decolonised of western captivity and incarceration. Melanie Kampen in her thesis, *Unsettling Theology: Decolonising Western Interpretations of Original Sin*, described the process of decolonising theology in her indigenous context in this way:

> The insistence of the particular theological doctrines and scriptural interpretations of European settlers as Truth led to the demise of many Others—a violence to which the Indigenous peoples of this land can attest. If, as I suggested, particular theologies were part and parcel of the western colonial project, then it follows that attempts at disarming the imperial machine must not only involve decolonizing dominant politics and cultural habits, but also decolonizing dominant western theologies.[26]

The decolonisation of theology is complex, and requires us to decolonise our minds and return to critical thinking and analysis typical of the *wānanga* (place of advanced education). And to use our mātauranga Māori to discern a process of decolonisation that best serves us as Māori. Graham Ward suggested that "To decolonize habits of mind, sensibility, and ways of feeling, experiencing and valuing, is a long process."[27] We as Māori must be prepared to walk the road to decolonisation, and to do the work required for change.

CONCLUSION

Like the road to Emmaus, the road to decolonisation is an opportunity to rediscover and regain a new perspective of and in theology. The road to decolonisation is an act of defiance and determination to bring about transformation and justice. We hope to meet Jesus along the road to decolonisation, to be guided and to deepen our faith. Moana Jackson situated the ethic of restoration that values place, tikanga, community, balance and conciliation in our journey for decolonisation—these may well be stopovers on the road to decolonisation and to transformative revolution.

NOTES

1. Taranaki chief Tinirau and his *tohunga* (diviner, healer, artisan, priest, educator) Kae had a disagreement after Kae cooked and ate Tinirau's whale (Tutunui) before fleeing. Tinirau sent a kapa haka group led by Hineteiwaiwa to entertain Kae and

his people. Upon identifying Kae with a smile that revealed his missing teeth, Hineteiwaiwa signalled the attack to enact Tinirau's retribution.

2. New Zealander of European descent settlers, or maybe more appropriately—squatters (as I have learned from Aunty Patricia Courtenay).

3. Te Tiriti o Waitangi (1840) was a treaty between Māori and the Crown that preserved the lands, forests and fisheries of Māori and made provisions for British settlers to establish themselves in Aotearoa. The treaty has been continually breached by the Crown and Pākehā from 1840 to present day.

4. Marae is a complex used for celebratory and ceremonial events with facilities.

5. Papa kainga is most often the village or settlement of a tribal group.

6. Tikanga are customary practices, derived from the word 'tika' meaning correct or right.

7. Kawa are Māori protocols, most specifically those that pertain to conduct on a marae.

8. Marae-ātea is most commonly identified as the courtyard in front of the meeting house of the marae complex.

9. God or ancestor of warfare and conflict, one of the many offspring of Ranginui and Papatūānuku (Sky and Earth personified).

10. Charles Te Ahukaramu Royal, *The Woven Universe—Selected Writings of Rev. Māori Marsden* (Masterton: The Estate of Māori Marsden, 2003), 88.

11. The story begins with Te Rauparaha who journeyed from Kawhia to seek alliances with other tribal groups, one of those being Tūwharetoa who lived in the Lake Taupō region. He was being pursued by a war party from Ngāti Te Aho, who wanted revenge for a previous incident involving *Ngāti Toa*. At Lake Rotoaira, Te Wharerangi reluctantly agreed to assist Te Rauparaha and as the war party closed on their quarry guided by the incantations of their tohunga (scholar, expert, priest) he instructed Te Rauparaha to climb into a *kumara* (sweet potato) pit and for his wife, Te Rangikoaea to sit on top. By combining the spiritual qualities of a woman and of food, Te Wharerangi was able to weaken the power of the Ngāti Te Aho tohunga.

12. Judith Binney, "Papahurihia: Some Thoughts on Interpretation," *Journal of the Polynesian Society* 75.5 (1966): 321.

13. Richard Taylor, 1868. *The Past and Present of New Zealand: With its Prospects for the Future* (Wanganui: Henry Ireson Jones, 1868), 4–5.

14. *The Annual Report of the Wesleyan Methodist Missionary Society 1830* (Auckland: Methodist Church in New Zealand Archives, 1830), 39.

15. A monthly journal publication by Wesleyan Methodist Missionary Society (WMMS) 1816–1903, formally known as *Missionary Notices relating principally to the Foreign Missions, first established by the Rev. John Wesley, A. M., the Rev. Dr. Coke, and others, and now under the direction of the Methodist Conference.*

16. Judith Ward, "The Invention of Papahurihia" (PhD Thesis, Massey University, 2016), 7.

17. Binney, "Papahurihia: Some Thoughts on Interpretation," 321.

18. Binney, "Papahurihia: Some Thoughts on Interpretation," 321.

19. Judith Binney, Vincent O'Malley and Alan Ward, *Te Ao Hou: The New World 1820–1920* (Auckland: Bridget Williams, 2018), 22.

20. Ward, "The Invention of Papahurihia," 1.

21. Mike Ross, "The Throat of Parata" in *Imagining Decolonisation* (Auckland: Bridget Williams, 2020), 30.

22. Royal, *The Woven Universe*, 79.

23. Ross, "The Throat of Parata," 38–39.

24. Moana Jackson, "Where to next? Decolonisation and the stories in the Land," in *Imagining Decolonisation* (Auckland: Bridget Williams, 2020), 149.

25. Ocean Ripeka Mercier, "What is Decolonisation?" in *Imagining Decolonisation* (Auckland: Bridget Williams, 2020), 42–43.

26. Melanie Kampen, "Unsettling Theology: Decolonising Western Interpretations of Original Sin" (Master of Theological Studies Thesis, University of Waterloo and Conrad Grebel University College, 2014), iii.

27. Graham Ward, "Decolonizing theology." *Stellenbosch Theological Journal* 3.2 (2017): 576.

PART II

Persevering with Tenacity, through Shitstems

Chapter 10

RastafarI and Domestic Labour
Roots in Menstrual Taboos and Western Inequality

Anna Kasafi Perkins

The roots of this essay draw upon the labour of several others:

> Original Rastafari is uncompromising in its commitment to "chant down Babylon," the capitalist system. However, it is bound by the "capitalist male deal." Sexism is the key defining feature distinguishing the old Rasta from the new. And it is also a fetter limiting the old Rasta to a black nationalist accommodation with capitalism. In contrast, the defining feature of new Rastafari is the affirmation that class consciousness cannot exist without gender consciousness.[1]

> The RastafarIan movement seeks to liberate black people from white oppression; ironically, it also promotes male domination and female subordination (Lake 199). They are to "spread their seed" without regard to their marital status, while their wives must remain faithful. At the same time, however, men are to be sensitive to the needs of their wives and develop a close relationship with their children. A woman becomes a Rasta through her man. She should wear a long dress and cover her head. She should not speak in church or talk directly to God, and is subject to menstrual taboos when she is "unclean."[2]

> A woman is the minister of home affairs and health, the husband the minister of foreign affairs and defense.[3]

> Sometimes the man feels superior if he does not take part in domestic work.[4]

Rastafari, which has become a global movement, emerged in 1930s colonial Jamaica as outcasts from the society due to their transgressive Afro-centric religio-cultural rejection of the oppressive Babylonian Shitstem, that is, "[the] corrupt, racist, and out-of-control society committed to the relentless pursuit of power, human and environmental exploitation, and mindless individual consumerism."[5] While not a uniform movement, Rastas share many beliefs and practices, in particular, their adoption of dreadlocks, which "symbolised both the construction of a greater social distance from Jamaican colonial society and the perception of Rastafari by the society as derelicts and outcasts"[6] and their belief in the divinity of Emperor Haile Selassie I.[7] Since the 1970s, Rastas' outcast status has changed significantly, and they have become increasingly secularised with continued attempts by the Jamaican state to co-opt the Movement, especially in the tourism arena.[8] At the same time, it is notable that Rastafarl has had "a dramatic impact on Jamaican culture even though it accounts for less than 1 per cent of the population."[9] Tafari-Ama maintains that Rastafarl has become part of the Jamaican cultural landscape and that the internationalization of its livity through migration and technological dispersal "has reshaped the character of this social movement beyond the confines of its Caribbean genesis."[10] In response, many Rastas resist this secularisation, accommodation and co-opting as a yielding to the Babylonian Shitstem in which true Rasta has no part. As Ras Dizzy I chants it, first clarifying that he wants out—and "no part of you":

> Sorry tall fellow, you may rule as you wishes
> But God [too] wants no part of you.[11]

One of the areas in which some Rastas determine to remain separate and separated from Jamaican society is in their refusal to work in the Babylon Shitstem, expressed in their emphasis on communal living, self-sufficiency, and cultivating and eating from the earth. Many Rastas continue to refuse wage labour and instead emphasise self-determination and self-sufficiency through a form of communal living and participation in the informal economy;[12] however, the means by which this self-sufficiency is realised has changed.[13] Entrepreneurism and innovation have become central values among Rastafarl as seen among the Nyabinghi in Montego Bay with their Rastafarl Indigenous Village[14] or the Bobos in Bull Bay, St Thomas, with their broom manufacturing and craft activities.[15] Similarly, Rastas who live outside Jamaica engage in a similar livity. The Fondes Amandes Community Reforestation Project (FACRP) in Trinidad is one such example.[16] Indeed, Nangwaya[17] proposes Rasta as catalysts for ecotourism development in Jamaica even though tourism is seen by many Rastas as "whore-ism."[18]

REJECTING WAYS OF UNDERSTANDING WORK

For many Rastas, both family and communal life are organised to reject ways of understanding work in the larger Jamaican society, which still maintains largely distinct spheres for females and males, though even that is changing as RastafarI itself is changing. Women continue to be the main home makers and carers (even when they engage in paid work) while men are providers and protectors.[19] To this end, Fox describes unions among Jamaicans as "largely economic arrangements to share sexually divided work, although this ideal is not as rigidly adhered to as it is described and husbands and wives often assist one another in their respective tasks."[20] However, in family life, in particular, it is claimed that some Rasta bredren generally remain distinctive; they take a more active and affective role in domestic labour than their non-RastafarIan counterparts while maintaining patriarchal norms of male headship and female inferiority and subordination. This distinctive male role in family life coupled with existing patriarchal norms gives rise to contentions both inside and outside of Rasta concerning the position of women within the Movement. Some researchers contend that such difficult conversations should best be had inside the community.[21]

Nonetheless, there is a fruitful conversation taking place both within and without the community. Indeed, there is an important conversation going on among Rasta sistren themselves, both theoretically and practically, which as an outsider I am simply listening in to. So, for example, Rasta sistren scholar and filmmaker Bianca Brynda argues that the presentation of RastafarI has mainly been undertaken by male sociologists and researchers, who dealt mainly with the male point of view which is projected as if it were that of the entire Movement.[22] She, therefore, seeks to foreground the voices of women as presented by the female researchers and adherents who have written about the Movement, particularly their experiences in RastafarI. Writing from the 1990s, Brynda is critical of the neglect or superficial treatment of Rasta sistrens' experiences in research. She, like others, maintains that there is a fundamental contradiction between the ideology of RastafarI with its emphasis on freedom and the social reality with its subordination and exclusion of women from leadership and central rituals. Nathalie Mountlouis, a more contemporary RastafarI sympathiser and researcher, on the other hand, argues for the agency of Rasta sistren to be recognised as she questions any notion of a universal subordination of Rasta sistren.[23] Certainly, the rich and complex range of the lived experiences of Rasta sistren and the continuing evolution of RastafarI cannot be captured in a single perspective. It is important, therefore, "to acknowledge acts of agency and self-determination, political and spiritual agenda-setting and individual subjectivities [among Rasta sistren]."[24]

This discussion explores the question of domestic labour within the Rastafarlan community, specifically the domestic roles in the Rastafarlan family. It argues that the apparently distinctive role of Rasta bredren within the household is the direct result of both the importance of the children ("yootz") and Rasta biblically based menstrual taboos, the most Orthodox form of which is seen among the Bobo Shanti mansion, which will be the focus of much of the discussion. In the Bobo Shanti mansion (officially, the Ethiopian African Black International Congress—EABIC), the Rastaman's woman ("daata"/empress) is relegated for a period of up to twenty-four days, including seven days before and seven days after her menses; she is not allowed to cook or mingle with the men or other non-menstruants. Each month, a seven-day period of interaction with her kingman becomes the window for sexual relations. This points to an underlying tension between recreational and procreational sex present within the Rastafarl community, which calls out for resolution.[25] The discussion maintains that some Rasta bredren, especially among the older generation, like Jamaican men generally, have internalized unequal gender viewpoints from the Bible while maintaining Western bourgeois notions of male as the head of the household/nuclear family with his woman and children dependent on his earning, guidance and teaching. It proposes insights from female Rasta scholars, including Imani Tafari-Ama, who undertook two studies of such questions among Rastafarl twenty-five years apart, on the role of Rasta sistren in the process of "imparting" (contributing and impacting) male-defined norms concerning domestic labour in Rastafarl. These Rasta sistren form part of the growing chorus of voices contesting various aspects of traditional Rastafarl belief and practice, especially regarding women's roles. Rasta sistren continue to contest, challenge, and subvert their subordination within the Movement. As a result, they claim "it is no longer possible to generalize about Rasta views of gender as the Movement is being changed by the differing perspectives of both private individuals and public organizations."[26] In undertaking this exploration, I try to take seriously the danger of a homogenizing or totalizing portrait of Rasta sistren or of the Movement itself.[27] Nonetheless, it is necessary to interrogate the roots of apparently contradictory messages in Rastafarl, which simultaneously elevate and denigrate women, as well as the accompanying practices, rooted in folk traditions, Western bourgeois notions and biblical perspectives.

WOMEN IN RASTAFARI

Rastafarl has never been a homogenous Movement, nor has it remained static over the seventy plus years of its existence, the beginnings of which can be marked by the Coronation of Emperor Haile Selassie in 1933. The Rastafarl

Movement seeks to liberate African people from white oppression and, unlike Pentecostal religion in Jamaica, is a largely male phenomenon. In making a comparison between Rastafarl and Pentecostalism, which both developed in the early twentieth century, Fox notes that both are "markedly gendered,"[28] with each redefining gender roles in ways that are at odds with the other. Hepner and Hepner maintain that, while Rastafarl grew out of resistance to colonial and neo-colonial ideals and structures, "it conflated the reclamation of black identity with male identity. In that regard, the subordination of women helped compensate for male powerlessness."[29] It is, therefore, a central paradox of Rastafarl that the oppression of women which is reflected in their own Movement remains fundamental to the very system they are attempting to subvert.[30]

Obiagele Lake, renowned Rastafarl researcher and pan Africanist, would maintain, however, that among the shared beliefs and practices of Rastafarl are major tenets regarding the relative status of men and women, which promotes male domination and female subordination.[31] She maintains, therefore, that one of the problems that preclude Rasta from assuming its role as a leading movement on behalf of African peoples is "their cultural ideology concerning women."[32] Barnett, however, notes that the Twelve Tribes mansion is distinguished by the equal roles of men and women within the livity; this makes Twelve Tribes distinctive among Rastafarl and the trend-setter for women's equality in Rastafarl.[33]

What is evident is that there continues to be much diversity, contradiction and evolution, even in ideas about the woman's traditionally undervalued role as mothers or female companions to Rasta bredren.[34] Grenadian Sehon M. Lewis is particularly strident in his critique of the unequal place that women occupy in Rastafarl, which he blames the "Holy" Bible for establishing.[35] He rejects especially the "language of grandeur" used by Rasta bredren to profess love for their women—"queen" or "empress." Such language he maintains "is enshrined in dominance."[36] And this is perhaps laid bare in the traditional day-to-day term used by a kingman for his partner—"daata" [daughter], who holds a childlike and subordinate status to the male. The designation of a woman as a *daata* originates in the early Movement when women traditionally entered through a male consort, who fashioned her in the Rastaman's ways, a process Yawney called "growing a daata."[37] In discussing their own self-image, some Rasta sistren expressed resentment of the use of *daata*.[38] There are indeed contradictions inherent in Rastafarl livity, which need to be articulated and resolved.[39] As such, Lewis[40] and others would reject the implied equality present in statements such as "every Rasta family is founded on the appropriation of a social order ruled by a benevolent king and queen, whose subjects are the willing, self-directed princes and princes," which renowned Rastafarl scholar Barry Chevannes made in arguing for the

RastafarI reclaiming of their African "royalness."[41] Such an idyllic picture is far from reality. Women are deified in the abstract but denigrated in reality, Lake argues.[42] Rather, Lewis emphasises that the important position occupied by women in RastafarI stems from her role in the family, where she has an important role in taking care of the children and the home, largely based on her valued maternal function.[43] Fox would agree with the valuing of women in the society mainly as mothers, both by men and women.[44]

Despite its resistance to Babylon, RastafarI "borrows heavily from Western liberalism, Christianity, and Judaism, all of which influence the popular belief in the livity that women have less authority than their male counterparts."[45] Men are, in most mansions, the designated spiritual leaders of the Movement, the heads of households and the rulers of women. Such hegemonic discourse, manifested by RastafarI, has been reproduced through the ideology and practice of the Movement. "By reinscribing these Babylonian perspectives in the livity, brethren exacerbate the oppressions that all Rastafari face in the wider society, because family relations suffer from the failure to even recognize this contradiction."[46] Indeed "Africans in Diaspora are parodying Western notions of gender relations that are based on the racist and sexist myth of man as the breadwinner (a central tenet of capitalism) and, by extension, head of the household."[47] Indeed, the European Christianity which became central to Jamaican notions of respectability "centr[ed] on the sanctity of marriage, the nuclear family, the patriarchal role of the husband as provider and the head of the family, and the wife as homemaker and mother."[48] Currently, "women have not been joining Rasta for a generation (at least now) in significant numbers. The jury is out on whether this is due to the patriarchal precedents/power structure in the livity."[49]

MENSTRUAL TABOOS IN JAMAICAN CULTURE

While identifying that the liberation of African people is the focus of RastafarI, Lake further contends that this freedom is a qualified one—reserved for RastafarIan men. The devaluation of RastafarIan women, she maintains, is "predicated on cultural notions of women's inferiority and their alleged state of pollution."[50] Lake makes the case that this ideology originates in pre-colonial African beliefs and practices as well as Judeo-Christian teaching and general notions of women's inferiority which permeate Jamaican society. She is adamant that concerns with pollution are significant because they have cultural, psychological and physical consequences for women's lived experiences even today. I support her arguments in my study of the origin of Jamaican curse words, which I found to be based on the menstrual processes of women;[51] as such, importantly, the belief in the power of menstruum "to tie men," that is compel their financial support and affection, giving rise to fear of the menstruating woman or her undergarments; such fears have led to acts of violence against women that have even ended up in the courts in Jamaica.[52] Journalist Mark Wignall reports on the pervasiveness of the cultural taboos on menstruating women, which he roots in ignorance supported by religion and a widespread lack of respect for women in Jamaican culture.[53] Unlike Rasta bredren and many other Jamaican men, Wignall's interlocutors refused to see any contradiction between purchasing food possibly prepared by a menstruating woman and refusing to eat from their female partner while she was menstruating.[54] Rasta bredren tend to be stricter in not eating food prepared by women since their menstrual status is not known. Wignall's arguments fell on deaf ears and one of the men remarked, "Yu can sey anything you want to sey. Mi nah eat from dem!"[55] Nonetheless, as will be discussed below, Mountlouis's research demonstrates that this taboo has undergone some evolution even among the Bobos.[56]

RASTA AND MENSTRUAL TABOOS

> She was told
> that she is bad omen,
> a bloody sanitary pad, useful but a disgusting topic.
>
> ("She was told!," Aruna Gogulamanda; see Chap. 2)

The menstrual taboos are deeply rooted in the origins and philosophies of Rasta. Several identifiable strands have knit together in the formation of menstrual rituals. Chevannes argues persuasively that dreadlocks symbolized a rejection of social control but also the triumph of male power over the female, who was considered to be the evil contaminating source of the Rastaman's confinement in Babylon.[57] Chevannes maintains that the RastafarI attempt at isolating the negative ideas about women, which were deeply rooted in Jamaican culture, and ritualizing them to establish distance from the contaminating source of their confinement in Babylon has not been entirely successful, however. Homiak adds another strand to the argument concerning female pollution with his discussion of celibacy among some younger Rastas in 1950s.[58] Their self-imposed celibacy temporarily countered the wide-spread and accepted attitudes of Jamaican males "sowing their seed widely."[59] Their spiritual quest represented a keyway of separating from the flesh. Even so, they replicated the ambivalent Jamaican male attitude towards women, especially notions of their menstrual pollution and ability to sap strength from mind and body through sexual intercourse. It is possible that their exclusion of women led to them needing to become independent in the domestic sphere in ways not ordinarily required of the Jamaican male.[60] This may be a strand in the deeper domestic involvement of Rasta bredren today.

Of course, not all Rastas hold to menstrual separation in the same way, if at all. Members of the Nyahbinghi observe the separation rule since menstruating women are discouraged from taking part in the 'binghi' ritual.[61] The reason for this is that the temple and the altar are to be kept pure. "No blood can enter the temple."[62] The ban is not limited to women, however, as men with sores or flesh wounds also cannot enter. As mentioned, Bobos are noted to maintain the strictest menstrual separation, which can last up to twenty-four days each month. (They too prevent men with wounds or sores from entering the temple or presiding.) The menstrual separation is seen as a time of purification which has both physical (health, cleansing) and spiritual benefits. The menstrual blood is considered to be a holy sacrifice and there is an entire ritual for offering it back to the earth.[63] Menstruating women are considered to be "under the influence and control of extensive powers" that are potentially dangerous to all males above seven years old and "transmissible into food through her vibrations."[64] Women generally live separately from men at Bobo Hill and the cooking is done by men at the communal kitchen, although notes that some women have begun to prepare meals for their children, who must leave for school and are not able to wait for the meals prepared in the communal kitchen.[65] While in their menstrual compound, women cook for themselves and have no contact with men, even boys as young as three are removed. During that time, they engage in craftwork for sale.

RASTA BREDREN AND THE FAMILY

Rastas are concerned to a high degree with cherishing and providing for "the youth."[66] Both Rasta men and women see the importance of being responsible for children and educating them well, including with a strong sense of African pride. Motherhood as often represented by Mother Africa, who is glorified and often seen to represent a lack of reproductive freedom. At the same time, Chevannes describes the Rasta bredren going beyond the concept of the "good father" which exists among Jamaican men; fatherhood for the Jamaican male mainly involves providing for the children's upkeep and education. Once this financial support is provided the job of actual upkeep and education rests with the mother. Many Rastafarlan fathers, on the other hand, are known to take personal interest and have a direct hand in raising and educating their children, especially the males. Women do not give up their natural maternal role but are responsible for general household chores like washing and seeing to the general comfort of her kingman. "But compared to the non-Rastafari male, the Dreadlocks is an affective part of the household grouping."[67]

Some insight into this experience from the woman's perspective is provided in a *Jamaica Gleaner* news story entitled "Female biology dictates family life in Rasta camp." Bobo Empress Sharon is cited as saying that her RastafarI faith holds that "the mother is the first teacher." However, at three years old, boys must be placed under the care of the "second teacher"—his father—during the period in which his mother is in menstrual confinement, which can last up to twenty-four days.[68] She further maintains that "A young boy should grow up with his father because that is who he is growing up to be."[69] "Girls[, however,] stay with their mothers learning how to do 'craft work and the things that will prove economically viable for her and her kingman.'"[70] Paradoxically, the increased role of the Rasta bredren in household affairs also results and reinforces the menstrual taboos. Since a Rasta bredren's empress is relegated during her menses and so is not allowed to cook during this time, the Rastaman generally takes over the cooking.

Yet that is not the full story as "in the sphere of domestic roles, taking care of children turns out to be the greatest and most consistent feature of a Rastawoman's life, despite the expectation that Rastamen will shoulder half the burden."[71] Furthermore, many Rasta bredren fall short of the ideal notion of fatherhood, particularly due to "secret polygamy," where they are involved with other, oftentimes, non-RastafarI women, thereby preventing them from spending adequate time with their children (evident even among members of the Bobo Shanti community).[72]

SHIFTS IN GENDER RELATIONS

Turner points out an irony in the development of RastafarI.[73] The origins of RastafarI are rooted in the spirit of Nyabinghi, above all the East African struggle against colonial oppression empowered by the Spirit of Queen Nyabinghi. This woman-centred spirit was lost in RastafarI, even as Rasta bredren began to refer to themselves as Nya-men and their drumming and reasonings called Nyabinghi. Consequently, these gatherings marginalised and subordinated women. Turner names the menstrual, reasoning and chalice prohibitions as expressions of this marginalisation and subordination. In addition, Turner points out the biblical warrants for such treatment of women, including limiting the woman's access to knowledge of Rasta through her kingman, a direct reference to 1 Timothy 2:11.[74] She, therefore, questions, what transformed the independent Jamaican woman of the post-slavery era into "the domesticated and idealized queen."[75] She argues that the Rastaman, like his non-Rasta counterpart, entered into a colonial "male deal" which privileged men and subordinated women; the implications of this deal remain today even as changes are happening.

Similarly, Imani Tafari Ama finds that there has been a shifting in gender relations of RastafarI over the last twenty-five years, particularly with women becoming more socio-economically independent.[76] She concurs that "RastafarI brethren[, unlike their non-RastafarI counterpart in the larger society] are active participants in domestic labor as well as being regular contributors to the maintenance of the household."[77] Sadly, she maintains that this active involvement in the domestic space is not due to any desire for gender equality. Rather, it is "a compensatory mechanism to maintain male dominance in the absence of the man being the breadwinner in the household."[78] The acceptance of man as the head of the household points to ways in which RastafarI brethren have internalized unequal gender viewpoints from the Bible but also Western bourgeois notions of male as the head of the household/nuclear family with his wife and children dependent on his wage. Even so, one group among whom changes in gender relations can be detected is the Bobo.

Mountlouis, who lived with the Bobos for several months, while conducting research, maintains that, contrary to popular perception, Bobo Shanti livity represents women on an equal footing with the men. "Female subordination is advocated neither in their theology nor in their conception of the body/temple, unlike the overtly negative portrayals found in what one may call mainstream Christianity."[79] In the Bobo Shanti community, the Woman Freedom Liberation League (WFLL), which was instituted in 1980 by King Emmanuel, oversees the elaborate menstrual regulations, which are styled as "the laws of Mama Omega."[80] Mountlouis demonstrates that it was at the behest of the WFLL that the period of purification was elaborated to twenty-one days. Prior to that, women were required to remain in-house only for fifteen days. However, one empress suggested to King Emmanuel that a longer period of purification could be beneficial as a form of birth control. Based on the female menstrual cycle, after the twenty-first day, fertility is at its lowest; this opens a space for non-procreative sex, which was formally taboo among many Bobos. Mountlouis, therefore, designates the laws of Mama Omega an exercise in Rasta sistren's agency over their own fertility and sexuality. They began by elaborating a process which allowed them to take control of their fertility in a natural way and in so doing they institutionalised the idea of non-procreative or recreational sex. This can be read as the subversion of a process of subordination to secure their interests in the face of patriarchal beliefs.

It is possible to see at play the inner workings of intimate relations between Rasta bredren and sistren, which involves much negotiation and strategizing on the part of the women. RastafarI sistren, Kandiyoti, would strategize within "a concrete set of constraints that reveal and define the blueprint of . . . the patriarchal bargain."[81] Such a bargain influences women's gendered subjectivities and the potential for and the forms of active or passive resistance in the face of patriarchy. Of course, as the Bobo Shanti sistren demonstrate, such bargains are not eternal or immutable, but subject to transformation, "open[ing] up new areas of struggle and renegotiation of the relations between [Rasta bredren and sistren]."[82] So, the patriarchal privilege of the "male deal" may not be the entire story.

CONCLUSION

In closing, it is no longer possible to generalize about Rasta views of gender as the Movement is continually changed by the differing perspectives of both private individuals and public organizations. Nonetheless, it is necessary to interrogate the roots of apparently contradictory messages in RastafarI, which simultaneously elevate and denigrate women, as well as the accompanying practices, rooted in folk traditions, Western bourgeois notions and biblical perspectives. So, while not homogenous or even static, RastafarI is known for generally subordinating women, particularly by reducing and restricting their role to the domestic sphere. This spiritual and cultural subordination is located in biblically supported menstrual taboos as well as adopted Western liberal bourgeois notions of male headship, including spiritual leadership. Some Rasta sistren identify the Bible as a major source for the imposition of an inferior and subordinate status on them.[83] They, therefore, challenge the authoritative status of the Bible and propose ways of interpreting it in liberative ways. They, like Karen Georgia Thompson chants in "grow up" (see chap. 2 of *Troubling [Public] Theologies*, forthcoming):

>   invite
>   new ways of reading that named holy
>   books
>   given power to decide
>   the
>   value of peoples humanity
>   interrogate
>   that Bible
>   strip
>   away the great divides
>   redefining
>   for today
>   respect,
>   worth and dignity.

Others, such as the Bobo Shanti sistren, negotiate "bargains" within the patriarchal situation that allows them some benefit while revaluing menstrual processes, which are also denigrated in the wider Jamaican culture. In so doing, they renegotiate sexual practices, opening possibilities for non-procreative intercourse.

In this complex of domination, resistance, and negotiation, they draw upon varying strategies to maximise their security and optimise their life options.[84] So, these sistren negotiate compromises based on the gains such as "having a King man as a valuable asset rather than remaining single and bearing the burdens this entails."[85] Such bargains in the face of patriarchy speak of strength which supports and calls forth life:

> No, if they really want to see your strength,
> They must not look to the rock that stands before them,
> But the daisy which grows out from under it,
> nurtured by the stream.
> It will never seek to destroy the rock that looms above it.
> It will simply,
> Persistently,
> Wonderfully,
> Gently,
> Kindly,
> Justly,
> Beautifully,
> Peaceably
> Grow.
> Not lashing out tendrils to crush,
> But sending its roots
> down,
> To places
> unseen,
> To drink
> deeply
> Of the Spring
> of the One
> who calls
> her
> to
> Life.
>
> ("Strong," Chad Rimmer—see chap. 2)

NOTES

1. Terisa E. Turner, "Women, RastafarI and the New Society: Caribbean and East African roots of a popular movement against structural adjustment." *Labour, Capital and Society/Travail, capital et société* 24.1 (April/Avril 1991): 67.
2. Diana J. Fox, *Cultural DNA: Gender at the Root of Everyday Life in Rural Jamaica* (Kingston, Jamaica: University of the West Indies Press, 2010), 119.
3. Nyabinghi elder in 1989 interview with journalist Alona Wartofsky in Barry Chevannes, *Rastafari: Roots and Ideology* (Syracuse, NY: Syracuse University Press, 1994), 255.
4. Imani Tafari Ama, "Resistance Within and Without: Reasonings on Gender Relations." In *RastafarI in the New Millennium: A RastafarI Reader*, edited by Michael Barnett (New York: Syracuse University Press, 2014), 212.
5. Tricia Redeker Hepner and Randall L. Hepner, "Gender, Community and Change among the RastafarI of New York" in *New York glory: Religions in the city*, edited by Tony Carnes and Anna Karpathakis (New York: New York University Press, 2001), 335.
6. Jean Besson, "Religion as Resistance in Jamaican Peasant Life: The Baptist Church, Revival Worldview and Rastafari Movement." In *RastafarI and Other African-Caribbean Worldviews*, edited by Barry Chevannes. (New Jersey: Rutgers University Press, 1998), 44.
7. Michael Barnett, "The many faces of Rasta: Doctrinal Diversity within the RastafarI Movement," *Caribbean Quarterly* 51.2 (2005).
8. Deborah A. Thomas, *Exceptional Violence: Embodied Citizenship in Transnational Jamaica*. (Durham and London: Duke University Press, 2011). Ajamu Nangwaya, "Rastafari as a Catalytic Force in Ecotourism Development in Jamaica: Development as Economic and Social Justice." Paper presented at The University of the West Indies conference series, 2007. (http://sta.uwi.edu/conferences/salises/documents/Nangwaya%20%20A%20.pdf).
9. Fox, *Cultural DNA*, 118.
10. Tafari Ama, "Resistance Within," 193.
11. Ras Dizzy I, "I wants no part with you," in *Rastafari*, edited by Rex Nettleford and Veronica Salter (Kingston, Jamaica: Caribbean Quarterly, 2008), 104.
12. Jovan Scott Lewis, "Rights, Indigeneity, and the Market of Rastafari," *International Journal of Cultural Property* (2017).
13. Thomas, *Exceptional Violence*.
14. Thomas, *Exceptional Violence*.
15. Nathalie Montlouis, *Lords and Empresses in and out of Babylon: The EABIC community and the dialectic of female subordination*. PhD Thesis, University of London, 2013.
16. Diana J. Fox and Jillian M. Smith, "Stewards of their island: Rastafari Women's Activism for the Forests and Waters in Trinidad and Tobago-Social Movement Perspectives," *Resilience: A Journal of the Environmental Humanities* 3 (Winter/Spring/Fall 2015–2016).
17. Nangwaya, "Rastafari as a Catalytic Force."

18. Lewis, "Rights, Indigeneity, and the Market of Rastafari."

19. Barry Chevannes, "What You Sow Is What You Reap: Violence and the Construction of Male Identity in Jamaica," *Current Issues in Comparative Education* 2.1 (2002).

20. Fox, *Cultural DNA*, 113.

21. L. Collins, "Daughters of Jah: The Impact of Rastafarian Womanhood in the Caribbean, the United States, Britain, and Canada." In *Religion, Culture, and Tradition in the Caribbean*, edited by Hemchand Gossai and Nathaniel Samuel Murrell (New York: St. Martin's Press, 2000).

22. Bianca Brynda, "'Roots Daughters': Rasta sistren and their Experiences in the Movement." In *Ay BoBo: Afro-Kaibische Religionen/African–Caribbean Religions. Part 3: Rastafari*, edited by M. Kremser, 77–100. (Vienna: WUV-Universitätsverlag, 1994).

23. Montlouis, *Lords and Empresses in and out of Babylon*.

24. Collins, "Daughters of Jah," 229.

25. Chevannes, *Rastafari*.

26. Hepner and Hepner, "Gender, Community and Change," 337.

27. Collins, "Daughters of Jah."

28. Fox, *Cultural DNA*, 118.

29. Hepner and Hepner, "Gender, Community and Change," 341.

30. Hepner and Hepner, "Gender, Community and Change"; Fox, *Cultural DNA*; Tafari-Ama, "Resistance Within and Without," (also describes the relations between sistren and bredren in Rasta as paradoxical.)

31. Obiagele Lake, "Cultural Ideology and RastafarI Women." In *RastafarI in the New Millennium: A RastafarI Reader*, edited by Michael Barnett (New York: Syracuse University Press, 2014).

32. Obiagele Lake, "The Culturalization of African Female Pollution: RastafarI Adaptations." In *Rastafari*, edited by Rex Nettleford and Veronica Salter (Caribbean Quarterly: The University of the West Indies, 2008).

33. Barnett, "The many faces of Rasta."

34. Hepner and Hepner, "Gender, Community and Change."

35. Sehon M. Lewis, *From Mythology to Reality: Moving Beyond Rastafari* (Raleigh, NC: Lulu Enterprises, 2013).

36. Lewis, *From Mythology to Reality*, 244.

37. Chevannes, *Rastafari*.

38. Chevannes, *Rastafari*.

39. Tafari-Ama, "Resistance Within and Without."

40. Lewis, *From Mythology to Reality*.

41. Barry Chevannes, *Betwixt and Between: Explorations in an African-Caribbean Mindscape* (Kingston: Jamaica, 2006), 294.

42. Lake, "Cultural Ideology and RastafarI Women."

43. Lewis, *From Mythology to Reality*.

44. Fox, *Cultural DNA*.

45. Tafari Ama, "Resistance Within and Without," 193.

46. Tafari Ama, "Resistance Within and Without," 212.

47. Leary in Tafari-Ama, "Resistance Within and Without," 212.
48. Fox, *Cultural DNA*, 210.
49. Imani Tafari Ama, Email communication with author (November 27, 2021).
50. Lake, "The Culturalization of African Female Pollution," 231.
51. Anna Kasafi Perkins, "Blood clot, ras clot and bun bow clot: Lovindeer takes on female bodily taboos in Jamaica." In *Breaking Down Binaries: Tidal shifts in the study of the languages, literatures and cultures of the Greater Caribbean and beyond*, edited by Nicholas Faraclas, et al., 63–78. Puerto Rico/Curacao: University of Curacao.
52. Perkins, "Blood clot."
53. Mark Wignall, "Religion, menstruation and mass ignorance." *Jamaica Observer* (Sunday, February 24, 2013).
54. Wignall, "Religion, menstruation and mass ignorance."
55. Wignall, "Religion, menstruation and mass ignorance."
56. Montlouis, *Lords and Empresses in and out of Babylon*.
57. Barry Chevannes, "The Phallus and the Outcast: The Symbolism of the Dreadlocks in Jamaica." In *RastafarI and Other African-Caribbean Worldviews*, edited by Barry Chevannes (New Jersey: Rutgers University Press, 1998).
58. John P Homiak, "Dub History: Soundings on Rastafari Livity and Language." In *RastafarI and Other African-Caribbean Worldviews*, edited by Barry Chevannes. (New Jersey: Rutgers University Press, 1998).
59. Homiak, "Dub History," 140.
60. Homiak, "Dub History."
61. Roland Henry, "Female biology dictates family life in Rasta camp," *Sunday Observer* (July 17, 2006).
62. Henry, "Female biology dictates family life."
63. Montlouis, *Lords and Empresses in and out of Babylon*.
64. Chevannes, *Rastafari*, 259.
65. Montlouis, *Lords and Empresses in and out of Babylon*.
66. Collins, "Daughters of Jah," 244.
67. Chevannes, "The Phallus and the Outcast," 122.
68. Henry, "Female biology dictates family life."
69. Henry, "Female biology dictates family life."
70. Henry, "Female biology dictates family life."
71. Chevannes, *Rastafari*, 258.
72. Montlouis, *Lords and Empresses in and out of Babylon*.
73. Turner, "Women, RastafarI and the New Society."
74. Turner, "Women, RastafarI and the New Society."
75. Turner, "Women, RastafarI and the New Society," 76.
76. Tafari Ama, "Resistance Within and Without."
77. Tafari Ama, "Resistance Within and Without," 217.
78. Tafari Ama, "Resistance Within and Without," 217.
79. Montlouis, *Lords and Empresses in and out of Babylon*, 130.
80. Montlouis, *Lords and Empresses in and out of Babylon*, 149.

81. Deniz Kandiyoti, "Bargaining with Patriarchy," *Gender and Society* 3.3 (1998): 275.
82. Kandiyoti, "Bargaining with Patriarchy," 275.
83. Chevannes, *Rastafari*.
84. Kandiyoti, "Bargaining with Patriarchy."
85. Tafari Ama, Email communication with author, November 27, 2021.

Chapter 11

Queer Arctivism
Talking Back to the Cis/tems

Ana Ester Pádua Freire

Religion—as a cultural system, a complex system of meanings, symbols, and behaviors related to a community of members[1]—re-elaborates the geographic space giving new meaning to the public space. The same public space that, "at least ideally, is the place of difference, heterogeneity, of meeting strangers,"[2] is the space that welcomes religious phenomena in their complexity and diversity. Marjo de Theije[3] affirms:

> Pay due attention to the religious lives of the city's inhabitants, to the symbols and social relations manifested in the religious activities of the urban population—and to the meanings they give to religion and the urban spaces that serve as its context; here is an anthropological care that would undoubtedly illuminate reflections on the processes of contestation, identification, and symbolization in the urban landscape.[4]

Thus, the prominence of religion in the urban landscape crosses themes dear to the contemporary public space, such as the monopoly of symbolic violence. According to Silvana Rubino, "the city is made up of borders, which prevent social actors considered inappropriate from entering, as well as the legitimate ones from leaving and thus disqualifying."[5]

Historically, art has been a way of breaking these boundaries of the public space, being, therefore, an instrument of resistance and an ally of political militancy. In this sense, the Metropolitan Community Church of Belo Horizonte (MCC BH), Brazil, makes use of art, through performances in order to give visibility to its activism and its struggle for LGBTQI+ rights. In this context, this essay presents some elements of this relationship between religion and art, through the case study of the Metropolitan Community Church in the III March against LGBTphobia in Belo Horizonte and the Metropolitan Region.

METROPOLITAN COMMUNITY CHURCH OF BELO HORIZONTE: FROM LOS ANGELES TO BELO HORIZONTE

Founded in the capital of Minas Gerais, Brazil, in 2006,[6] the Metropolitan Community Church of Belo Horizonte is part of the Universal Fellowship of the Metropolitan Community Churches, founded in Los Angeles, USA, by the Reverend Troy Perry, in 1968. MCC is a self-proclaimed inclusive church. Inclusive church is a terminology that has been used in recent decades to refer to churches commonly known as "gay churches." According to Marcelo Tavares Natividade, this is a religious "self-denomination," which proposes to be an alternative when elaborating its own hermeneutics that allows "the conciliation between Christianity and forms of exercising sexuality that are dissonant from the heterosexual norm."[7]

Based on the values of inclusion, community, transformation, and global justice, MCC intends to be a church for Human Rights. This is the case also in Belo Horizonte; there the church makes alliances with civil society in search of the maintenance of guaranteed LGBTQI+ rights and new achievements.

WE EXIST AND WE DESERVE RESPECT: III MARCH AGAINST LGBTPHOBIA IN BELO HORIZONTE AND THE METROPOLITAN REGION

In the context of political alliances, MCC BH joined the "Fight Center for Free Sexual Orientation of Minas Gerais" (Cellos MG) to coordinate the "March against LGBTphobia" at the city. The march is a political act that has been consolidated in several cities in Brazil since 2010, and takes place on May 17, when people around the world mobilize for the "International Day Against Homophobia, Lesbophobia and Transphobia" (IDAHO). The date was chosen in reference to May 17, 1990, when the World Health Organization (WHO) removed homosexuality from the International Classification of Diseases (ICD).

> The first significant and nationwide achievement of the Brazilian LGBT movement occurred in 1985 and is the result of a decision by the Federal Council of Medicine (CFM), which removed homosexuality as a pathology, as was the case until then in terms prevailing in the International Classification of Diseases

(ICD), prepared by the World Health Organization (WHO). WHO itself began to have the same understanding as of May 17, 1990, a date that became a historic landmark to the point that this day is now internationally recognized as International Day Against Homophobia. This landmark has also recently been endorsed by the Federal Government, which, based on demand from the LGBT movement, instituted, through Presidential Decree of June 4, 2010, May 17 as the National Day Against Homophobia.[8]

The III March against LGBTphobia in Belo Horizonte and Metropolitan Area took place on May 14, 2016, with a concentration in "Praça Sete," a milestone representing militancy and resistance in the downtown of the capital of Minas Gerais and the symbolic city center of Belo Horizonte's main political activities. Traditionally, Praça Sete has been the stage for dissonant voices, attracting diverse audiences, both for its easy access and for its symbolical, political, and historical character. Regarding the dynamics of this public space, Juliana Gonzaga Jayme and Magda de Almeida Neves state that "Praça Sete is a space for interactions and coexistence between strangers and, also, an identity place, which has vitality."[9]

That year, the March was held on the 14th (Saturday), and not the 17th (Tuesday), as the Organizing Committee preferred that the event would take place on a Saturday so that more people could join the demonstration. The theme chosen for 2016 was "We exist and deserve respect." The program of the event was: 14h—Concentration in Praça Sete; 16h—March through downtown; 18h—final act at Praça Raul Soares. Ten people from MCC BH attended the March. The group was small but represented almost 50% of the active members of the community (at the time, twenty-two members). Of the participants, some were directly involved with the organization: the pastor, in the coordination, and three members in the cultural part, through presenting performances.

The March against LGBTphobia is a plural, non-violent political action that presupposes a variety of dissident bodies and sexualities representing their positions. The central issue is the visibility of violence against LGBTQI+ people, in the sense of mobilizing society in the struggle to maintain already acquired rights and to obtain new rights, such as, for example, the approval of Bill 5002/2013 in Brazil, known as "João W. Nery Bill"[10] or "Gender Identity Law."

The march advocates for embodied collective rights. It defends against precarity, from singular and plural perspectives, that is, from the experiences of individuals and the community. According to Judith Butler, "even a life devoid of rights is still within the sphere of the political and, therefore, is not reduced to mere existence, but is often angry, indignant, revolted and opposing resistance."[11] It is the vocalization of "anger" and "indignation" which, according to the philosopher, takes people to the streets. The bodies that come out in assembly are sexualized bodies, which persist in taking over the public space, even though they are the target of the eradication of the State. Going out on the streets is, according to Butler, a performative break in the *status quo*. It is the representation of a gesture that is, at the same time, a movement in the corporal and political sense.

Going to the streets is a plural and performative exercise to appear when the meeting itself means persistence and resistance. The march begins when people start gathering in Praça Sete, which Butler calls "public assembly."[12] This is a mass demonstration, in which people come together in a public space to demand one or more specific outcomes. In an exercise of freedom of assembly, these mass demonstrations occur as a collective rejection of socially and economically induced precarity. Butler elucidates that

> the assembly is already speaking before any word is spoken, meeting in assembly is already a representation of popular will; this representation means, quite differently, the way in which a singular and unified subject declares his/her desire through a vocalized proposition.[13]

Thus, there is no need for a claiming vocalization for the assembly to take place. The right to freedom of assembly is different from the right to free expression:

> If we consider why freedom of assembly is different from freedom of expression, we will see that it is precisely because the power that people have to come together is itself an important political prerogative, quite different from the right to say whatever they have to say once people are gathered. The meeting means beyond what is said, and this mode of signification is a concerted corporeal representation, a plural form of performativity.[14]

Acting together does not mean acting in concert, after all, as it happens in the march, different agendas can be raised. However, there is a desire prior to a demand for a political agenda that unites them: to create forms of coexistence characterized by equality and minimized precarity, through alliances that are formed. There is a linguistic performativity and a bodily performativity in the assemblies, which in addition to uniting around an agenda, perform the right to appear, which is a bodily demand for a set of more livable lives. Thus, going to the streets is a plural and performative exercise of appearance. Appearance of their bodies, their common goals, their resistance to precarity.

For Butler, precarity is the biopolitical situation to which populations are subject. It is a situation of insecurity and hopelessness, which is usually induced and produced by the government and economic institutions. It is a non-viable way of life and "implies an increased feeling of being expendable or being discarded that is not evenly distributed in society."[15] It is a condition imputed to the human being by the oppressive relations of political and economic control in which, in a maximum requirement for personal accountability, responsibility is redefined as "the requirement to become an entrepreneur of oneself in conditions that make a dubious vocation impossible."[16] After all, individualizing morality requires unattainable self-sufficiency.

Thus, in a singularity of its purposes in the march, MCC BH does not go to the streets just to talk about itself, but to coexist in an ethical exercise in relationality. Relationships that were once banned are a mark that touches stigmatized lives, like those of sexual dissidents. Many LGBTQI+ people experience relational exclusion in their families, because they do not accept them; in their work environment, because they are stigmatized; in their affective life, for trying to live a celibate life; in their religious life, for not believing they are worthy of a relationship with the Sacred. Leaving the temple to the city center, takes MCC BH to a relational encounter with others who share emancipatory ideals, which go through the claim of maintaining acquired rights and new civilian protections. Thus, individual responsibility is replaced by an *ethos* of solidarity.

PERFORMANCES: THE RELIGIOSITY OF "ABJECT BODIES"

Praça Sete was the stage for the performances of members of MCC BH. Sexuality and corporeality that could be considered protected through what may be seen as a "ghetto" church, which "hides" LGBTQI+, was giving visibility to its members. It is what Christine de Alencar Chaves[17] would call a "resonance box" in describing the Brazilian "National March of the Landless" (*Marcha National dos Sem-Terra*), which took place in 1997. According to the author, the National March, having become prominent in the media, with the creation of facts and news, has become a resonance box of clashes with the State. In this sense, the III Minas Gerais March against LGBTphobia, through its political agenda that generates mobilization and news, would work as this resonance box, giving visibility to MCC BH.

Among the performances was Simone Star, a drag queen performed by the actor Marcelo Oliveira, the spouse of the pastor of MCC BH (See Figure 11.1). The picture below shows Simone Star lying on a kind of stage that exists on that street, with a mesh that hid pieces of raw beef steaks that would be used later, wearing a butcher's apron, lying between barbed wire and photos of murdered transvestites. Simone Star looks at the nothing, and, as if she were dead, she remains there for a few minutes.

Figure 11.1. Simone Star (2016). *Photo provided by author*

The march had a certain initial tension, as the date coincided with the passing of the Olympic Torch in Belo Horizonte. The organizers were notified by the Municipality of Belo Horizonte, requesting a change in the date of the event. But the Organizing Committee decided to keep the date and, therefore, there was only permission to start the march after the Olympic Torch had passed through Avenida Afonso Pena, one of the main avenues in the capital.

Meanwhile, Simone Star's performance continued silently, between getting up, sitting down, and smoking a cigarette, and waiting almost two hours, until she received the microphone and the right to speak (see Figure 11.2).

Some people gathered trying almost unsuccessfully to hear what was being said on the microphone. With cellphones in hand, the performance was recorded by people who were there to follow the march. Curious people also stopped, listened to what was being said and continued, since Praça Sete is a transit point, due to its local commerce and the countless public transportation lines that merge there.

Some passersby went by without showing any interest in what was happening. Running, they crossed the small group that gathered there and ignored the performance. Some people who would march with the group also did not pay attention to what was being presented, continuing to talk in their small groups, laughing, greeting one another, and taking selfies. Other people sat on the stage, with their backs turned to Simone Star, disinterested in what was happening there. Simone Star's presence was a picture framed by the people's personal interest. According to Butler,

Figure 11.2. Abject bodies (2016). *Photo provided by author*

any photograph or any series of images would undoubtedly have a frame or a set of frames, and these frames would function as a potentially exclusive designation, including what is captured by establishing a zone of what is not likely to be captured.[18]

This perspective can be analyzed from the point of view of Roland Barthes' *punctum*. The concept is in opposition to another, namely, the *studium*. Barthes—in his classic work "Camera Lucida: Reflections on Photography" (1980)—coined the terms *studium* and *punctum* in the context of photographic theory. According to Rodrigo Fontanari, "*punctum* comes from the Latin verb *pungere*, 'prick,' 'drill,' 'perforate.' What is poignant, that cuts, hurts, pricks, pins and amortises."[19] Fontanari points out that the *punctum* is the invisible that is in the photo, it is what is not seen, the intentionality. *Punctum* can be the detail, the drama, the supplement.

As Butler stated, the photographic framing includes and excludes at the same time. There is an intentionality in what is registered objectively. The image of a drag queen in the center of the city, in a demonstration against LGBTphobia, is something that breaks with what is expected, creating a favorable space for breaks and continuities. As an example of continuity here, we can see the location chosen for the demonstration, the use of a sound car, slogans, a march that crosses the city center.

On the other hand, there are important ruptures that must be perceived from the point of view of the *punctum*, that is, the subjective that appears in the photo and beyond. The political role of a Christian church on the streets generates tension in the idea of *laïcité*, which is often understood as secularism.

The presence of the Church in the streets carries a sense of tension in the assembly. But it is on the streets that the identity of the nation is formed.[20]

On the streets Simone Star was performing a political and religious liturgy. According to Marvin Carlson, one of the emphases of performance is the body:

> One typical performance art is solo art, and the typical performance artist makes little use of the scenic surroundings elaborated by the traditional stage; but sometimes it uses a few elements and some furniture; any outfit (sometimes even nudity) is better suited to the performance situation.[21]

In the case of Simone Star, her body was the center of her performance, and even the chosen theme "abject bodies," was a critique of society's indifference to the bodies of travestis and transsexual people. *Travesti* is a gender identity from Latin America that is usually recognized as a transgender woman. However, the word *travesti* says more than gender identity, taking into consideration other intersectionalities, such as race and class. In the past, *travesti* was used to refer to transgender women who were sex workers; today it is that too, but it is also a political position.

QUEER ARCTIVISM: TALKING BACK TO THE CIS/TEMS

Benefiting of the Praça Sete as a post-structured stage,[22] MCC BH used art as a ritualistic way to speak about itself. Choosing not to walk in unity nor carry the denomination's flag, the church showed that, during the III March against LGBTphobia, their mission was, similar to the community's interpretation of the mission of Christ, to take a prophetic message to the streets. Through art as a denunciation, art as arctivism, MCC BH was concerned with giving visibility to what it considers to be a political agenda for travestis and transgender people.

Between the "sacred and the urban,"[23] religion and art intercross in a complex relationship in which, in principle, the desacralization of the rite is not perceived. On the contrary, performed by discursive bodies, the rites bring new meanings to the religion of the LGBTQI+ community. The departure of members from the temple, through performances in the center of the city, would also imply an "exit from the closet" of their religion.

The presence of MCC BH in the public space shows the arctivism of MCC BH as a social language which challenges cisgender and heteronormative systems. The case study reveals that the active and artistic use of liturgy, as a ritualistic way this faith community identifies itself, is a fundamental mechanism to experience the world, while subverting the precariousness of being sexual and gender dissidents. Religion and politics can be found in the religious temple, and on the streets, through art as an emancipatory activity that resists the cis/tems.

The uniqueness of MCC BH's queer activism lies precisely in how religion and sexuality go through its political action. Upon leaving the temple to the city center, members bring their faith, hope and idea of justice from the construction of the Kin/dom of God. Religiosity is an inseparable condition of the lives of these LGBTQI+ people who transform the public space through the affirmation of identity categories that do not dissociate faith, politics, and sexuality.

The purpose of the march is to ask: "What are the possible lives to be lived?" There is a need to know, first, the conditions of interdependence that will guarantee the struggle for the achievement of political goals. It is the construction of the idea of community and community life that enables interdependence between people who collectively build their sense of meaning.[24] The ideal of solidarity is what moves this community of faith from the temple to the city center. However, it is important to note that collectivity, solidarity, and interdependence are also built on the path between the temple and the city center. After all, Butler expounds that,

> sometimes it is not a question of first having the power and then being able to act; sometimes it is a matter of acting, and in action claiming the power you need. This is performativity as I understand it and it is also a way of acting out of precariousness and against it.[25]

Thus, the experiences of sexual and gender dissidents within traditional and hegemonic Christianity are subverted by political encounters and desires that reconfigure religion by affirming differences and allowing precarity to become a reality conducive to resistance.

NOTES

1. Clifford Geertz, *A interpretação das culturas* (Rio de Janeiro: LTC, 2008).
2. Juliana Gonzaga Jayme, Magda Almeida Neves, "Cidade e Espaço Público: Política de revitalização urbana em Belo Horizonte," *Caderno CRH* 23.60 (Sep–Dec 2010): 605–617.
3. Marjo de Theije, "Religião e Transformações Urbanas em Recife, Brasil," *Ciências Sociais e Religião* 8.8 (Out 2006): 63–84.
4. Marjo de Theije, "Religião e Transformações Urbanas em Recife, Brasil," 66.
5. Silvana Rubino, "Enobrecimento Urbano," in *Plural de Cidades: Novos léxicos urbanos*, ed. C. Leite; R. P Fortuna (Coimbra: Edições Almedina, 2009), 37.

6. Léo Rossetti, *Borboletas tropicais:* O *caminho brasileiro das Igrejas da Comunidade Metropolitana* (Rio de Janeiro: Metanoia, 2016).
7. Marcelo Tavares Natividade, "Uma homossexualidade santificada? Etnografia de uma comunidade inclusiva pentecostal," *Religião & Sociedade* 30 (2010): 90.
8. Luiz Mello, Camilo Braz, Almeida De Freitas, Fátima Regina, Rezende De Avelar, Bruno, "Questões LGBT em debate: sobre desafios e conquistas," *Sociedade e Cultura*, 15.1 (Jan-Jul 2012): 152.
9. Juliana Gonzaga Jayme and Magda Almeida Neves, "Cidade e Espaço Público," 610.
10. João Nery was a trans man who pioneered claims about the rights to gender identity.
11. Judith Butler, *Corpos em aliança e a política das ruas:* Notas *para uma teoria performativa de assembleia* (Rio de Janeiro, RJ: Civilização Brasileira, 2018), 89.
12. Butler, *Corpos em aliança e a política das ruas*, 173.
13. Butler, *Corpos em aliança e a política das ruas*, 173.
14. Butler, *Corpos em aliança e a política das ruas*, 14.
15. Butler, *Corpos em aliança e a política das ruas*, 21.
16. Butler, *Corpos em aliança e a política das ruas*, 21.
17. Christine de Alencar Chaves, "A marcha política como ritual," in *Rituais ontem e hoje*, ed. Mariza Peirano (Rio de Janeiro: Jorge Zahar Editor, 2003).
18. Judith Butler, *Corpos em aliança e a política das ruas*, 182.
19. Rodrigo Fontanari, "A noção de punctum de Roland Barthes, uma abertura da imagem?" *Paralaxe* 3 (2015): 66.
20. Roberto DaMatta, *A casa e a rua: Espaço, cidadania, mulher e morte no Brasil* (Rio de Janeiro, RJ: Rocco, 1997).
21. Carlson, *Performance:* Uma *introdução crítica* (Belo Horizonte: Editora UFMG, 2010), 17.
22. Macdonald, *Theater at the Margins*: T*ext and the post-structured stage* (Ann Arbor: University of Michigan Press, 1993).
23. Zeny Rosendahl, "O Sagrado e o urbano: Gênese e função das cidades," *Espaço e Cultura* 1.1 (1996): 26–40.
24. Peter L. Berger and Thomas Luckman, *Modernidade, pluralismo e crise de sentido: A orientação do homem moderno* (Petrópolis, RJ: Vozes, 2018).
25. Butler, *Corpos em aliança e a política das*, 65.

Chapter 12

The Bacchus Lady as The Parable of "Promiscuous Care"

Nami Kim

If you visit the Topgol Park (once called the Pagoda Park), located in Jongro in the central district in Seoul, South Korea, you may run into women in their 50s, 60s, or 70s who are contemptuously called the "Bacchus *ajumma* or *halmoni*." This park, known as an "elders' park," is where older men hang out; but no "decent" women would venture there.

RUNNING INTO THE BACCHUS LADIES

Named after the Roman god of wine and fertility, Bacchus is an energy drink that contains taurine and caffeine. Supposed to improve energy level and stamina, the Bacchus drink was popularized in the early 1960s in South Korea, during which the country had entered a state-run economic developmental phase through rapid industrialization and urbanization.

The word *ajumma* is commonly used to refer to a woman who is married or who no longer "looks young," whereas *halmoni* literally means granny. The Bacchus ajumma/halmoni (Bacchus ladies hereafter) sell bottles of Bacchus to elderly men and solicit them for sex in the park and its vicinities where the elderly men stroll, chatting with other elderly men, playing chess, or sitting idly. The Bacchus ladies and their male clients go to nearby motels or any places available. The women get paid 20 to 40 U.S. dollars for their sexual services. The Bacchus ladies are "despised" women who "sell sex" in their old age for daily survival in a society where elderly people with no resources or safety net struggle inordinately. The Bacchus ladies do not fit the image of a "respectable" grandmother, who has "gracefully aged." As elderly sex workers, the Bacchus ladies are subject to humiliation, stigma, policing, or imprisonment for prostitution. Their nonnormative activities and lives place them outside the category of decently aged women who are no longer sexually active and who conform to socially prescribed gender roles and relations as "grannies."

The Bacchus Lady (*The Killer Woman* in Korean title) is a South Korean film that came out in 2016.[1] The film is about the life of So-young Yoon, an elderly sex worker, played by Youn Yuh-jung. "The Killer Woman" connotes a woman who "slays" with her sexual services, but the protagonist becomes a "prostitute-turned-killer" when she assists the suicide of three former clients who are old and ill. This is an evocative film in multiple aspects. As David John Graham says, film itself is a "powerful affective medium," engaging the viewers "at the level of the feelings and emotions."[2] As a "type of text," film also makes us question and reflect on various theological ideas and practices. Based on John Dominic Crossan's distinction between parables and myths, Graham maintains that films may function either as myth or as parable. In order for film to be effective, Graham insists that it must function as "parable." Films as parable, unlike myth, "expand and broaden our understanding of the world by questioning our world-view."[3]

The Bacchus Lady as a "parable" exposes systems of domination and exploitation and challenges theology to attend to the lives of poverty-stricken elderly women, who not only bear the brunt of the society but also defy the normative understanding of aged women as "virtuous and decent." As a parable, *The Bacchus Lady* also compels us to consider "promiscuous care"[4] as an integral part of feminist theoethical praxis. While exposing the dubiousness of "filiative family" that is based on biological, heterosexual nuclear unit, the film explores the possibility of forming "fictive family" that extends care to strangers. It further urges us to think about the difficult question of euthanasia or "assisted suicide," a taboo issue in larger Korean society that is harsh to impoverished, sick, elderly people who are no longer "productive" and/or "independent."

THE BACCHUS LADY: PARABLE OF "PROMISCUOUS CARE"

The Bacchus lady in the film is So-young, a woman in her 60s, wearing shoddy, flamboyant clothes with makeup. The movie starts with a scene in which So-young sees a male gynecologist for contracting gonorrhea. She asks for a fast treatment because she has to go back to work. On her way out of the hospital, she runs into a boy, whose Filipina mother has just been taken by the police for stabbing the boy's father with a pair of scissors over the issue of paternity. The boy's father is the medical doctor whom So-young just saw for her treatment. So-young takes the boy, a "Kopino"[5] child who only speaks Filipino, to her place and feeds him. The boy's name is Min-ho and he stays with So-young. So-young asks her housemate, Do-hoon who has a prosthetic leg, and her transgender landlady, Tina, to take care of Min-ho while she is working outside. The film shows So-young's mundane daily life of going to the Jongro area and its neighborhood to solicit men for sex. It also briefly shows some tense moments between So-young and other Bacchus ladies. The story makes a surprising turn when So-young learns about the illness of one of her former clients, who she recalls as well-dressed and kind. This is when the double meaning of the film's Korean title, "The Killer Woman," starts making sense.

In the meantime, the Emergency Support Center for Migrant Women has been searching for Min-ho, whom they thought was kidnapped. When So-young, Min-ho, and Do-hoon finally meet up with the staff person of the Center, So-young gives the photo that she found inside Min-ho's book that can serve as key evidence to prove paternity: Min-ho's mother, the baby Min-ho, and his Korean father posed together in the photo. The Center's staff and a lawyer say they can speed up a paternity suit against Min-ho's father. They also take a DNA test of Min-ho. If they win, Min-ho's mother will receive child support from Min-ho's father, despite his denial of his paternity.

As William Herzog says in *Parables as Subversive Speech*, the parables are "not earthly stories with heavenly meanings but earthy stories with heavy meanings, weighted down by an awareness of the workings of exploitation in the world of their hearers."[6] Comparing Paulo Freire's education program to Jesus' public activity, Herzog argues that some parables correspond largely with what Paulo Freire calls "first-level codifications," the primary purpose of which is "unmasking the world of oppression."[7] Such codification is "a means to an end, not an end in itself," enabling people who are caught up in the larger realities to step back and gain perspective. The social analysis and theological reflection that emerge in this process begin with "the perplexities of daily life," not with "the mysteries of God."[8]

What if we view *The Bacchus Lady* as one of those parables that are not meant to be a story with "either a clear moral or a single meaning that could be gleaned" by watching it "correctly," but that serves as "discussion-starters, whose purpose was to raise questions and pose dilemmas" to the viewers?[9] *The Bacchus Lady* as a parable exposes the details of exploitation in our times and the regimes of normativity and conformity that regulate and confine people to certain classification where values are also attached. It raises a series of questions regarding the older and neglected population in Korea and poses dilemmas to the viewers. Among many questions raised in *The Bacchus Lady* are the following: Why do elderly women sell both the Bacchus drinks and sex in their old age? What kind of end-of-life care is available? What kind of society is it that the protagonist is asked to assist the suicide of elderly men? Why is So-young taking care of a Kopino boy, a stranger, whose biological father denies his parentage? What are the ways in which disability affects masculinity? What is family and for whom does it exist? In relation to these questions, four major themes emerge: "surrogate/prosthetic labor," fictive family, (un)caring of elderly people, and suspension of judgment. These themes guide us to see critically how the intersecting structures of exploitation and domination work, to consider "promiscuous care" as a feminist theoethical praxis, and to reimagine public space as a "place of solidarity in difference."[10]

Considering these themes will compel feminist theology to attend to "indecent" women who live "unholy" lives as elderly sex-workers and defy the respectability required of elderly women. The stories of women like So-young, including her fictive family formed with a person with disability, a transwoman, and a child of mixed Korean and Filipino ethnicity, are not readily found in feminist theology or queer theology. *The Bacchus Lady* tells us stories that cannot be easily categorized by any one aspect of elderly sex workers' socioeconomic conditions, and therefore compelling feminist theology to expand its horizons. Such stories can also help queer theology to broaden "queer" subjects, for they allow us to understand "queer" as a "politics that eschews gender and sexual normativity" rather than as an "identity category" only.[11]

Surrogate/Prosthetic Labor

The abridged story of So-young's life emerges when she reluctantly agrees to be interviewed by a documentary filmmaker, who initially approached her pretending that he was a potential client. Sitting on a bench in a park, So-young tells him that she came there—where she is currently working—about five years ago. She says she is not ashamed of "making a living," but doesn't want to "let the whole world know either." She continues, "It is easy to judge, but there aren't many options for an old woman like me," adding that she couldn't allow herself to pick up the wastepaper on the streets, which is one of the few options available for impoverished elderly women to make a living in South Korea. So-young tells the documentary filmmaker that she had to earn for her own living all her life. "I worked as a house maid when I was little. I worked at a factory too. Then, even at a U.S. army base in Dong-doo-chun (one of U.S. military base towns in Korea). I became a prostitute for the American soldier."

The Bacchus Lady helps us see sex work as a necropolitical labor through So-young's life. In her book *Service Economies*, Jin-Kyung Lee argues that necropolitical labor is the "most disposable labor," and sex work and the sex worker is one of the "most disposable (labor) commodities."[12] Lee defines necropolitical labor as "the extraction of labor" that is premised on "the possibilities of death, rather than the ultimate event of death itself," and calls a particular type of service work—military, military sex work, and sex work—"surrogate/prosthetic labor."[13] Surrogate/prosthetic labor, which is a necropolitical labor, is work that "enables someone else to live" on the basis of "difference or hierarchy of race, class, and gender."[14] Lee explains that sex work "exists in an inherent continuum with 'sexual violence,' which always carries the risk of death" under economically, physically, and psychologically coercive conditions. The worker's ultimate disposability is "an integral element of prostitution as an occupation."[15] Lee contextualizes her definition of prostitution as a surrogate/prosthetic labor in the specific context of South Korea's "miraculous" economic development under military dictatorships from the 1960s until 1980s, which I also call the period of hypermasculine developmentalism.[16] While noting the discontinuity between domestic prostitution and military prostitution for the U.S. military in the South Korean context, Lee also argues that there is the continuity between these two categories of prostitution.[17] Lee further points out the "interchangeability" or "evident connections" between sex work and factory work by young women as labor force from the 1960s through the 1980s. As she explains, the connections between the economic exploitation of factory workers and the sexual exploitation of working-class women in the sex industry are palpable, for both exploitations took on "patriarchal constructions of femininity and feminine sexuality."[18]

So-young's history of labor attests to "the porous and ambiguous boundaries between the broader female working-class labors":[19] starting as a housemaid, then a factory worker, a military prostitute serving U.S. military clientele, and then a "domestic prostitute" as an elderly woman. So-young's labor history shows not only "the flow of working-class female labor from factories to sexualized service and prostitution industries," but also "another kind of interchangeability and 'migration' between domestic prostitution and other kinds of transnational working-class female labors" by contesting the firm line drawn in sex work for U.S. male soldiers and for elderly Korean men.[20] Her story reveals how a young military prostitute has become an elderly domestic prostitute, as she has no social resources or family support. Women like So-young are not included in the category of "aggressive modern wives" in sociologist Haejoang Cho's study of three generations of middle-class women in Korea from the colonial modern to postmodern period.[21] The cheap labor provided by So-young-like women as domestic servants and as other service workers made possible the rise of "aggressive modern wives" who are So-young's contemporaries through "the process of housewifization" in the 1970s.[22] *The Bacchus Lady* challenges us to pay attention to the stories that do not align with this kind of typology of women in Korea and with the positive portrait of the middle class elderly women as "gracefully" aging grandmothers.

The film shows the kind of work So-young performs as an elderly sex worker and exposes elderly men's sexual exploitation of their female counterparts. So-young is engaged in "surrogate/prosthetic labor" that satisfies sexually "deprived" elderly men. Upon her former clients' requests, she further performs "surrogate/prosthetic" labor by assisting the ailing elderly men who cannot or will not end their lives by themselves. Her other "surrogate/prosthetic" labor is also dangerous because assisting others to end their lives with dignity puts her own life at risk. The consequence of her assistance is severe. She is incarcerated and subsequently dies alone in a prison cell.

Her surrogate/prosthetic labor as a domestic servant, factory worker, and military sex worker took place in the context of hypermasculine developmentalism in South Korea. Her surrogate/prosthetic labor as an elderly prostitute who also assists the suicide of elderly men takes place in the shadow of post-hypermasculine developmentalism in South Korea, in which the issues of various forms of migration from other Asian countries, "multicultural family," homophobia, transphobia, transnational sex tourism of Korean men, and the aging population with no safety net. As a parable, the film challenges us to see how society relies on surrogate/prosthetic labor and who bears the consequences of such labor.

Filiative versus Fictive Family

So-young rents a room in a house where the landlady Tina and her fellow tenant Do-hoon live. Tina calls So-young *unnie* (a Korean term for an older sister used by female siblings) and Do-hoon calls So-young *noonim* (an honorific and endearing term for an older sister used by male siblings). So-young's "fictive family" is comprised of two "siblings," Tina and Do-hoon, and Min-ho, along with a street cat she feeds everyday by leaving food outside of her room. Because Min-ho's Filipina mother is in prison, So-young temporarily becomes a "surrogate" mother for Min-ho. Three socially marginalized people—So-young, an old sex worker, Do-hoon, a young man with a prosthetic leg, and Tina, a transwoman—live together in a house with a courtyard. They don't mind each other's business and they take care of Min-ho when So-young goes out to work. So-young offers Do-hoon two boxes of cigarettes for taking care of Min-ho as a gesture of appreciation. When So-young asks him a favor to accompany her to meet the staff and a lawyer at the Emergency Support Center for Migrant Women, he is reluctant at first but agrees to go with her and Min-ho. When Min-ho disappears while Do-hoon is cooking, both So-young and Do-hoon search their neighborhood together. Min-ho is found by a Filipino man who is able to communicate with him. Do-hoon asks the Filipino man to take Min-ho with him, for they can communicate in Filipino as co-ethnic people, but to his disappointment the Filipino man says he can't. He only tells Min-ho to stay with So-young and buys him some snacks. So-young, Do-hoon, and Min-ho visit Min-ho's imprisoned mother together, and So-young tells Min-ho's mother that she will take care of Min-ho until she is released. Min-ho's mother profusely thanks So-young.

So-young with her fictive family takes a day trip riding in a car that Tina drives, enjoying their time together. They spend time at an amusement park and go to the Imjingak, the closest area to the DMZ, where they can peek into North Korea from an observation deck. The viewers learn that when she was a young child, So-young crossed the 38 parallels that has separated the South from the North. She was one of those whose families have been separated along with the North and South division. In a restaurant where So-young treats her family to a nice dinner, they watch the TV news report of an elderly man found overcome by sleeping pills, accompanied by hotel security camera video footage of him and an old woman entering a hotel room. The anchorperson implies that the woman killed the old man, and that money is the motive. When Tina disparagingly says how anyone could kill another person for as little as $1,000, So-young, looking utterly unsettled by the news, says there must be a story that is not revealed. As the last stop to wrap up their trip, they go to the bar where Tina works and enjoy watching Tina's singing performance. In the meantime, police are searching for the "killer" of the elderly man (Jae-woo) and comes after So-young. In the middle of Tina's singing, they show up and arrest So-young on the charge of murder. So-young might have intuitively sensed how her "assistance" of three elderly men's suicide would come to an end, because she suggested for a "family trip" after she unintentionally assisted Jae-woo's suicide.

Two filiative families are juxtaposed against So-young's fictive family. One is Min-ho's filiative family consisting of Min-ho, his Filipino mother, and his Korean father who denies his paternity. As a nurse who works at Min-ho's father's hospital bitterly criticizes, some Korean men's irresponsible sexual behaviors and practices have created devastating situations for Filipina women whom they had intimate relations with while traveling or studying in the Philippines. There are a few number of women like Min-ho's mother, some of whom don't have an option other than staying in their own country while raising children by themselves without paternal support.[23] The other filiative family is the family of the first elderly man whose dying So-young assists. He has a son, daughter-in-law, and their two teenage children, visiting him from the United States. Their obligatory visit of him in hospital is brief, and his son promises to visit him again next year. When his son and daughter-in-law see So-young visiting their father, his daughter-in-law suspects that So-young might be a "gold-digger." She tells So-young not to visit him again and that he doesn't have any money. Referring to his son and his family, the bed-bound man says, "They are cold-hearted."

So-young also had a "family" when she was in a relationship with an American soldier. Through her interaction with a young Black GI who was eating at a local restaurant, So-young's conversation with her former colleague, and a picture of her baby boy, the viewers learn that she had a son who she had given up for transnational adoption. The young Black GI at the restaurant reminded her of her son, who would have grown up like him. The film touches on the thorny issue of transnational adoption that is entangled with the history of the Korean War, Christian "benevolence," the ongoing presence of U.S. military troops in South Korea, and the patrilineal Korean society that is averse to adoption.

As a parable, *The Bacchus Lady* challenges us to ask what family is. So-young's fictive family is counter-normative in an ethnocentric, heteronormative, ableist society where poor, sick, elderly people, people with disability, transgender people, migrants, or foreigners from "less developed" regions often don't have "family" to depend on. So-young's fictive kinship or family of choice is antithetical to a heteropatriarchal nuclear family consisted of male provider, female caregiver, and ideally their biological children in the context of "legal" marriage, in which the mother-wife is responsible not only for building a "moral" family, but also for keeping the man/father "safe" from other women including prostitutes.

The Un-Caring of the Elderly people

Upon learning that one of her former clients is bed-bound at a hospital, So-young visits him. He begs her to help him end his life with dignity. So-young determinedly rejects his request at first but decides to assist him. In his hospital bed, her former client who was always well-groomed and generous to So-young tells her how humiliating his life is as a debilitated person. He says, "What good is living if you're only lying for a few more years?" The film shows a professional caretaker cleaning him as he is helplessly laid on the bed after he defecated on the bed. So-young buys a bottle of herbicide and pours it into his mouth. The Next day he is found dead. Without knowing So-young's involvement in his death, another former client, Jae-woo, tells So-young about his suspicious death and his son's rushed burial of his father without an autopsy. Upon listening to Jae-woo, So-young murmurs, "I helped him go . . . (He) desperately wanted to leave . . . I knew I shouldn't have . . . I thought it would be better for him to leave as soon as possible. For God's sake, I helped him go. I must be insane." As he was listening to her, Jae-woo says in a low voice, "Why did you do that? Why did you do that?" Referring to his friend who is suffering from what he calls "filthy disease," dementia, Jae-woo mumbles, "How have we become this old?" "What is the best way to die . . . That is the question."

Jae-woo visits So-young again and takes her to his friend's shabby place. Jae-woo's friend is suffering from dementia, with no one to take care of him. Jae-woo asks So-young to assist his friend's suicide. At first, she reacts angrily, adamantly saying no. But the movie shows the three of them going to a mountain together. At the top of the mountain, So-young assists his suicide by pushing him to death. She is finally caught when she is inadvertently involved in Jae-woo's suicide, who has long suffered from depression since his wife's passing. Jae-woo takes So-young out to a fancy restaurant and afterwards to a hotel where he tells her about his depression and his plan to end his life. He takes sleeping pills and does not wake up the next day. So-young hastily leaves the hotel room in the morning. Though Jae-woo left money to her, So-young places all the money except two bills into an offering box in a Buddhist temple. In a police car after she is arrested, So-young asks if the police can lock her up when spring comes because she can't stand cold. She murmurs, "I can't afford the nursing home . . . and they [prison] feed you three times a day. How's the food there nowadays? Hope it doesn't get too cold this winter." The film briefly shows her unfocused, haggard face sitting in the prison courtyard and eating in her prison cell. Soon after, her dead body is shown covered by a sheet and carried out on a metal cot by two female prison guards. The camera shows the close-up view of the box with her information that says "no family" with her real name and age. So-young died at the age of sixty-seven in a women's prison. There is no "happy" ending.

While *The Bacchus Lady* brings to the forefront a serious issue of euthanasia or assisted suicide of elderly people who are debilitated or have no family support and care, a fundamental issue is the lack of caring of the elderly people who have no safety net in a society, including end-of-life care. Though in different ways and degrees, So-young and her male clients' generation bore the weight of hypermasculine developmentalism in South Korea. In addition to selling Bacchus and sex in her old age, So-young bears the burden of assisting elderly men's suicide at a great risk to her own life. So-young, who has labored in all her life, cannot afford the nursing home. She even gets to the point where prison is like a nursing home where she can spend her end-of-life. The image of South Korea as a "prosperous" country that has made a miraculous economic development betrays poverty-stricken elderly people who struggle daily for survival and those who cannot afford proper end-of-life care.[24]

Who Judges?

The last theme that arises from *The Bacchus Lady* as a parable is suspension of judgment. In addition to So-young's comment on people judging her way of making a living, one brief, but important, conversation that cannot be overlooked in this film occurs between Tina, the transwoman, and Do-hoon, the young man with a prosthetic leg. In the small courtyard of Tina's house, Do-hoon is lifting weights. Tina asks him about his sex life, and Do-hoon responds unenthusiastically. Startling at his prosthetic leg, though it was not her first time seeing it, Tina adds that she can't get used to his prosthetic leg. Do-hoon insinuates that he doesn't have a "girlfriend" because he is an amputee. Do-hoon teases Tina saying that she must well understand how he feels about his dismembered leg because she also had a "similar" experience. Reminding Do-hoon of his late rental payment, Tina says she can go to heaven because she is so kind that she lets Do-hoon stay even though he is four months behind in his rental payment. Do-hoon further teases Tina, saying that he isn't sure if Tina can go to heaven because she has changed at will what God has created. Tina responds saying, "My pastor says people like me go to heaven too." Do-hoon continues, "you went and messed with what God created," to which Tina says, "He said the judgement is up to God." Do-hoon later becomes sexually intimate with Tina.

The conversation between Tina and Do-hoon disrupts gender and sexual normativity, and God's "creation order," according to which God presumably created "male and female" who are "cisgender and heterosexual." As opposed to following "paradigmatic markers of life experience—namely birth, marriage, reproduction, and death"[25]—Do-hoon and Tina can be seen as living in a "queer time and place." If "(hetero)normative time, space, and the life achievements" are denaturalized, as Lisa Cacho contests using Jack Halberstam's notion of alternative temporalities in queer subcultures, suspending judgement of people who "live outside the logics of capital accumulation and bourgeois reproduction"[26] might become not just possible but imperative.

IMAGINING PROMISCUOUS CARE AS A FEMINIST THEOETHICAL PRAXIS

William R. Herzog says that parables' conclusions are "often minimal and may be unsatisfactory for many readers."[27] *The Bacchus Lady*'s conclusion is vexing and unsettling. Like a group of villagers in the parable of the friend at midnight (Luke 11:5–8), who were "fools" because they feed a stranger instead of saving food for hard times, So-young also seems a "fool" because she takes care of a boy who is not related to her, and assists the suicides of elderly men, which leads to her own imprisonment. She provides surrogate motherhood and surrogate labor, and faces her own death in a prison cell. In the parable of the friend at midnight, however, Jesus turned "the dominant negative value judgment into an affirmation of village hospitality."[28] What kind of dominant values and assumptions are challenged and what is affirmed in the parable of promiscuous care?

The Bacchus Lady as a parable challenges us to imagine promiscuous care as a feminist theoethical praxis. The UK-based Care Collective offers an ethics of promiscuous care in their manifesto. This ethics of promiscuous care is based on the work of Douglas Crimp, the ACT UP activist and academic. The Care Collective defines "promiscuous" as "indiscriminate," not as "casually or indifferently," and providing "promiscuous care," then, means not discriminating when we care.[29] It also means "caring more and in ways that remain experimental and extensive by current standards" and that anyone can "potentially care for, about and with anyone."[30] When we consider promiscuous care as a feminist theoethical praxis, three interrelated issues are noticed for further reflection and action.

First, So-young's "fictive family" that is more expansive than "filiative family" helps us to imagine a "promiscuous care" that experiments with who we care and how we care.[31] So-young's care of Min-ho who is not related to her is an example of promiscuous care as she spends her meager resources to extend care to a stranger. When Do-hoon takes care of Min-ho, he also participates in promiscuous care. The collective childcare arrangement made in So-young's "fictive family" helps change our understandings of "caring kinship" and "forms of care." The kind of care provided by So-young's fictive family for Min-ho can be called the care for "strangers like me," that is, "forms of care carried out by strangers whose lives resemble our own."[32] All members of So-young's fictive family—So-young, Do-hoon, Tina, and Min-ho—are strangers to one another. So-young's feeding of a street cat is another indicator of her care, extended to a non-human being.

As the Care Collective contends, "caring for children who are not your own, caring for the community and caring for the environment are equally valuable tasks that must be adequately resourced and appreciated."[33] Referring to the children who were separated from their families at the U.S. border against their will, the Care Collective maintains that "caring for migrants and refugees should carry the same significance that our culture places on caring for our own."[34] A feminist theoethical praxis of promiscuous care that urges us to extend the circle of people for whom we care can be a real challenge in a society where strangers, refugees, migrant workers, or society's despised populations are deemed underserving of care.

Second, when understanding promiscuous care as extensive, experimental, and indiscriminate, a difficulty arises. Can we say that So-young's assisting of elderly men's suicide is a form of "promiscuous care"? She was not paid for doing it. She might have felt pressured by their dire situations, but she was not intimidated or forced to do it. It seems that she helped them because she felt empathy for them and understood their predicament. But the cost was too high. So-young was accused of killing those frail old men for money and died lonely in her prison cell. Instead of providing care to those in need due to their age and illness, the state imprisoned So-young who extended her "care" to those debilitated, depressed elderly men. Instead of providing the resources to those who need care, the state punished So-young who tended to their urgent needs, probably the last want in their lives.

What does this film expose about the society in which So-young and her debilitated former clients live? While So-young engages in dangerous work that eventually led her to her imprisonment, the kind of "promiscuous care" that she provided challenges us to see how elderly people with illness live in a society that does not provide needed care to them before judging readily and categorically what she did as wrong. The provision of end-of-life care is wholly inadequate. Having a "biological family" doesn't necessarily make aging and illness bearable. It can even add more pain, because some family members are unwilling to help, or are unable. So-young's "care" for three elderly men through assisted suicide is not redemptive but urges us to imagine what kind of care needs to be delivered by kinfolk, society, faith communities, nation, and the globe. In other words, this film as a parable shows us that promiscuous care should be carried out in "every scale of social life."[35] The stigma and the burden of the life that So-young bears urge us not to turn away from exposing and interrogating the ways in which society is operated by heteropatriarchal filiative family, surrogate/prosthetic labor, ableism, xenophobia, neoliberal capitalism, and U.S. militarism in South Korea.

Third, instead of sensationalizing the treacherous image of elderly sex workers, the film discloses several pervasive problems of society: its glaring overlook of poverty among elderly people, the taboo of euthanasia, lack of end-of-life care, transphobia, ableism, and "multicultural" family in subimperial South Korea. In relation to these problems, the film provides an opportunity for us to reimagine a public space that is not based on exclusivity but on an "imagined community" where "the texture of our interactions shapes and forms who we are and how we live together."[36] This is the space where the "we," our narrative identity, is challenged and reexamined by those who tell their stories. Feminist theologian Rebecca Chopp argues that such public space should be formed as "a place of solidarity" that is a "polyglot texture of different bodies, different voices, different people," because "the 'we' of the public is not and cannot be one singular voice, cannot be reduced to a least common denominator, cannot promote sameness as the basis for our interactions."[37] Such public space is "a network of interrelations among multiple and overlapping or contending public spheres,"[38] which urges us to reimagine care in indiscriminate ways and in multi-scalars in society. *The Bacchus Lady* as a parable pushes us to "hear and understand our narrative identity" or the "we" in new ways, by remembering elderly women, people with disability, transgender people, migrants, and strangers who have been marginalized by society and ecclesial communities.

EPILOGUE

Women like So-young are socially despised because they fall into "indecency," which, according to the late feminist theologian Marcella Althaus-Reid, is "to fall outside the tenuous definition of men respecting women's lives, a dangerous development, especially for poor women."[39] The social system of decency controls permissible behavior of women including elderly women like So-young. According to Althaus-Reid, however, being "indecent" or "indecency" as a "social gesture" that is subversive of social, economic, sexual, and even religious identities can not only debunk and uncover sexual assumptions but also challenge the "multiplicity" and "incoherence" of oppression.[40] In so doing, women like So-young alert that what they need is not regulation, policing, stigmatizing, shaming, or sympathy but decriminalization of sex work, affordable health care, and other forms of care, including end-of-life care, that are indispensable for living as aged people, particularly those who are with little to no resource.

While *The Bacchus Lady* does not provide an inspiring or positive picture of aging and its related matters, it generates meaning through its unabashed exposure of a care-less social structure, gender and sexual normativity and conformity, poverty, ableism, and the limits of filiative family. As a parable, *The Bacchus Lady* will continue to challenge us to reimagine care, family, social relations, aging, illness, dying with dignity, (in)dependency, and social resources, and to reconsider our skewed value systems and the meanings attached to them that are antithetical to promiscuous care.

"So-young," a name she gave to herself while working as a military sex worker, is ironically juxtaposed to her aged self when it is spoken in English. She was indeed "so young" when she renamed herself many years ago. Those of us who were or are still "so young" will meet our aged selves, if we are fortunate enough to live long. When we meet our aged selves, probably with some forms of debility, we, too, will need promiscuous care, a care that does not discriminate. Such indiscriminate care is not what we can expect in our current world. *The Bacchus Lady* as a parable invites and pushes us to start imagining what we could not.

NOTES

1. *The Bacchus Lady* (*Jugyeojuneun Yeoja* in Korean title) is a South Korean film directed by E J-yong (2016). *Jugyeojuneun Yeoja* is translated as "The Killer Woman."
2. David John Graham, "The use of film in theology" in *Explorations in Theology and Film: Movies and Meaning*, ed. Clive Marsh and Gaye Williams Ortiz (New York: Wiley-Blackwell, 1997), 38.
3. Graham, "The use of film in theology," 39.
4. The Care Collective, *The Care Manifesto* (Verso, 2020, Kindle Edition).
5. The word "Kopino" refers to a person of mixed Korean and Filipino descent.
6. William R. Herzog II, *Parables as Subversive Speech* (Grand Rapids: Westminster John Knox, 1994), Kindle Location 13.
7. Herzog II, *Parables as Subversive Speech*, 99.
8. Herzog II, *Parables as Subversive Speech*, 324.
9. Herzog II, *Parables as Subversive Speech*, 316.
10. See Rebecca S. Chopp, "Reimagining Public Discourse" in *Black Faith and Public Talk: Critical Essays on James H. Cone's Black Theology and Black Power*, ed. Dwight N. Hopkins (Maryknoll, NY: Orbis, 1999).
11. Grace Kyungwon Hong, *Death beyond Disavowal: The Impossible Politics of Difference* (Minneapolis: University of Minnesota Press, 2015), Kindle Locations 508–509.
12. Jin-Kyung Lee, *Service Economies: Militarism, Sex Work, and Migrant Labor in South Korea* (Minneapolis: University of Minnesota Press, 2010), 7.
13. Lee, *Service Economies*, 6.
14. Lee, *Service Economies*, 13, 14.
15. Lee, *Service Economies*, 7.
16. Hypermasculine developmentalism characterizes South Korea's "miraculous" economic growth and the explosive expansion of Korean Protestant Christianity from 1960s until late 1980s. See Nami Kim, *The Gendered Politics of the Korean Protestant Right: Hegemonic Masculinity* (New York: Palgrave Macmillan, 2016).
17. Lee, *Service Economies*, 81.
18. Lee, *Service Economies*, 87.
19. Lee, *Service Economies*, 84.
20. Lee, *Service Economies*, 88–89.
21. The three generations of middle-class women represented in Cho's study are the grandmother's generation, the mother's generation, and the daughter's generation. See Haejoang Cho, "Living with Conflicting Subjectivities: Mother, Motherly Wife, and Sexy Woman in the Transition from Colonial-Modern to Postcolonial Korea," in *Under Construction: The Gendering of Modernity, Class, and Consumption in the Republic of Korea*, ed. Laurel Kendall (Honolulu: University of Hawai'i Press, 2002).

22. Lee, *Service Economies*, 84.
23. "Helping Kopino Kids Fight Poverty, Prejudice." *The Korean Herald* (August 14, 2011). (http://www.koreaherald.com/view.php?ud=20110814000224; accessed April 28, 2021).
24. As of 2019, South Korea has the highest rate of elderly suicide (24.6) among OECD member countries (https://data.oecd.org/healthstat/suicide-rates.htm; accessed 20 March 2021). The income poverty rate among elderly population is also the highest among OECD member countries, and elderly women at the higher rate than elderly men (https://www.oecd-ilibrary.org/sites/fb958d50-en/index.html?itemId=/content/component/fb958d50-en; accessed 20 March 2021).
25. Jack Halberstam, *In a Queer Time and Place: Transgender Bodies, Subcultural Lives* (New York: New York University Press, 2005), 2—cited in Lisa Marie Cacho, "One, Racialized Hauntings of the Devalued Dead," in *Strange Affinities: The Gender and Sexual Politics of Comparative Racialization*, ed. Grace Kyungwon Hong and Roderick A. Ferguson (North Carolina: Duke University, 2011), 47.
26. Cacho, "One, Racialized Hauntings of the Devalued Dead," 47.
27. Herzog II, *Parables as Subversive Speech*, 316.
28. Herzog II, *Parables as Subversive Speech*, 260.
29. The Care Collective, *The Care Manifesto*, 35.
30. The Care Collective, *The Care Manifesto*, 35.
31. The Care Collective, *The Care Manifesto*, 29.
32. The Care Collective, *The Care Manifesto*, 32.
33. The Care Collective, *The Care Manifesto*, 36.
34. The Care Collective, *The Care Manifesto*, 36.
35. The Care Collective. *The Care Manifesto*, 37.
36. Chopp, "Reimagining Public Discourse," 160.
37. Chopp, "Reimagining Public Discourse," 162.
38. Chopp, "Reimagining Public Discourse," 162.
39. Marcella Althaus-Reid, "On Wearing Skirts Without Underwear: 'Indecent Theology Challenging the Liberation Theology of the Pueblo.' Poor Women Contesting Christ." *Feminist Theology* 20 (1999), 42.
40. See Marcella Althaus-Reid, *Indecent Theology: Theological Perversions in Sex, Gender and Politics* (New York: Routledge, 2000), 168–169.

Chapter 13

Glimpses of God's Dis/Abled Domain

Rising Up against Empire in Small Steps / Huge Leaps

Graham Adams

In this personal exploration of dis/ability, arising out of various examples in my context, I explore the way in which people are 'glimpsed': that is, we see each other only partially, and on the basis of such partial glimpses, we measure one another, reducing our humanity in the interests of those with most power. This is particularly illuminated here in terms of dis/abilities, exposing the System's bias towards measurable versions of reality—versions which are untrue precisely because they edit the relational truth of a person. Out of contexts of dis/ability, relational truth re-emerges: its glimpses of people, even if they are little and apparently weak in power, tell us of a different story; a rising up in small steps in a solidarity of the immeasurable. This is God's alternative realm in our midst.

INTRODUCTION: CONTEXT

Dis/ability has touched me since I was eight, when my mother was diagnosed with multiple sclerosis. In different versions of this introduction, I have altered the sequence, sometimes telling of her disability first, sometimes of her abilities, an ambivalence which reflects my experience—and her own understanding—of her identity, personally and socially, depending on the circumstances of the context. After all, when situations made things difficult, the 'disability' was heightened; but when there were no obstacles to the exercising of her abilities, the 'disability' was lessened. This reflects the social model of disability,[1] in which the commonality amongst people with dis/abilities is their exclusion, on various fronts and to varying degrees. Such ambivalence is also at the root of why I tend to speak of 'dis/ability,'[2] an intentionally disruptive term, because 'disability' is never the whole story—as I shall explore further.

Nonetheless, returning to my mother's condition, it would go on to affect her mobility significantly, such that she became a wheelchair user. Over several years, she had many operations, certainly over twenty, so we were very familiar with hospitals. It affected life at multiple levels, because of everyday decisions, helping out with a wide range of personal and domestic tasks, as well as awareness of what may be called micro-injustices—all the ways in which people with dis/abilities have to negotiate not only the management of their own condition, but also access to the world around them, and the systems designed to support them. This can feel all-consuming, or at least as though it is an omnipresent framework within which life is lived. On the one hand, however, as she would have said herself, "you just get on with it," because it is your 'new normal'; so my experience of it was that, even though I was conscious that friends' lives were not framed in this way, it was nevertheless simply "life as we knew it." On the other hand, it was also apparent that certain moments or issues prompted a more vocal response from Mum, and indeed from us as her family, occasionally and directly speaking out of the experience of dis/ability to challenge a situation or structure. It was not that she saw herself as political, but her own experiences of dis/ability meant that she became an advocate for accessibility in church and beyond.[3]

These formative experiences shaped in me a sense of injustice, from a particular perspective, and as I look back on their impact, also an awareness of the ambiguities of 'dis/ability.' After all, Mum was significantly defined by her abilities, not her limitations; she was independent in many ways, a skilful craftworker, musician, worship leader, children's worker, with high standards for herself and others. In her later years, too, she was effectively my father's carer, because he had developed dementia—and the irony is that it was not her own medical condition which caused her death, but effectively it was his, because while negotiating the demands of his condition and reaching the point of painful realisation that he needed to be in residential care (which we supported, for the sake of them both), she unknowingly developed pneumonia and suddenly died.

Dementia is not the same as dis/ability, but they share certain features and impacts. They both lead the person and their relationships into a 'new normal,' which in some respects is defined by particular limitations, but at the same time, the identity of the person is still crucial. So while his identity was certainly affected, such that he was not 'fully' the person he had been, at the same time there were powerful glimpses of who he always had been, even more intensely than before: notably the disarming silliness and wit. As I will go on to argue, it is vital that identity is understood in terms of the wholeness of the narrative, rather than viewed in terms of fixed moments or perspectives—because although we deal in 'glimpses' of ourselves and one another, they give us access to something more than what is immediately present, and this 'storied truthfulness' is intrinsic to the demands of social justice and the possibility of God's new realm, in which the dignity of all is upheld.

There is also a little boy with a rare genetic condition who is part of my life. Let us call him Daniel. As a result of a rare genetic condition, known as Joubert Syndrome, his brain development has been 'delayed,' affecting him in a number of ways, especially in terms of communication, mobility and sensory processing. Now aged six, it has been amazing to see videos of him walking independently at school, while he still uses a frame elsewhere. This is a repeated pattern: learning a new skill in a particular space but taking ownership of when and where he will exercise it, so demonstrating his own agency. When he began to contribute independently to conversations, it highlighted for me how each new skill is identifiable as a tiny step in itself, which would not be so noticeable in those of us lacking in dis/abilities. It is as though he draws out of us attentiveness to the miracle of detail, showing us how, whenever he does something new, the world is reshaped just a little.

I want to reflect on these experiences in the light of the systems within which people with dis/abilities are 'glimpsed,' that is, how people are measured and reduced, even as they open up the possibility of glimpsing each other more truthfully, more wholly and more justly, for the sake of a reshaped world.

WHAT IS TRUTH?

In order to access support, in meeting the needs of those with dis/abilities, government bureaucracy inevitably requires forms to be completed. This process effectively involves the person concerned being defined by all the things they 'cannot' do, all the benchmarks they 'have not' met, all the milestones they are struggling to reach. It is a process which reduces people to 'deficit'—what they lack, what they are missing, what has not yet been seen, or glimpsed. It does this in order to quantify the support that people need from the State, or rather, to delimit the support that is given. While of course it is the case that the support given by governments varies considerably, and some are not in a position to give much at all, the notion of quantifying and objectifying people and their stories is systematically dehumanising—often demoralising—and fundamentally untrue.

It is untrue because it consists of objectification: defining someone by only part of the story, in order to fit with the institutional and economic boxes shaped by the system. Even where such processes deliver some social goods, the problem is still there: people are 'edited' in order to prompt a quantifiable outcome.

And the many problems with the system—where it shows itself to be the Shitstem, a power-dynamic lacking in humanity and defined by vested interests—are far more numerous than I can address here. When trying to access support to help with her care for my father, my mother found the system to be so difficult to navigate—and this is after she learned to get over her own reluctance to ask for help, having been proudly 'sufficient' in the face of so many challenges. Dementia, of course, is famously difficult for systems to negotiate, often being confused with mental illness, which has also suffered from institutional and social lethargy: it is as though something which cannot be 'seen' so clearly is less deserving of support. It seems now to be seen more explicitly and widely in terms of organic mental disorder, that is, as a condition caused by one or other specific disease impairing the functioning of the brain; and hopefully this truer account of it may help to generate better understanding and better outcomes. Even so, the ignorance around it and fear of it are deeply ingrained, often affecting how we glimpse and relate to people who live with it. There is a clear sense of the 'loss' of the person, how the disease 'edits' them but how the system's handling of this continues to edit and objectify them—even as practitioners urge us to hold on to the whole person, no matter how rarely they are glimpsed. Our best efforts can, of course, be hugely affected by grief: for the person may be 'slipping away,' affecting our own capacity to engage fully. It is exhausting.

These questions, however, concerned with the measuring, limiting, quantifying, objectifying of people in light of their conditions, prompt me to ask, "What is truth?" It is as though two different truths co-exist and struggle against one another. On the one hand, this struggle could be characterised as being between disability and ability, deficits and assets, milestones and, alternatively, inchstones. Rather than succumbing to the system of deficits, we may choose to focus on the assets, the abilities, all the achievements there have been, no matter how small they may seem. But in a sense, even this more positive approach in the face of the deficit-shaped Shitstem finds itself dancing to the tune of a world of measurement. Of course, it is good to affirm what people can do, to recognise and celebrate their assets (rather than focusing on the deficits), and to rejoice with every inchstone reached (helping us to take nothing for granted). But this can still be exhausting—constantly on the alert to seek out the positive to counteract the burden of the negative as understood by the Shitstem. In fact, it still runs the risk of dealing in a person's measurability, the 'economics' of truth, even as it focuses on what is in credit rather than in deficit.

So might there be another way of telling the story, another truth, which holds the ambiguities together, the pain and joy, the miles and inches? After all, *how* we measure is itself an ideological decision, a conditioning—so who decides that a small achievement is actually small, or that a huge leap is genuinely huge? This is the problem with the Shitstem: its editing of a person's truth determines that a small step is a small step, cut off from its relational reality, or a milestone remains unreached, as though other achievements are not 'more' powerful.

The system may believe itself to be, or may rather present itself as, 'objective,' but the 'truth' may be less clear. Rather, when seen from another perspective, a 'third space' in a sense, defined neither by assets and deficits nor by inches and miles, the reality may actually be illuminated more sharply, or more broadly. After all, truth is genuinely relational, not merely a matter of millimetres walked, or words pronounced, but something so much more. So even an achievement which seems 'tiny,' but which those who experience it know it's true scale, is a glimpse of the greater truth. Whilst the Shitstem focuses on numbers—measurements of achievements or non-achievements, deficits or assets, abilities and disabilities, and indeed on the money required to support these things—there is a greater truth which cannot be quantified, or even encapsulated. An 'ecology' of truth, telling the story of the webs of relationships which constitute reality as a whole.

As Ngugi sees it, "Our lives are a battlefield on which is fought a continuous war between the forces that are pledged to confirm our humanity and those determined to dismantle it."[4] This insight relates to the systems of colonisation conditioning our experience of the world—but it applies starkly to dis/abilities too. People with dis/abilities, and their relationships, become a battlefield between different truths: those defined by measurement, and those defined by something less quantifiable. Drawing on theology concerned with Empire, I see how this struggle between different truths is itself conditioned by 'coloniality' or 'the colonial matrix of power':[5] Mignolo here identifies the 'four interrelated domains' of control—that is, control of economy, of authority, of gender/sexuality and of subjectivity/knowledge—and how, together, they frame the limitations and constraints of our lives. In other words, it is not simply that socio-political or economic structures and practices demonstrate the biases of the system, but that these biases are normalised within our psyches, our relationships, our interpretations of the world. They are not just there in the policies of government, but we see them there because we are conditioned to expect them. There is an interplay between our internal and external realities, reinforcing the colonial matrix as a whole. At the heart of this, in terms of the control of our subjectivity, is how we are conditioned to see each other as selves, with the Western-conditioned epistemological bias towards measurement prevailing, which shapes the very battlefield on which the struggle is fought. To see this as Empire is to begin to decolonise.

The British theologian Andrew Shanks speaks of a contrast between 'truth-as-correctness'—the more limited and limiting notion of truth, but the one with which we tend to operate, each with our own ideologies and experiences, editing the truth of reality to fit what we deem to be correct—and 'truth-as-openness,' which is the higher truth, open hospitably to ever new glimpses, troubling our more exhaustive correctness.[6] This contrast can be seen also in the two kinds of truth battling over the lives and relationships shaped by dis/ability: the supposed correctness of the Shitstem, which tries to characterise people by way of their edited or objectified selves, attracting or limiting monetised support, and by contrast, the 'openness' of the more relational ecology of truth, which holds together the complexity, wonder, pain, joy, ambiguity, tears, laughter, of the self who is a story in progress, in relationship, held by love.

To turn from the colonial matrix, which is satisfied with objectified glimpses of people, towards the storied truthfulness of whole lives, is to begin to name the colonisation which conditions our mindsets and our social structures. To begin to name it is to step towards decolonisation.

Seeing Differently

What, then, might it look like to see—or glimpse—each other more truthfully, not merely in terms of measurements and money, but in terms of the whole story of who we are, in particular in relation to people with dis/abilities, but seeing how dis/ability enables the development of a wider conversation about perceptions and enactments of self and other, and relationships and systems?

The first step, from the focus on 'deficit' to a recovery of 'asset,' is a contribution to the whole story, affirming people's giftedness and multiple achievements in the face of complex obstacles. But it should not be romanticised, as though the whole truth can be understood in terms of such beautiful resilience. This would overlook the pain, the disappointments, and the reality of the overbearing structures which make such struggles necessary. It is, after all, wholly unjust to expect people with dis/abilities to be superhuman, as though it is down to their own formidable achievements to transform exclusionary structures.[7]

The second step, then, is vital: to note the contrast between two truths— one, rooted in the epistemology of the colonial matrix, concerned principally with measurement, thereby editing and objectifying the self and relatedness; and another, which demonstrates open regard for the wholeness of who a person is. David Horrell speaks of 'other-regard,'[8] which applies not only to the otherness of who someone is, but arguably can relate also to the otherness of who each of us may *become*. That is to say, since our own identities are in progress, including those of people with dis/abilities, we continue to grow into the otherness to which such openness has proper regard. We are not confined by this moment, but will 'become' the Other to whom we may have open regard—just as *other people* may also grow into an otherness to which we too should be open. To see this openness in identity is both to see and to challenge how the colonial matrix of power conditions our self- and systemic perceptions, recognising that such a system tries to measure and objectify us, whilst the alternative ecology of truth is attentive to the storied truthfulness of our complex identities. This second step, then, is not simply about naming a different way of seeing, beyond the binary of deficit and asset, and towards a richer account of who we are *in defiance* of a world of measurement, but is also to begin to subvert and dismantle such assumptions and frameworks which delimit our growth.

However, even this alternative vision must not be romanticised. After all, there is nothing easy about it at all. It is hugely demanding—to be committed to the truth that no-one is merely a series of ticked-boxes, but always so much richer and intrinsically more valuable. It can be painful to glimpse and embrace the whole of the person, including the person with dementia, or the whole of the person with dis/ability. Of course, it prompts a question, as it must: how can we even conceive of what 'the whole' is anyway? Rather, the very point is that what we currently glimpse, through whichever particular lens, conditioned by whatever colonial matrix, is not the whole. Instead, we affirm the need to remain open in light of our ignorance. We cannot say that a tiny step is genuinely, only, tiny, or that a huge leap is measurably huge. The reality of such experiences is not capable of being reduced to a number. Rather, storied truthfulness requires imagination—revolutionary and rebellious imagination—to conceive of other people, but also ourselves, as 'more' than any measurement, without quantifying the 'more.'

Ironically, theories from the world of mathematics may help to dethrone the supposedly objective nature of the world of measurement, as it is seen to reduce people to edited versions of themselves—even if I am co-opting these theories consciously for particular purposes. For example, chaos theory, understood commonly as 'the butterfly effect,' reckons with the real possibility that small acts can cause disproportionate effects; whether it is a butterfly fluttering its wings, or a child with dis/ability taking a tiny step, it is not possible to predict the exact outcome, because the event is embedded in relationships, a complex web of realities, through which the event can ripple and expand, logically but unpredictably. In other words, the event is not merely the event before us, but the web of connections which give it its significance and meaning; so a single number cannot capture the entirety of the truth of it. A small step can be huge.

Or as complexity theory (overlapping with 'chaos') explains, following a radical change in a system brought about by even the smallest of inputs, any previous equilibrium in that system can never be recovered, because the system now has a new equilibrium: which means that the reference-points for the system's previous measurements may no longer apply; the story of the system-of-relationships has moved on; identity has moved on, not losing what once was (it remains part of the story) but being incorporated into the new. In other words, the *means* of measuring in any given moment can lose its very meaning, because the structure of the very system can be altered beyond recovery due to the smallest (so-called) of acts. So it is not only that a small step may be a huge leap, but that the very notion of determining its size may be problematic!

As I suggested above, my own use of chaos/complexity is not objective—though my very point is that any such aspiration would itself be conditioned by the matrix of measurement. Nonetheless, it reflects a theological and political truth. God's domain—the kingdom—is a realm marked by the significance of small things: seeds, yeast, hidden pearls, children. In these the capacity of smallness to reconfigure the system is deeply affirmed. That is intrinsic to the gospel: the power of weakness to subvert systems of strength.[9] But not only is smallness in terms of size upheld, but so too smallness in terms of 'apparent power': that is to say, dis/ability, not least the dis/ability of a child, is loaded with chaos-capacity, potentially generating effects on a much larger scale. So measurement is always problematic: a milestone is an inchstone, an inchstone is a milestone, depending on the location of the event in a series of relationships, or the position from which we see or glimpse such realities. So, while the Shitstem looks down from its position of authority and wealth, inculcating in us a way of seeing each other, objectifying us according to measurements and money, a dis/abled child has this capacity to wreak holy havoc on such a system. My point is not to romanticise dis/ability, but to destabilise the epistemological norms, and political biases, of a system of reductive measurements.

Being Seen

The story in Mark 8:22–26 brilliantly illuminates the question of our location and perspective, when glimpsing how the world measures and objectifies people. In the episode, people bring a blind man (a person with dis/ability) to Jesus—so the unnamed man is 'measured' by the world, including those who bring him, as in deficit and in need of change. Jesus, though, led him out of the village, perhaps as a way of drawing him out of relationships which had defined him, and objectified him, for too long, such that he had internalised the pain of being measured. But Jesus also presumed to heal him, without apparently asking him whether that is what he wanted—and put saliva in his eyes, barely respectful of the man's space or agency; and yet the story testifies to an ambiguity, because Jesus asks him, "Can you see anything?" It is a strange question, because, from a seeing perspective, it presupposes that the man could conceive of seeing in terms which Jesus understood; and yet it was also a turning-point, seeking to take seriously the man's own experience, free to answer in his own way.

But it is the man's response which deserves particular attention: "I can see people, but they look like trees, walking." It raises so many questions: firstly, we could ask why it is that in this healing story, Jesus' power has not been entirely effective immediately, rather gradually—but actually, that is not the key issue here, though part of the answer may indeed be that the man's agency is seen to be integral to the unfolding of the story. There is, though, a more intriguing question: how can the man conceive of both people and trees, to know that the walking-things are people and not trees? It seems the man has more insight than the seeing-world may have glimpsed; he has recourse to a way of mapping the world, and to creative metaphors. But he is also helping the seeing-world to see themselves anew, in three senses.

First, he helps the seeing-world to recognise that it is not only people with dis/abilities who are 'seen'—measured and edited—but that temporarily able-bodied people are also seen, measured, edited. Secondly, that this event of being seen, by others, is like a potential chaos-event, a seed, opening up the possibility of deeper empathy amongst people-glimpsed-partially-by-each-other, so that we may unpick such partiality and learn to see 'through' the limitations of the colonial matrix which conditions us. In other words, in the event of our *realising* we are all 'being seen,' the butterfly flutters its wings and the potential for something bigger emerges: a realm in which we practise empathy amongst ourselves. But thirdly, let us sit for a moment with the mystery of being seen as walking trees.

On the one hand, to be seen as a tree is to be objectified; it is not only an act of editing, but 'untrue'; so it prompts us to think how we 'un/see' others too, not least those with dis/abilities, how they can be mis-characterised, misunderstood, defined by one thing and not so many others. On the other hand, however, to be seen as a tree is to be seen as something intrinsically life-giving, an oxygen-provider, a home to wildlife, a sanctuary; in its very 'untruth' there is such chaos-capacity, opening up a vision of something so much more than the truth, something into which the walking people may grow. It is, therefore, an awesome metaphor, bringing together the 'is' of truth and the 'is not' of untruth in order to create something illuminating—and it comes from the dis/abled person, the un/seeing one, whose identity is in progress, who does not cease to be what was but who grows into a new chapter of storied truthfulness.

To capture this, without limiting it, when Jesus does further laying-on-of-hands, he then tells the un/seeing seer, "Do not even go into the village." It is as though, in order to find his home, which will now be a new home, 'seen' anew, he must disentangle himself from the frameworks within which his dis/abled identity had been limited; he is free to exercise his agency on his terms, to take tiny steps, or huge leaps, in his own time, along his own path, unimpeded by those who measured him and found him in deficit, yet free to engage with them as trees walking, mis-seen but so much more than they knew they were. He cannot go back the same way, because things can never be the same again: the equilibrium of the old world of measurement no longer stands; it is a new world, defined by walking trees, a genuine ecology of truth in which the capacity for people to be life-giving towards each other has been unearthed. In Molly Haslam's terms, this is about "participation in relationships of mutual responsiveness,"[10] reminiscent of my affirmation of 'mutual humanisation':[11] how we become more fully human in and through relationship with each other.

Rising Up

In these glimpses of dis/ability, we begin to see what God's domain may look like: a world not defined by the colonial matrix and its epistemological bias towards measurement, since such a framework does not only entrench obstacles to the flourishing of people's full humanity but also quantifies people according to their deficits in the face of such obstacles/flourishing. Nor is it a world defined even by best efforts to celebrate or accentuate assets, because the truth of experience in all its complexity and ambiguity must be grappled with, queering the measurement of deficit and asset, the scale of milestones and inchstones, the ways in which people are compared or in which their stories are objectified as fixed moments in time. So this alternative vision must include the potential for any such measuring to be seen from multiple angles—where smallness is glimpsed for the potential greatness (chaos-capacity) which may be present, and the greatness of the system is relativised accordingly, reduced to the partial perspective it really is, its imperial majesty humbled, its colonial matrix dismantled and its pride scattered.

To enter into this new domain, a domain owning its dis/abilities in contrast to the complacency of the prevailing order, we are invited to do so as children—as the relatively powerless of the world, those who do not seem to possess such agency, or such self-possession, but who can erupt with chaos-capacity; those like people with dis/abilities, or who live with dementia, who are glimpsed partially, but in whose stories there is richer truth, which breaks the illusions of 'normalcy,' security, economic usefulness; who may see others as 'trees, walking,' ambiguous symbols of life-giving potential. But as illuminated by Chad Rimmer's poem, *What the child knows* (presented at the eDARE 2021 webinars):

> Not a soul stayed to ask
> What the child knows.

Whereas if we did stop to ask, and to 'become' in light of such experience, we would find how reality is opened up quite differently, deviating from norms imposed by the colonial matrix, and generating alternative space. In this spirit, we are indeed invited to rise up, to recognise our own mix of deficit and asset, smallness and greatness, how none of these things is ever the whole story, and how any moment has within it the potential to change all our reference-points, all our frameworks of measurement and monetisation, as a child wreaks holy havoc on systems which would limit them.

Just as a dis/abled child demonstrates a new skill, which from one angle is a 'small' achievement, but from another, is a light-year of movement, so illuminating for us how the whole web of life is constituted by huge interactions which seem small, lost in the detail, but which are world-shatteringly immense, each a miracle of im/possibility; just as a person with dementia defies expectations, emerging from the mist of their new normal with an occasional glimpse of their true glory, even in the tiniest of smile or a reminiscent quip; just as the un/blind man reflects back to the seeing-world how people are mis-seen, misunderstood, while simultaneously revealing to us the potential to be life-giving trees, in motion, heading away from old habits of objectification, towards new relationships of dignity, justice and wholeness; *so we are invited to rise up*—to defy systems which would contain us, reducing us to an equation of deficits and assets, overlooking the deeper truth on the basis of partial glimpses, misinterpreted; to defy such systems, such a Shitstem, in solidarity with the child, the adventurous risk-taker whose life asks 'why?' when others tell them to play it safe; in solidarity with a child with dis/abilities who relishes the opportunity to mess up people's expectations and assumptions; in solidarity with the person with dementia, who does not fit, who 'sees' the world differently, glimpsing people as something like trees walking.

It is a new domain which encourages such rising up, such defiance, such deviance in the face of apparently ordered measurements in a Shitstem whose vision is limited and limiting. It is a new domain of dignity, a world where our stories are not constituted by one life-defining, life-limiting moment or perspective, but are valued in all their incomplete wholeness. It is a world which is 'home,' but the route there is not familiar—it is walked, by people and trees, in defiance of what previously conditioned us, in solidarity with all who cry out for recognition, whose agency and chaos-capacity demand attention, away from sites of objectification and towards new ways of seeing ourselves and one another, unromantically but holistically, each of us perfectly flawed, generously small, and deeply integrated with each other.

Where might this lead? Can you glimpse it? Dare we live it?

NOTES

1. See, for example, Nancy L. Eiesland, *The Disabled God: Toward a Liberatory Theology of Disability* (Nashville: Abingdon, 1994), 23–5.

2. There are no ideal terms. I could have used 'different abilities,' but as I explain, it is the ambiguity of 'dis/ability' which speaks out of my family context and speaks to the relational and disruptive nature of what I am proposing. Indeed, my mother's abilities were not necessarily 'different' from the abilities of those of able-bodied people; rather she experienced limitations in particular ways, which impeded the exercise of some skills but did not prevent her exercising skilfulness in many spheres. I recognise, though, that the '/' could appear to separate the disabilities from a person's abilities, as though to deny their connectedness—but the intention is to show the overlap between the two words and two realities: disabilities and abilities. I appreciate, on the other hand, that this could seem to diminish the distinctiveness of disability, as though viewing someone's disability from an able-bodied perspective, which could allow my best intentions to 'overlook' the difficulty of the reality—but while it is important that I recognise that danger, my aim is to affirm that 'dis/abilities' are complex, their presence is such that they cannot really be 'bracketed' out, but neither may it be helpful to read them as the entirety of the story, though the relationship between the two sets of conditions will vary considerably from person to person, social context to social context, moment to moment. However, when it comes to describing people, personhood always precedes condition: so I speak of 'people with dis/abilities'—and indeed, I am struck by the term 'temporarily able-bodied' persons (Eiesland, *The Disabled God*, 24) for those who, in my terms, shape the system within which dis/abilities are constructed and glimpsed.

3. See also Chad Rimmer's poem "Strong" (Chap. 2).

4. Ngugi wa Thiong'o, *Devil on the Cross* (Portsmouth: Heinemann, 1987), 53.

5. Walter Mignolo, "Introduction," *Cultural Studies* 21.2–3 (2007): 156.

6. Andrew Shanks, *Hegel and Religious Faith: Divided Brain, Atoning Spirit* (London and New York: Bloomsbury T&T Clark, 2011), 50; Andrew Shanks, *Hegel versus "Inter-Faith Dialogue": A General Theory of True Xenophilia* (New York: Cambridge University Press, 2015), 54.

7. As Miriam Spies argues in "Cripping the Failed Body of Christ" in *Decolonizing Church, Theology, and Ethics in Canada* edited Néstor Medina and Becca Whitla (Montréal: McGill/Queen's University Press, forthcoming)—contexts of 'compulsory able-bodiedness' require bodies to perform as 'supercrips.' She notes Alison Kafer's

definition of 'supercrip': "products of either extremely low expectations (disability by definition means incompetence, so anything a disabled person does, no matter how mundane or banal, merits exaggerated praise) or extremely high expectations (disabled people must accomplish incredibly difficult, and therefore inspiring, tasks to be worthy of nondisabled attention)" (Kafer, *Feminist, Queer, Crip* (Bloomington: Indiana University Press, 2013), 90).

8. David Horrell, *Solidarity and Difference: A Contemporary Reading of Paul's Ethics* (London: T&T Clark, 2005).

9. In my forthcoming work, *Holy Anarchy* (London: SCM, 2022), I speak of God's 'awesome weakness' as the power through which the system of False Order is exposed, subverted, and potentially transformed.

10. Molly C. Haslam, *A Constructive Theology of Intellectual Disability: Human Being as Mutuality and Response* (New York: Fordham University Press, 2012), 104.

11. Graham Adams, *Christ and the Other: In dialogue with Hick and Newbigin* (Farnham: Ashgate, 2010).

Chapter 14

Temporarily Abled or Permanently Differently Abled

Rising to Life with Disability

Wanda Deifelt

> Our life is a walk in the night, we know not
> how great the distance to the dawn that awaits us.
> And the path is strewn with stumbling blocks
> and our bodies are grown tyrannous with weeping
> yet we lift our feet.
> We lift our feet.[1]

Our times are shaped by an economy of absence and void. We focus on what we lack, what we don't have. In pastoral care, there is a delicate practice of addressing absence and loss, to process grief and death. This is not the type of void and absence I am talking about here. What I am addressing and problematizing is the type of void—a lack—which leads to a need to compensate, to fill the physical and emotional emptiness with objects and material goods. We fill the void of physical contact by binge watching Netflix, the absence of youth with makeup tricks or plastic surgery, and the lack of meaning in one's own life by focusing on the lives of others. The void is temporarily filled because it is fed by a consumerist society based on a capitalist economy.

My reflection in this chapter is to think of an incarnate, enfleshed, embodied spirituality that starts from an economy of grace and abundance. Instead of focusing on the lack and void that is filled by consumerism, what would a spirituality built on who we are and what we have to share look like? Using a framework of embodiment, mediated through gender analysis and disability studies, I ponder on the contributions that can be made precisely by those who do not appear to benefit from the abundance, whose lack and deficiency seem to define their existence, and from that space rise to life.

EMBODIMENT

A poem by Brazilian feminist theologian Ivone Gebara:

> The body is my story and my destiny; it's my life and death. The body is my love, my passion, freedom, equality, fraternity, sorority, hope, and longing. The body is my flesh, my sex, my job, my city, my country, my world, my planet, and my galaxy. The body is my equal, my different, my indifferent, my plus, my minus, my multiplied, my subtracted. The body is my theorem, my hypothesis, thesis, antithesis, synthesis, dialectic, demonstration, hallucination. The body is my letter, language, literature, reading, writing. The body is my pain, anguish, tears, saliva . . . The body is my son, my mother, my father, my grandmother. The body is my myth, my rite, my ethics, poetics, religion, invention. The body is my war, my peace, wind, calm, nostalgia.[2]

Embodiment is synonymous with life itself. As Hugo Assmann already wrote, our embodiment is the creator and articulator of "the real."[3] Embodiment overcomes the dichotomy and dualism between mind and body, inside and outside. To approach embodiment is to unveil the mysteries and mechanisms of the functioning brain-mind and its relationship with health, happiness, and wellbeing. Embodiment refers to the house, the many spaces we inhabit and that sustain life: the personal body, the social and political body, the cosmic body.[4] Embodiment is not the attempt to shape bodies according to aesthetic, athletic or fashion precepts. Rather, it is the ongoing process of a holistic vision for human life and for the future of our threatened planet. Embodiment does not mean putting the body in a mold of conformity and normativity but developing a broader perspective of the body and its multiple facets and interfaces—within oneself, between each other, from oneself to the world, and vice-versa. Instead of molds, the emphasis is on the quality of life and on the understanding that life is simultaneously deteriorating and dying while also being recreated and born anew.

The quest for quality of life is a constant in embodiment and disability studies, in contextual, intersectional, and contemporary theologies, and in multiple spiritual and religious practices. An ableist society equates quality of life with bodies and minds devoid of diversity, labels disabilities based on typical or standardized performances, and often perpetuates stereotypes. For instance, it is assumed that all disabled people want to be cured, that wheelchair users also have intellectual disability, that visually impaired people have special forms of insight, etc. To reflect on quality of life invites us to consider embodiment as it connects the physical and the spiritual, finding meaning and joy in the diversity of human lives.

The problem is that we have inherited a Greco-Roman culture that insists on polarities and operates on dualisms: mind-body, spirit-flesh, male-female, inside-outside, white-black, rich-poor, active-passive, strong-weak, perfect-imperfect, pretty-ugly, healthy-sick, alive-dead. The first is always better (superior) than the second and there is no room for ambiguity. In this either-or, there is no place for what the Brazilian novelist João Guimarães Rosa, in his book *Grande Sertão: Veredas*, described as the space in-between, the hyphen that connects and bridges both sides, thus becoming the third margin (or bank) of the river.[5]

To see the connection between different bodies, that is, how the personal, social, and cosmic bodies are intertwined, let us take the word "head" as an illustration. If I say "head" and think hierarchically, then the head is placed in opposition to "the rest" of the body, operating in such a way as to keep it under control. I treat the head with deference because it determines where the body goes, and the body's purpose being that of taking the head from one place to another. The word "head" comes from the Latin *caput*, which can mean both the extremity of the body or the upper part of something. There are multiple ways in which a dualistic framework imposes a hierarchy of values among and between different bodies.

From *caput* (head) comes the word capital, where the administrative headquarters of a state or country are located. Those who do not grow up in the capital but in the interior (or countryside), like me, know that there is a social hierarchy. The capital (at least in Brazil, where I come from) is always the largest, busiest, and richest city. In my childhood, being from the capital implied superiority. The capital is where cultural events take place, where political decisions are made, and power is found. Being from the capital was to be refined; being from the countryside, crude.

From *caput* (head) also comes the noun capital, about which Karl Marx wrote extensively about in *Das Kapital*. Marx addressed the capitalist mode of production and explained how the workers are expropriated of the material goods they produce. In modern economy, capital is a synonym for money, the accumulated assets invested, properties acquired, or income generated. Finally, capital makes our heads by placing profit and greed above collective, communal, and environmental interests and social welfare. We place bodies at the service of capital. A single word exemplifies the complexity of the multiple bodies we inhabit and the power dynamic in which these bodies are treated.

In a dichotomous perspective, the real body is hijacked. The real body—with its strengths and weaknesses—is replaced by an imaginary (projected) version of the body—an edited, digitized, and unrealistic version that submerges real bodies—of historical subjects who feel, laugh, suffer, cry, live and die. The suffering body, or the body in pain, is scandalous. For this reason, it is either hidden (in institutions such as hospitals or nursing homes) or exposed, as a target, to nevertheless keep it under control (as pain is commonly treated by athletes). In one way or another, the body becomes an exotic commodity. Bodies, however, are transient and liminal. Bodies have stretch marks, scars, and muscle pain. They are impermanent and have limitations. Bodies have sensitivity, respond to stimuli, and enjoy pleasure. The real body is perfect in its imperfection.

Embodiment serves as a fundamental reference in all ethical, political, economic, educational, theological, and philosophical questions.[6] Not only because embodiment keeps us engaged in the life processes and its vitality (as the Hebrew reminds us, we are *nephesh chayyah*, living beings), but also because, in this living embodiment, we are extremely complex, unique, and relational in our process of life. Only when we realize this can we also recognize the interdependence between real bodies and the world, between living and non-living beings of the planet.[7] This awareness that we are interconnected enables us to embrace an attitude of active solidarity. I call this perception, this awareness, embodied spirituality.

DISABILITY STUDIES

Here is a kyrie, addressing disability:

> We lift to you, o Lord, our cry for this world to see you as Your image and likeness. We cry out for less looks of prejudice and more looks of compassion and care. We cry out for fewer barriers that prevent us from coming and going and for more accessibility to enable our autonomy. We cry out to be seen less for our shortcomings and more for our gifts and talents. We cry out for less incapacitating attitudes and more encouragement to exercise our citizenship and build a more inclusive world. Kyrie eleison![8]

Disability studies carry a creative tension between the personal and the political, the existential and the relational: the sequelae that mark the mind and body of a child due to a labor without the necessary medical assistance meets the unquestionable reality that this same child is also a source of life and daily renewal of hope and joy. Disability studies have shown that disability is not just a physical or mental issue, but is also a social construct. For a long time, medical and psychiatric practices placed emphasis on psychomotor limitations, and the solution was often medicalization or institutionalization. If a cure cannot be provided, a disability is considered "chronic" or, in instances when an individual is born with a disability, "congenital." As Brenda Brueggemann points out, under this paradigm "disability is a property of human bodies, a deficit or lack in the human body that belongs to the individual whose body it is. The medical model views disability as a departure from the normative functioning of healthy human bodies."[9] In the medical field, disability is addressed as an illness or disease.

More recently, the perspective has shifted toward the social dimension, with an emphasis on inclusion and rights.[10] A disabled person is not reduced to their disability, as an impairment. Rather, by acknowledging that disability itself is a social construction—after all, who deems what normal is?—different dimensions of the experience of disability can be emphasized, leading to different approaches as to what disability means. How we interact with disability in our world reveals the way we understand embodiment. We are simultaneously temporarily abled and permanently differently abled.

One of the fallacies about the human body is that it is similar to a perfect machine, always healthy and responsive to the will of the mind. But the truth is that bodies—the many bodies we inhabit—are also fragile. Each one is unique and the template of what normalcy entails is more open to different abilities, such as neurodiversity among human beings.[11] Realizing that people experience, interact, and interpret differently helps reduce stigma and welcomes diversity. These bodies are resilient, yes, but they are also vulnerable, and it would do us good to realize that, in fact, all of us are only temporarily abled. Our individual bodies will not always be autonomous, the stability of our social and political bodies can be shaken by fascist authorities, the cosmic body—our ecosystems—are at risk in light of the omnicide caused by climate change.[12] Wellbeing is not and cannot be taken for granted.

Disability studies are built on the foundation of vulnerability. The reality of disability—whether it is perceived as incapacity or impediment—can be better understood from an anthropological/theological/philosophical notion of difference and otherness. In other words, it is not a question of minimizing or making disability exotic, but of recognizing that difference is always a reality. Everybody is different, but social constructions deem some differences as reason for exclusion. This continues to be a challenge and a constant object of debate (for instance, the current debate in the Brazilian education system about the inclusion of students with disabilities in regular classrooms). It is an ongoing challenge to fully integrate the multiplicity of capabilities and creativities we find in our encounter with others. It is a fine balance to reflect theologically on suffering without, however, reducing disability to passivity. It is also important that the pendulum not swing in the opposite direction, expecting that every person with a disability be an inspirational model for self-improvement—as if their lives were only validated by winning a medal at the Paralympic Games, for example. Again and again, it is necessary to question and deconstruct.

Some of the contributions in this direction are found in feminist family therapy. This model starts from a deconstruction of normative (dualistic) values and proposes a redefinition of social roles based on feminist theory, using the framework of gender and power relations. Common attitudes are questioned. For example, in cases of people who require special attention, it is expected that mothers be the primary (and oftentimes exclusive) care giver. This expectation is engendered by a culture (and why not say a theology) that blames the woman, fosters the dependency of children who are disabled, leads to paternal distancing and, not infrequently, a distancing from the extended family as well. In short, instead of emphasizing the potential and capabilities of people with disabilities, their existence is reduced to their special needs.

What the field of disability studies teaches us is that embodiment is much more than the human body in its full vitality. We are reminded that, like a movie, physical strength and mental acuity are just a few images from the scroll of our lives. For this reason, we emphasize the need for dignity at each stage, establishing the contrast between the ideal and the real. On the one hand, no human being can "fit" into a notion of the perfect body, and this relativizes all bodily forms—including the bodies of people with disabilities. On the other hand, we acknowledge that the variety of bodies and experiences is part of the diversity of creation. What permeates our relationships is not the aesthetic ideal, but the appreciation of the real body, suffering, painful, but also happy and full of life.

AN EMBODIED SPIRITUALITY

A poem by Brazilian poet Cora Coralina entitled "Aninha and her stones."

> Don't let yourself be destroyed . . .
> assembling new stones
> and building new poems.
> Recreate your life, always, always.
> Remove stones and plant roses and make sweets. Restart.
> make your life mean
> a poem.
> And you will live in the hearts of the young
> and in the memory of generations to come.
> This fountain is for the use of all thirsty ones.
> Take your share.

> come to these pages
> and do not hinder its use
> to those who are thirsty.[13]

I have always admired Cora Coralina's poems for their simple language and conversational tone, as if she were giving advice in a space of intimacy and sharing. I imagine her as my grandmother, sitting in her chair on the porch, thinking about life and trying to find joy in the midst of life's challenges. My grandmother was born with one leg shorter than the other, caused by a hip displacement resulting from a difficult birth. She never complained or spoke bitterly about her condition. She took it as a fact of life. As in the poem "Aninha and her stones," my grandmother instilled in us the same resilience that Cora Coralina insists on. Despite setbacks, it was necessary to try again, never giving up or letting go. It is in the midst of this process, the in-between of birth and death, that the mystery of life unveils itself.

Even when we seem to have no strength left, we find strength in those who carry us and support us. When the personal, individual body is lacking, it is the social, collective body that cradles us. As Mayra Rivera observes, "The constitution of my body in relation to the social-material world entails action—reaching toward others, interpreting what I perceive, and responding."[14] I imagine this care like a hammock set up in the shade of two trees, in which we lull ourselves on lazy summer afternoons. Sometimes, others care for us, rocking us in a soft lull; other times, it is our turn to care for others, gently swinging the hammock, caring for their wellbeing.

We recognize that disability itself is a social construction, and this allows us to identify and name as sinful the social exclusion caused by derogatory attitudes and systemic barriers that prevent people from flourishing. An embodied spirituality reminds us that embodiment is much more than the human body reduced to functional limitations or impairments, or celebrated for its vitality and athleticism. This is why we emphasize the need for dignity in each stage, for every age, and all places. What permeates our relationships is not the normative ideal, but the appreciation of the real—with all its limitations and potentialities.

It is possible to envision an embodied spirituality by reinterpreting our bodies as being only temporarily abled while also celebrating the permanent diversity among us. Our bodies are not unbreakable machines. We spend so much time trying to hide the places where we feel unsteady, covering our vulnerability as if it were a shame. The idea of a body and a mind that cannot falter leads us to hide our frailties and weaknesses. We go to great lengths to try to look like we have got it all together, as if we did not need others to care for us. In the name of this self-sufficiency, we can also exempt ourselves from caring for others.[15] This is true also in the church, with a pressure to "measure up" to other members of the body of Christ. The church is a place to be real, honest, broken, and vulnerable. Church should be the place where we can embrace our own, one another's, and the world's messiness, and open ourselves to God's wholeness. Healing, here, takes the shape of restoring relationships.

This is one of the contributions of disability studies. Everybody has disabilities because we are human, each one perfect in our imperfections. Although we want permanence and certainly, life is filled with the unexpected. Hopefully we live in the fulness of this diversity. Some disabilities are visible, some invisible. The methodological relevance of disability studies shows us the power of vulnerability and resilience, as well as the need for cooperation and greater demand that public policies meet human limitations.

An embodied spirituality teaches us that it takes a village to educate a child, a network to support and welcome those with special abilities or needs, and a whole world in search of the common good to save the planet we call our home.

NOTES

1. Rachel Kadish, *The Weight of Ink* (Boston: Houghton Mifflin Harcourt, 2017), 50–51.

2. Ivone Gebara, "Caminho da torre, caminho das aldeias," in *Tempo e Presença* 322 (março/abril de 2002): 28–29 (My own translation).

3. Hugo Assmann, *Paradigmas Educacionais e Corporeidade* (Piracicaba: UNIMEP, 1995), 67–68.

4. See Wanda Deifelt, "Bodies, Identities, and Empire," in Jione Havea (ed.), *Vulnerability and Resistance: Body and Liberating Theologies* (New York: Lexington Books/Fortress Academic, 2020), 107–122.

5. João Guimarães Rosa, *Grande Sertão: Veredas* (Rio de Janeiro: Editora Nova Fornteira, 1988), 538.

6. See Giorgio Agamben, *The Use of Bodies* (Stanford: Stanford University Press, 2016).

7. See Kiara A. Jorgerseon and Alan G. Padgett (eds), *Ecotheology: A Christian Conversation* (Grand Rapids: William B. Eerdmans, 2020).

8. This kyrie is part of a liturgy elaborated for the Week of the Persons with Disabilities in Brazil: https://aplicativosieclb.org.br/docs/Semana%20da%20Pessoa%20com%20Deficiencia_em_alta.pdf).

9. Brenda Jo Brueggemann, "Introduction, Background, and History," in *Arts and Humanities*, edited by Gary L. Albrecht (Thousand Oaks, CA: SAGE Reference, 2012), 2.

10. For an overview of disability studies and changes in the field, see Lennard J. Davis (ed.), *The Disability Studies Reader* (New York: Routledge, 2017).

11. See Steve Silberman, *NeuroTribes: The Legacy of Autism and the Future of Neurodiversity* (New York: Avery/Penguin Random House, 2015).

12. See Elizabeth Kolbert, *Field Notes from a Catastrophe: Man, Nature, and Climate Change* (New York: Bloomsbury, 2015).

13. Cora Coralina, "Aninha e suas pedras," in *Vintém de Cobre: Meias Confissões de Aninha* (Goiânia: Universidade Federal de Goiás, 1985), 139 (my own translation).

14. Mayra Rivera, *Poetics of the Flesh* (Durham: Duke University Press, 2015), 149.

15. See Serene Jones, *Trauma and Grace: Theology in a Ruptured World* (Louisville: Westminster John Knox, 2009).

PART III
Unending

Chapter 15

Rising to Life (John 11:38–44)

Politics, Contexts, Illusions, Oxymorons

Sainimili Kata Rockett

[. . .] a subjective but not individual system of internalised structures, schemes of perception, conception, and action common to all members of the same group or class [. . .][1]

We read biblical texts through our own experiences, and we read from particular locations. Everything comes from, and through, pre-conceived viewpoints. This is to say that we as readers are conditioned to see certain details, and in the same way we are conditioned to not see other details. Sociologist Pierre Bourdieu would say that this is down to *habitus*, or different aspects that people have been exposed to over the course of their life. It is an ongoing relationship between social structures and free-will, that can and may possibly change over time.

My understanding of the Bible is based largely on my evangelical upbringing. I am the grand-daughter of Pentecostal missionaries and a daughter of Fiji—a country that was not only colonised and largely influenced by white European male missionaries, but also by our Pacific Island neighbours, Tonga, although the Tongan influence is less reported on.[2]

I am an indigenous iTaukei woman, a believer of Christ and an anthropologist. I was born and bred in two vastly different societies and worlds. My reading of biblical texts, and this text (John 11:38–44) in particular, presents an opportunity and challenge to turn what I have always been taught on its head in an attempt to dissect the mainstreamed interpretations of the Bible and its lessons because, as an anthropologist, I know that life is more nuanced and is not always linear in trajectory. I argue that situations and experiences are not autonomous, they are part of a series of choices and actions, and my understanding of life experiences as an indigenous person supports this greatly.

Up until now, my perception of the Bible has been greatly influenced by my habitus. How my family, society and ancestors have been taught to interpret it, a lot of which is literal and naive, and leaves no room for an alternative, interdependent narrative. This alone reflects how the family setting has become restraining in terms of re-producing and re-acting coloniality without even acknowledging one's own position and experiences. It is also possible that due to the deep internalisation of colonialisation, we have become unaware of the regurgitation and re-production that is occurring.

Through this necessarily brief reflection, I read and interrogate the narrative presenting the resurrection of Lazarus in John 11 through my own cultural and social contexts, as well as my personal experience and background, in an attempt to place the resurrection of Lazarus in today's world. In my world, and in the world around me. But more specifically, as an indigenous iTaukei woman in a mid-Covid-19 world.

NA RAILESU AND *VAKANANUMA LESU*

> As soon as they had brought them out, one of them said, "Flee for your lives! Don't look back, and don't stop anywhere in the plain! Flee to the mountains or you will be swept away!" [. . .] But Lot's wife looked back, and she became a pillar of salt. (Genesis 19:17 & 26 NIV)

Na railesu is a Fijian term that translates as reminiscing or looking back into the past (in *railesu*, "rai" means "to look" and "lesu" means "back"). The term *vakananuma lesu* expresses the same longing: *vakananuma* means "think" and thus *vakananuma lesu* is about "thinking back" or remembering. Together, *na railesu* and *vakananuma lesu* refer to the act of wistfulness, a desire and longing for what was, and retrospect.[3]

Although John 11 is linked to resurrection and life-after-death or what is to come, it can be argued that being resurrected also means to return to what was left in the past. The story is about glancing back or *vakananuma lesu* but doing so in a way that one looks forward, meaning to let go of all that was not life affirming or life giving. There is a movement between past, present and future when resurrection occurs. We see the same movement between past, present and future in the story of Lot's wife who, rebelled against the advice of the angels and looked back at Sodom, and therefore turned into a pillar of salt. Lot's wife was punished for glancing back at her former life because she was instructed not to. Some argue it was an act of disobedience, others may see that it is part of being human because *to err is human*—no? Perhaps Lot's wife looked back as a last nod to her former life, wanting to release everything that was no longer life-fulfilling for her and her family. If that was the case, should allowances not have been made so that she did not turn into a pillar of salt—that seems quite extreme for me.

Many times, in my own life I have looked back, gone back and reminisced on aspects of my past that no longer serve me, yet I have not been turned into a pillar of salt. God provides me with more mercy than he did Lot's wife—and my question is why? What is to say that those who are resurrected are not and should not be punished for looking/coming back too? Questions as such continue to drive the narrative of who determines what is punishable, who can look back, and who will not be turned to a pillar of salt.

GLORY OF GOD

> When peace, like a river, attendeth my way,
> when sorrows like sea billows roll;
> Whatever my lot, thou has taught me to say,
> It is well, it is well, with my soul.
>
> (Philip P. Bliss, 1876. copyright: public domain)

In April 2020, I lost my best-friend—my Tutu Jone, my grandfather, Revd. Jone Kata. He was a keen diver, a believer of the word, an encourager, and eloquent speaker, a friend to many and a fighter for the marginalised in our society. He was also an Assemblies of God missionary who contracted malaria in the mission field, and a victim of diabetes. It was on his last mission trip to a prison in Papua New Guinea where he hurt his foot. I am here reminded of a position attributed to Frederick W. Hickling about how in the Caribbean, colonial administrations created two institutions to control the "natives"—an asylum (for rebellion and apparent madness) and a prison (for the economic and socially deprived, or those who revolted).

The cut that my grandfather got on this prison visit was the beginning of his demise, and as a result, he needed to have his toe, and later his leg, amputated. My grandfather was 77 years old when he died—the narrative does not say how old Lazarus was, but in my mind, I believe he was younger than my Tutu. This is perhaps due to my habitus, where some part of me feels that only those who are young, children, or yet to have "lived their full life" are deserving to be resurrected. It is the misfortune of the young to not have been able to experience life in all its seasons.

Focusing on the attacks on Tutu Jone's health and well-being could raise questions on whether God loved him. The same questions that Job could have asked when God allowed / invited ha-Satan to test him. Job lost everything and everyone he loved, and likewise for families who have lost loved ones to Covid-19, for the people of West Papua facing genocide, and for the Kingdom of Tonga when the Hunga volcano erupted and tsunami waves surged across the islands (on Jan 15, 2022). For here is a man/people/country who dedicate(d) their whole life to fighting for the voiceless and sharing the word of God, and yet he faced so much turmoil throughout his lifetime.

Faith believers expect that God does not promise a life free of turmoil, however, what is to say that God could spare them of too many. In the world today, there are many factors that may cause believers and non-believers to question the existence and faithfulness of a higher being. However, somehow, the story of Lazarus being raised from the dead continues to bring hope and reassurance to those questions. Just like British rapper Dave said, in the first round, he thought he was dead, but it brought him back to life like Lazarus. Jesus raising Lazarus to life provides hope to those in "dead" situations, where they feel buried by life, suffocated by a lack of freedom, restricted to confined space.

LOVE OF JESUS

At the beginning of John 11, we are reminded of Jesus' love for the forgotten, the lonely and the sinful. It was Jesus' love for Lazarus, Mary and Martha that moved him to raise Lazarus from the dead. It was his love for them that caused him to wait two days before visiting Lazarus. *In this connection, I feel that it was also Jesus' love for my grandfather that allowed him to die at that specific time in his life.*

Is the last statement as justifiable by Jesus' love as the former? Yes, and no. Arguably, the latter statement requires much more wisdom (over time) than the former. Love is a trait that is associated with positive outcomes, joy, salvation, friendship. To associate love with actions and results that bring pain, hurt and turmoil truly takes wisdom. This kind of wisdom can come with time—old age, having lived through life and all its experiences, and it can also come with trust—the innocent trust of a child, trust that your best intentions are always at the core of every decision. It can be argued that to see something that causes pain and hurt, as a blessing and gift from God, is to really understand the mystery of the creator and everything that God is (which is to say that it shows how we rationalise God). Prompting us to then ask, does God's love allow death? Or is death simply a part of the human life-cycle and it's God's love that embraces and carries us in times of loss?

Later in John 11 we read that Jesus asks God to hear him because this is for the "benefit of the people standing" there. This raises questions such as, did Lazarus "rise to life" because of Jesus' love for him? Or was it because of God's love for Jesus and his people? Surely if Jesus were focused solely on Lazarus, he would have healed him before his death. For Jesus to wait until Lazarus was dead suggests that Lazarus' death was intentional. Lazarus was meant to die so that Jesus could then raise him from the dead. It was one death for the glorification of God. A possible lesser of two unfavourable situations—healing from sickness which can be seen as chance or luck, or resurrection from dead which ultimately reflects the Lord's power and strength. Loss for the greater glorification of God and his Kingdom and his teachings. This is a common characteristic of God that we see throughout the Bible, and it is similarly reflected through the lives and stories of Job, Noah, and Moses.

I believe that to separate Jesus' love for Lazarus from his love for God is to reduce who Jesus is and to view him as merely human, like you and I. Whereas the arguably appropriate way to understand this is to see Jesus as being focused on the overall outcome or the final result. Focused on questions such as, will this cause people to turn to God? Will more people believe in God and his power if Lazarus is resurrected from the dead? Will they finally view Jesus as the son of God after this miracle? How will this glorify the father in heaven? These were the questions that concerned Jesus.

We (you and I, Lazarus and my grandfather) are part of the process or pieces of the puzzle. Our sights can be and are often limited to the moment that we are living in, and when it involves pain, loss and death, it is possible to become hyper-focused on that moment. It is only human to transitorily forget the end-goal, and become wrapped up in the moment. We cannot and it is possible, will not, ever fully understand the reasoning for our processing and why we go through certain discomforts until we have reached the outcome. And for Lazarus, his process, death, was arguably unfair. However, the outcome is what continues to give Christian's hope. And for many, like Tutu Jone, they would say, whatever my lot in life, through His teachings, *it is well with his soul.*

DISABLED BODIES

> The fact is, returning to the old normal would be the worst thing to happen to us.[4]

In being dead, Lazarus' body became dis-abled. However, through Lazarus' belief, Jesus' ability as son of God and knowledge of the outcome, he was able to turn a dis-abled body back into an able body, and glorify his father in heaven. An outcome that ultimately provides relief, respite and reassurance from the grief and pain of bodily death. It is this hope that Christians and faith-believers so often cling to when facing turmoil; however, it also causes me to wonder, is it the case that only abled-bodies can praise God?

To change contexts and place myself in Martha and Mary's position, I do not know if I would want to see Tutu "rise to life." This is not to be confused with my wish to see him again—as that is something I yearn for every day. However, there is something about "rising to life" and allowing a deceased and dis-abled body to become able, that troubles me.

Understanding that the act of being resurrected is the ultimate reflection of God's strength and promise for his people, on a personal level, I still struggle to understand why you would want that to happen to someone you love. Why do we assume that resurrection from death, from "resting in peace," is good? Have we ever considered what it would be like for those who have died and their loved ones? For people who have died from cancerous disease, in tragic accidents, or peacefully in their sleep—what if death was the ultimate relief and respite from their pain? If we were to bring this into the context of 2021, a world "post" but truly mid-pandemic, how do we explain the consent behind being risen to life, and the uncovering and up-lifting of bodies that are not only no longer "abled" but that have been dead for four days?

Na vakananuma lesu would cause us to think about the life of the dead, before they passed. Was it a fulfilling life and a life well lived? Did they experience pain, loss, and tragedy? What were their last moments or final living weeks like? Did they have Covid-19 and struggle to breath? Did they search the world for a joy that was ultimately never found, and was death a welcome rest? Did they drown whilst swimming to higher ground or were they beaten because of their race? Like Reddie shares in his reflection on "Not returning to the old normal," going back to what it was like before would be terrible, because it would mean returning to systemic racism, pain, loss, a life-killing virus, and other life-inhibiting factors.

I know that for my Tutu, his last moments were not filled with constant praise. It certainly was not always well with his soul. Many of his last nights were spent crying out to God, asking God why he was experiencing so much pain, and what he had done to go through such loss. Cries akin to why O Lord, has thou forsaken me? To say that he spent his last moments in praise, is to romanticise his death. Yes, there was praise, but there was also tremendous pain—pain that for some reason, we refuse to acknowledge, admit or accept. Disregarding the hurt that comes with death and loss, is to rob life of its joys, and reduce all of life's experiences, to a heavenly goal that those in the living are yet to experience because just like life and death, pain and joy are not autonomous from one another.

ROMANTICIZING DEATH

I often believe that death is romanticised in order to help the living cope with pain. Those (un)fortunate to have faith, and believe in something greater than now may be more willing to accept their lot. However, we must not take away from the fact that those who die are also human beings who are filled with disappointment, sadness, and fear for those they will leave behind. The Bible doesn't share Lazarus' thoughts, but I wonder whether we worried for Mary and Martha in his last moments. Did the thought of their future, without him, trouble him? When you think of those you love experiencing life without/after you, what emotions does it evoke?

With this in mind, *na vakananuma lesu* functions as a practice that benefits the living and the human desire for reasoning. By looking back at a person's life, their relationships and experiences, the inner voice of reason can begin to justify their death. We can attest their demise to certain actions and allow reasoning to replace the matter of the fact that they are dead. It is used as a way to deter the attention from the loss, to what once was.

To that affect, it is possible that our voice of reason causes us to imagine that Lazarus was an abled-body person. Could he have been disabled? If so, did this have anything to do with Jesus taking his time to come to meet the family? Are the dis-abled not worthy of being saved too? Is there a discrimination against what is seen as "not normal"? In today's Covid-ridden context, the word "normal" has somewhat lost its meaning.

I am drawn to Tinyko Maluleke's "graveyard man" (based on the story of the demoniac in Mark 5:1–20)—who lived in the graveyard, had impeccable strength, felt no pain, was nameless, and walked about naked.[5] If we take time to consider it, many of us living in Covid stricken world have adopted the features of the graveyard man. Maluleke's reflection stirs us to consider whether, if we too are like the graveyard man in Mark 5, and he was worthy of restoration and mercy; surely all those who are abled and disabled, are also worthy. With that being said, may we be challenged to question the immediate (mis)conceptions that arrive in our minds when presented with situations pertaining to life, death and who is deserving of both.

ROMANTICIZING LIFE

The observations on the story of Lazarus have shown that life is multifaceted and there is no one-for-all rule. With that being said, we must be cautious not to oversimplify death, and in the process, oversimplify God. Yes, I was raised in a Christian home and identify as a Christian, but there are teachings of other faiths that I agree with. In my identity, being a person of faith means being able to respect all faiths and their respective teachings. To this reason, I will maintain my argument that life and death are nuanced, and likewise is the death and the "rising to life" of Lazarus.

Why do we mourn death, but celebrate life and resurrection, when surely, to be resurrected, means to die again? If we are to consider all those who have lost loved ones during this pandemic, to Covid-19, to old age, and to other means, although we mourn their loss and the inability to grieve in unison, would we want them to be resurrected? What does the resurrection of a dis-abled body mean? How does "rise to life" relate to us in our current context?

As we consider this text, and the resurrection of Lazarus after 4 days, let us think about how we would respond if that were our brother, son, father, grandfather. Our sister, mother, daughter, grandmother. Would we rejoice in their "rising of life," or would we also ask, "could not he who opened the eyes of the blind man have kept them from dying?" (John 11:37).

LOOKING AND THINKING BACK

To conclude, it is fair to say that John 11 is a complex passage that can be read and reinterpreted from many different contexts and viewpoints. None of which are better than the other, all having their own merit and holding their own weight. What can be said is that if a certain reading of this scripture resonates with you, then for you, that is your truth. For me, I will continue to question the desire to resurrect loved ones, and return to the old normal. My retrospect or *railesu* will be to glance back at what was left behind, appreciate it for what it was, and then move on. I cannot, for my own personal wellbeing, dwell and desire in the past, because for me, the past is something I can never change. It would be futile.

During my grandfather's burial, a favourite anecdote of his was shared, and it was as follows: *There is only one flower that you will find growing out of the sod and the mud and that is the lily. So, when you ask, can something beautiful come out of the sod, the answer is yes.*

The anecdote reflects the living human need for hope and reassurance. Lot and his family ran out of sod(om), Lazarus was raised from under the sod, my grandfather is now under the sod; and out of the sod, a beautiful lily can grow. All rising to life in one way or another. As we all navigate this new normal, the pandemic, death and loss, can hope be such a bad thing? If we as people of faith can cling onto something, then why not cling onto a passage that teaches us that Jesus has the ability to save us from what we want to escape? I for one, will continue to question mainstream teachings and why my habitus, or conditioning causes me to perceive the Bible, the world, and experiences in such a way. And in my spirit, I too will be singing, it is well with my soul whilst looking for my lily.

NOTES

1. Pierre Bourdieu, *Outline of a Theory of Practice* (Cambridge: Cambridge University Press, 1977), 86.
2. The influences, coercions, and invasions between neighboring islands are stories that await telling.
3. *Lesu tale mai* (said to someone who is leaving, inviting them to return) is also associated with these terms. They express longing for someone / something to come back.
4. Anthony G. Reddie, "Not Returning to the Old Normal," in Jione Havea (ed), *Doing Theology in the New Normal* (London: SCM, 2021), 254.
5. Tinyko Maluleke, "Beyond the Graveyard and the Prison, a New World is Being Born," in Jione Havea (ed), *Doing Theology in the New Normal* (London: SCM, 2021), 327–343.

Chapter 16

Chant Down Christian Shitstems
Then What?

Michael N. Jagessar

eDARE 21, out of which this collection arose, was held the week prior to the COP26 gathering in Glasgow which saw a series of protests and 'public square' activism. Prior to COP26 an insulate group embarked on a series of protests involving traffic obstruction (gluing themselves to the road in some instances) beginning on 13 September 2021. Labelled variously as 'eco-warriors,'[1] anarchists or protestors with their public activism viewed as justified by some though disruptive and annoying.[2] For some the activism or taking to the public square or public spaces is very costly with abuse and death threats via social media.[3] The biblical prophets knew, and contemporary prophets know this very well.

CONTEMPORARY PROPHETS

On 27 October 2021, British-Trinidadian visual artist Zak Ové and award-winning Caribbean-born novelist Monique Roffey unveiled a poster evoking the return of paradise after the collapse of "Babylon." Created by XR Writers Rebel and designed by Ebon Heath, the image formed part of their street presence during the COP summit in Glasgow. The images caught my attention as timely for our purpose. While one carried the dream "When Babylon Falls, Paradise Will Thrive Again," the other chanted: "Big oil is the Poison. Action is the antidote."[4]

Sticking with the COP Summit theme, the protests outside of the COP26 gathering in Glasgow and what was happening inside the Summit demonstrated a massive dissonance. Inside has been characterised as "blah-blah-blah" rhetoric, political manoeuvres, greenwashing pledges by Big Oil, alongside lobbying/negotiating for voice and fair deal. Greta Thunberg voicing the sentiments of the protestors describe the summit as "two-week long celebration of business as usual and blah, blah, blah" to "maintain business as usual" and "create loopholes to benefit themselves." She sums up the situation in these words:

> The people in power can continue to live in their bubble filled with their fantasies, like eternal growth on a finite planet and technological solutions that will suddenly appear seemingly out of nowhere and will erase all of these crises just like that [. . .]. All this while the world is literally burning, on fire, and while the people living on the front lines are still bearing the brunt of the climate crisis.[5]

Thunberg's observation that "we cannot solve a crisis with the same methods that got us into it in the first place" is not only spot on; it also has bearing on the long-haul work of talking back to the theologies of empire and what needs to happen to facilitate a move from rhetoric to action. For the young activists and protestors, the words used is 'failure' by a leadership of 'naked emperors.' And the fact that the make-up of the 'inside' gathering's largest representation came from the fossil fuel industry[6] is not insignificant. The importance of and the ongoing task of church in the public square should not be underestimated.

The late Archbishop Desmond Tutu knew and understood this. Tutu was not only a voice chanting down the 'shitstems.' Tutu was also an activist-priest who embodied an uncompromising faith and spirituality for the larger good of humanity and creation. Upon learning of his passing (December 26, 2021), there was an outpouring of admiration and a sense of loss across the media platform from people across all walks of life and of the political and religious spectrum. The outpouring reminded us of a man of a relentless pursuit for justice with compassion, of an uncompromising opposition to violence, walking humbly, laughing at the stupidity of exclusion, and living out the belief that all are made in the image of God. The eye-watering number of quotes attributed to Desmond Tutu—priest, prophet, and activist in the public square—from a multiplicity of voices, would be enough to make any system and hegemony quake, tremble, and fall. Apartheid in South African did fall, yet the 'shitstemic hegemonies,' often endorsed and blessed by religious powers, continue to reign with each rebirth making it more difficult and complex to take-on. This includes the post-apartheid South Africa of Tutu and Mandela. The disappointment of Desmond Tutu, champion of the people and for justice could not be contained. He wrote:

> If you go anywhere today in the world, many of our friends ask, "What has happened to you? What has happened to you, South Africa? We struggled with you and together we won this great victory, and we believed that we didn't have to worry, that South Africa would be on the side of victims, opposing dictators, seeking to uphold human rights." We are destroying our legacy; we have tumbled from the moral high ground. We are the pits.[7]

Desmond Tutu went on to hint that perhaps a reason for the states of affairs he was critiquing may have been that they "imagined that the idealism, the altruism, the being concerned about others more than ourselves, all of those things would carry over automatically into the post-apartheid era."[8] In letting their "guard down" Tutu noted, they "were surprised how quickly we seemed to forget."[9] Amnesia took over.

So, the question remains an urgent one: what follows the chanting down of the shitstems, including the Christianised ones? What can we learn from prophetic voices such as Desmond Tutu and others so that change and transformation do follow and happen after the 'chanting down'? If as is attributed to Desmond Tutu[10] we need to go beyond pulling victims out of the river and instead travel upstream to find out who are throwing them into the river, or what is causing them to fall into the river, then surely there must be steps alongside the 'laments' and 'chanting down'?

DISSENT

Arundhati Roy was on to something when she wrote:

> What we need to search for and find, what we need to hone and perfect into a magnificent shining thing, is new kind of politics. Not the politics of governance, but the politics of resistance. The politics of opposition. The politics of forcing accountability. The politics of joining hands across the world and preventing certain destruction. In the present circumstances [. . .] the only thing worth globalising is dissent.[11]

Can dissent, resistance, chanting down force accountability and solidarity towards transformative change? Certainly, what should follow cannot be 'civility.' Not that being 'civil' is not important. The challenge is that civility leans too heavily towards unity as a goal and respect for the sides of the aisle while compromising what is systemic while providing more food for those wishing not to see transformative change. To critique civility is not to suggest the embracing of violence. The critique is intended to move beyond chanting down shitstems (including the Christianised ones) to create strategic spaces to interrogate motivations, oppressive polices, theologies, ecclesiologies and missional practices so that we keep in focus the ultimate end—full and flourishing life for all. Arundhati Roy's call for a way of resistance and solidarity towards holding all accountable will mean that it would be inevitable to be eternally vigilant in order to deploy disruptive public action in order to support full emancipation.

MADNESS

Let us consider another African prophet. This one, however, was assassinated because of their ideological threat to Capitalism. I am referring to the late Thomas Sankara. I wonder why theological discourse on the various public squares of Africa and beyond tend to overlook him. Sankara was one of Africa's most important anti-imperialist leaders of the late 20th Century. His insight and advocacy that fundamental socio-political change would require a "certain amount of madness" is perhaps one of the most honest nailing of the challenge before us. In an interview in 1985, Sankara contended that one "cannot carry out fundamental change without a certain amount of madness" which he suggests "comes from nonconformity" and determination and boldness "to turn your back on the old formulas" and, "to invent the future." Sankara goes on to note that "we must dare to invent the future."[12] Transformative change will only come through "undaunting audacity, preparedness and enthusiasm for decisive and radical action to overturn existing ways of doing things and thinking."[13] This means that we cannot give the agents of the shitstems "a monopoly over thought, imagination, and creativity."[14] The revolutionary model of Sankara around human rights, debt, gender justice, food sovereignty, health, literacy, extractive and textile industries produced more enemies than friends. No wonder he was crucified. For me this is the shape and cost of public theology.

A COLLECTION OF RESISTANCE

The essays, poetry, and art in this volume underscore that public God-talk in the square is an intentional location of faith and faithfulness, beyond rhetoric and symbolic action. What is critical public theology if not towards liberation and transformation? Its aim and gaze must be towards liberation.

Poetry

One senses this reminder in the hymn of John Bell and Graham Maule's on Jesus waiting, raging, healing, dancing, and calling which is located "in the streets," the public spaces, so to speak.[15] In those numerous places and spaces where oppression relentlessly sacrifices lives "in the service of the land, the hut, the master" and where the dry hallowed eyes of the Dalit Women "bear silent witness to hundreds of deaths of her mothers, daughters, sisters" (Aruna Gogulamanda, Chap. 2), the call to "rise like silver flying fish over clean waters of living oceans" and rise-up "with hearts leaping to do right" (John Robert Lee, Chap. 2) remain urgent and necessary.

As evident from the contributions in this volume and elsewhere, can the "seeds of hope" we sow result in "a harvest" of seeing transformation and hearing 'yes' and 'amen' (Anna Jane Lagi, Chap. 2)? How can our "god-talk to inspire" so that "righteousness prevails" and "justice will flow" "to cleanse and to heal all brokenness" (Karen Georgia Thompson, Chap. 2)? If the life, work, and writings of Desmond Tutu suggest anything it is this: that the resilience, strength, and sustenance for what continues to be a long haul lies in drawing from the nourishing "font of life" with "roots down to places unseen" drinking "deeply of the Spring of the One who calls [us] to life" (Chad Rimmer, Chap. 2).

All the poetic contributions remind us of the need to pay attention, to see, to listen, to act, to keep naming and calling out injustice, to continue naming the near dead and the dead, and to sing from right here, right now where we are situated.

Art Work

In drawing from this font and fount of life we dare to hope another world into being. Such hope calls for action and our actions are motivated by hope. Neil Thorogood's art piece "There must be a God somewhere" (Figure 1.1 on page 5) aptly sums up the contextual realities in which such hope needs to take root. Thorogood's depiction arises from the toppling of the statue of the slave trader Edward Colston in Bristol (June 7, 2020). The image takes the viewer gazing through prison iron bars with what looks like a list of ship names for transporting enslaved on inside (or is it outside?) the right wall. Outside (or inside?) on the plinth where Colton stood is Thorogood's depiction of Marc Quinn's sculpted model of Jen Reid, a black female protestor with her arms in a Black power salute. There is much to contemplate through this depiction. Perhaps, those prison-like bars can serve as an image to awaken us to the challenging task of not only undoing chains, but also the need to be mindful that the undoing is only the beginning to the larger work of costly eternal vigilance towards full freedom. The shitstems may have quickly removed the Jen Reid statue. But that started the moment that a white man (Quinn) immediately capitalised on the Black woman, with the ensuing conversations in the public square turning from Jen Smith and Colston to focus on Quinn. Olivier Marboeuf poignantly observes:

> By capturing the image of a Black woman, Quinn instrumentalizes it for his own projections, ignoring the lapse of time necessary for a re-composition of collective thought regarding the now toppled statue and the ghost of Colston—also ignoring the fact that this vacant space could engage people in the delicate process of exploration of the invisible part of this heritage in the very infrastructure of the city, of the country; in sum, how the statue functions as a system with the artist's action whatever the motivation serving as a useful motif that informs us about the tensions and stakes concerning subaltern representations and representations of subalterns.[16]

Those prison bars may be more pertinent than Thororgood intended.

The artists whose works are included in this collection (see Chap. 1) use their tool and gift to disturb our indifference and inaction and to serve as a means of resistance and (a)rising to lay claim on one's humanity, giving agency especially to despised and marginalised bodies and opening-up alternative possibilities to expose, and strip embedded ideologies. Thorogood's depiction signifies on the reality that black-bodies, especially women, continue to be crucified.

The CWM eDARE event, in giving intentional space for theology to be in conversation with art and poetry, is underscoring that beyond the 'chanting down' such an interdisciplinary dialogue may open-up possibilities for transformative change. Art and poetry carry the capacity to bear witness to something 'beyond the hills' which our theologising as currently practiced can benefit from in that dialogue. Art and poetry depict our realities as they are (here and now) while enabling us to catch a glimpse of the emancipatory possibilities present, available, and possible. However, as Thomas Sankara's life and work remind us—the task ahead will be radical, revolutionary, and costly.

Prose

The essays in this volume collectively testify to Christianity's contribution to building Babylon and to justifying Babylon's shitstems, especially in relation to race, women, and dis/abilities. It is not enough to simply "remove the stone" (read: chant down Babylon). A critical question is what of the Lazarus(es) who come out of the tomb? Why should we assume that such resurrection and rising is a good thing for Lazarus(es)? Would their life and circumstances be different? Resurrection will mean nothing if there are no reversals to what we currently have, and to the spaces into which they are raised. Our theologising and knowledge production will be no different from social media postings which hardly ever do anything to reverse injustice as we continue to highlight the mess of free market capitalism which continues to fail and produce death all around us. What kind of life do we desire: just existing, or living worthy, meaningful, and flourishing lives?

The task before us is going to be transgenerational and may not happen in our lifetime. But we have a responsibility to be 'good ancestors' to future generations yet to be born. So collectively we are saying that we exist in both present and the future. There is a future for the marginalised. How this future will be made real will demand of us to be strategic more than reactionary. We may have to use the colonial infrastructure to undo the epistemologies which the infrastructure is normatively associated as we carry out the work of epistemic disobedience. In the end what lasted for, and will outlive, Desmond Tutu, Thomas Sankara and all of us—are the bits of 'small goodness' (Levinas' idea of la petite bonté).[17] As Jojo Varakukalayil put it (reflecting on this idea of Levinas):

> No matter how good is the effort to bring about it, the monsterocity of the systemic evil subverts the good. The good has no records! Alas. No matter however the structural evil is, there is still a ray of hope. That's the humanity of humans! Nothing is more sublime and saintly than the humanness as manifested in the little "Goodness of the everyday life." It is the Goodness without witness! One's bearing witness to the glory of the good that announces its height from above. The freshness of the human Goodness bears witness to the little one's across the globe who are last, least and the lost! This is the glory of the infinite incarnate in the human flesh as being-there-for-the-other. "The Other is what I am not. [. . .] The other is, [. . .] the weak and the poor, the widow and the orphan." An excess of small Goodness is the way of being fully human—a path toward human flourishing![18]

NOTES

1. Barney Davis, "Insulate Britain blocking Parliament Square in latest rush-hour road protest." *Evening Standard* (04 Nov 2021) https://www.standard.co.uk/news/london/insulate-britain-parliament-square-protest-cop26-b964313.html.

2. Owen Jones, "Insulate Britain's protests are disruptive, annoying—and justified." *The Guardian* (4 Nov 2021) https://www.theguardian.com/commentisfree/2021/nov/03/insulate-britain-protests-protesters-direct-action-climate-emergency.

3. Laura Foster, "COP26: Amazon activist Txai Suruí 'got death threats' after speech." *BBC News* (5 Nov 2021) https://www.bbc.co.uk/news/av/world-latin-america-59166607.

4. Marceline Powell, "British-Trinidadian writer-artist team unveil Iconic COP image slamming Big Oil." *Urban Kapital* (27 Oct) https://www.powellandbarnsmedia

.com/post/british-trinidadian-writer-artist-team-unveil-iconic-cop-image-slamming-big-oil.

5. "COP26: Greta Thurnberg tells protest that COP26 has been a 'failure.'" *BBC* (5 November 2021) https://www.bbc.co.uk/news/uk-scotland-glasgow-west-59165781.

6. Matt McGrath, "COP26: Fossil fuel industry has largest delegation at climate summit." *BBC* (8 November 2021) https://www.bbc.co.uk/news/science-environment-59199484.

7. Desmond Tutu, *God is not a Christian: Speaking Truth in Times of Crisis* (London: Random House, 2011), 212.

8. Tutu, *God is not a Christian*, 216.

9. Tutu, *God is not a Christian*, 216.

10. I use attributed as I have been unable from any of my reading of Tutu's work or writings to locate this comment which may most likely be anecdotal or in a speech.

11. Arundhati Roy, *The Algebra of Infinite Justice* (Flamingo: London, 2002), 191.

12. As quoted by Amber Murrey and Nicholas A. Jackson in their blog https://www.plutobooks.com/blog/lives-afterlives-thomas-sankara/#_ednref4]. See also: https://www.thomassankara.net/interview-de-jean-philippe-rapp-realise-en-1985-oser-inventer-lavenir/.

13. Ama Biney, "Madmen, Thomas Sankara and Decoloniality in Africa" in *A Certain Amount of Madness: The Life, Politics and Legacies of Thomas Sankara*, Murrey A. (ed). (London: Pluto, 2018), 136.

14. Thomas Sankara, Thomas Sankara Speaks (New York: Pathfinder, 2007), 87.

15. John K. Bell and Graham Maule, "Jesus Christ is Waiting" in *Church Hymnary* (London: Canterbury, 2012), 360.

16. See, Olivier Marboeuf, "Towards a de-speaking cinema [1] [A Caribbean Hypothesis]" in *Non-Fiction: The Living Journal* 3 (2021). (https://opencitylondon.com/non-fiction/issue-3-space/towards-a-de-speaking-cinema1-a-caribbean-hypothesis/).

17. See also Arundathi Roy's *The God of Small Things* (New York: Random House, 1997).

18. Jojo Varakukalayil CST, "Small Goodness (la petite bonté) as Human Flourishing: Overcoming Structural Goodness through Ethical Transcendence" in *Jnanadeepa* (24/2 July-December 2020), 55–56.

Bibliography

Adams, Graham. 2010. *Christ and the Other: In dialogue with Hick and Newbigin.* Farnham: Ashgate.
Adams, Graham. 2022. *Holy Anarchy: Dismantling Domination, Embodying Community, Befriending Strangeness.* London: SCM.
Agamben, Giorgio. 2016. *The Use of Bodies.* Stanford: Stanford University Press.
Aguilera, Jasmine. 2021. "More Migrants Die Crossing the Border in South Texas Than Anywhere Else in the U.S. This Documentary Depicts the Human Toll." *Time* (August 20; https://time.com/6091742/migrant-deaths-texas-documentary/).
Alencar Chaves, Christine de. 2003. "A marcha política como ritual." In *Rituais ontem e hoje*, edited by Mariza Peirano, pp 28–36. Rio de Janeiro: Jorge Zahar Editor.
Alexander, Paul. 2013. "Raced, Gendered, Faithed, and Sexed." *Pneuma* 35.3: 319–34. https://doi.org/10.1163/15700747-12341364.
Althaus-Reid, Marcella. 1999. "On Wearing Skirts Without Underwear: 'Indecent Theology Challenging the Liberation Theology of the Pueblo.' Poor Women Contesting Christ." *Feminist Theology* 20: 39–51.
Althaus-Reid, Marcella. 2000. *Indecent Theology: Theological Perversions in Sex, Gender and Politics.* New York: Routledge.
Assmann, Hugo. 1995. *Paradigmas Educacionais e Corporeidade.* 3rd. ed. Piracicaba: UNIMEP.
Aston, Emma. 2014. "Part-Animal Gods." In *The Oxford Handbook of Animals in Classical Thought and Life*, edited by Gordon Lindsay Campbell, 366–83. New York: Oxford University Press.
Bacon, Benjamin W. 1930. *Studies in Matthew.* New York: Henry Holt.
Baffes, Melanie S. 2011. "Jesus and the Canaanite Woman: A Story of Reversal." *Journal of Theta Alpha Kappa* 35.2 (Fall): 12–23.
Bailey, Kenneth E. 1976. *Poet and Peasant: A Literary and Cultural Approach to the Parables of Luke.* Grand Rapids: Eerdmans.
Barnett, Michael. 2005. "The many faces of Rasta: Doctrinal Diversity within the RastafarI Movement." *Caribbean Quarterly* 51.2: 67–78.
Basser, Herbert with Marsha B. Cohen. 2015. *The Gospel of Matthew and Judaic Traditions: A Relevance-Based Commentary.* Leiden: Brill.

Baverstock, A.H. 1937. "The Parable of the Unjust Steward: An Interpretation." *Theology* 35, 206: 78–83.
Beavis, Mary Ann. 1992. "Ancient Slavery as an Interpretive Context for the New Testament Servant Parables with Special Reference to the Unjust Steward (Luke 16:1–8)." *Journal of Biblical Literature* 111.1: 37–54.
Bell, John K. and Graham Maule. 2012. "Jesus Christ is Waiting." In *Church Hymnary*. London: Canterbury.
Berger, Peter L. and Thomas Luckman. 2018. *Modernidade, pluralismo e crise de sentido: A orientação do homem moderno*, translated by Edgar Orth. Petrópolis, RJ: Vozes.
Besson, Jean. 1998. "Religion as Resistance in Jamaican Peasant Life: The Baptist Church, Revival Worldview and Rastafari Movement." In *Rastafarl and Other African-Caribbean Worldviews*, edited by Barry Chevannes, 43–76. New Jersey: Rutgers University Press.
Bhabha, Homi. 1994. *The Location of Culture*. London and New York: Routledge.
Biney, Ama. 2018. "Madmen, Thomas Sankara and Decoloniality in Africa." In *A Certain Amount of Madness: The Life, Politics and Legacies of Thomas Sankara*, edited by A. Murrey, 127–146. London: Pluto.
Binney, Judith, Vincent O'Malley, and Alan Ward (eds). 2018. *Te Ao Hou: The New World 1820–1920*. Auckland: Bridget Williams.
Binney, Judith. 1966. "Papahurihia: Some Thoughts on Interpretation." *Journal of the Polynesian Society* 75.5: 321–331.
Birch, Bruce C., Walter Brueggemann, Terence E. Fretheim, and David L. Petersen. 1999. *A Theological Introduction to the Old Testament*. Nashville: Abingdon.
Bornkamm, Gunter. 1963. "The Stilling of the Storm in Matthew." In *Tradition and Interpretation in Matthew*, edited by Gunter Bornkamm, Gerhard Barth, and Heinz-Joachim Held, 52–57. Philadelphia: Westminster.
Bourdieu, Pierre. 1977. *Outline of a Theory of Practice*. Cambridge: Cambridge University Press.
Bruce, James R., Winfried Blum, and Carmelo Dazzi. 2013. "Bread and Soil in Ancient Rome: A Vision of Abundance and an Ideal of Order Based on Wheat, Grapes, and Olives." In *The Soil Underfoot: Infinite Possibilities for a Finite Resource*, edited by J. Churchman and E. Landa, 153–73. Boca Raton, FL: CRC Press.
Brueggemann, Brenda Jo. 2012. "Introduction, Background, and History." In *Arts and Humanities*, edited by Gary L. Albrecht, 1–62. Thousand Oaks, CA: SAGE Reference. https://link-gale-com.proxy.luther.edu/apps/doc/CX4193500011/GVRL?u=luther_col&sid=GVRL&xid=70952699 (accessed March 27, 2020).
Brynda, Bianca. 1994. "'Roots Daughters': Rasta sistren and their Experiences in the Movement." In *Ay BoBo: Afro-Kaibische Religionen/African-Caribbean Religions. Part 3: Rastafari*, edited by M. Kremser, 77–100. Vienna: WUV-Universitätsverlag.
Butler, Judith. 2018 (2015). *Corpos em aliança e a política das ruas: Notas para uma teoria performativa de assembleia*. Rio de Janeiro, RJ: Civilização Brasileira.
Cacho, Lisa Marie. 2011. "One, Racialized Hauntings of the Devalued Dead." In *Strange Affinities: The Gender and Sexual Politics of Comparative Racialization*,

ed. Grace Kyungwon Hong and Roderick A. Ferguson, 25–52. North Carolina: Duke University.
Cadwallader, Alan H. 2013. "Surprised by Faith: A Centurion and a Canaanite Query the Limits of Jesus and the Disciples." In *Pieces of Ease and Grace: Biblical Essays on Sexuality and Welcome*, edited by Alan Cadwallader, 85–100. Adelaide: ATF.
Carlson, Marvin. 2010. *Performance: Uma introdução crítica*. Belo Horizonte: Editora UFMG.
Chen, Mel. 2012. *Animacies: Biopolitics, Racial Mattering, and Queer Affect*. Durham: Duke University Press.
Chevannes, Barry. 1994. *Rastafari: Roots and Ideology*. Syracuse, NY: Syracuse University Press.
Chevannes, Barry. 1998. "The Phallus and the Outcast: The Symbolism of the Dreadlocks in Jamaica." In *RastafarI and Other African-Caribbean Worldviews*, edited by Barry Chevannes, 97–126. New Jersey: Rutgers University Press.
Chevannes, Barry. 2002. "What You Sow Is What You Reap: Violence and the Construction of Male Identity in Jamaica," *Current Issues in Comparative Education* 2.1: 51–61.
Chevannes, Barry. 2006. *Betwixt and Between: Explorations in an African-Caribbean Mindscape*. Kingston: Jamaica.
Cho, Haejoang. 2002. "Living with Conflicting Subjectivities: Mother, Motherly Wife, and Sexy Woman in the Transition from Colonial-Modern to Postcolonial Korea." In *Under Construction: The Gendering of Modernity, Class, and Consumption in the Republic of Korea*, ed. Laurel Kendall. Honolulu: University of Hawai'i Press.
Cho, Paul K-K. 2019. "'I Have Become a Brother of Jackals': Evolutionary Psychology and Suicide in the Book of Job." *Biblical Interpretation* 27.2: 208–34.
Cho, Paul K-K. 2019. "Job the Penitent: Whether and Why Job Repents (Job 42:6)." In *Landscapes of Korean and Korean American Biblical Interpretation*, edited by John Ahn, 145–74. Atlanta: SBL.
Chopp, Rebecca S. 1999. "Reimagining Public Discourse." In *Black Faith and Public Talk: Critical Essays on James H. Cone's Black Theology and Black Power*, ed. Dwight N. Hopkins, 150–166. Maryknoll, NY: Orbis.
Clines, David J. A. 2011. *Word Biblical Commentary: Job 38–42*. Nashville: Thomas Nelson.
Clines, David J. A. 1989. *Word Biblical Commentary: Job 1–20*. Dallas: Word.
Coakley, Sarah. 2013. *God, Sexuality, and the Self: An Essay "On the Trinity."* Cambridge: Cambridge University Press.
Cochrane, James R. 1999. *Circles of Dignity: Community Wisdom and Theological Reflection*. Minneapolis: Fortress.
Collins, L. 2000. "Daughters of Jah: The Impact of Rastafarian Womanhood in the Caribbean, the United States, Britain, and Canada." In *Religion, Culture, and Tradition in the Caribbean*, edited by Hemchand Gossai and Nathaniel Samuel Murrell. New York: St. Martin's Press.
Coralina, Cora. 1985. "Aninha e suas pedras." In *Vintém de Cobre: Meias Confissões de Aninha*. 3rd ed. Goiânia: Universidade Federal de Goiás.

Coren, Anna, Jessie Yeung, Abdul Basir Bina. 2021. "She was sold to a stranger so her family could eat as Afghanistan crumbles." *CNN* (01 Nov 2021) https://edition.cnn.com/2021/11/01/asia/afghanistan-child-marriage-crisis-taliban-intl-hnk-dst/index.html.
Dallas, Joe. 1998. *A operação do erro: Confrontando o movimento "gay cristão."* São Paulo: Editora Cultura Cristã.
DaMatta, Roberto. 1997. *A casa e a rua: Espaço, cidadania, mulher e morte no Brasil.* Rio de Janeiro, RJ: Rocco.
Davies, W. D., and Dale C. Allison. 2004. *Matthew 19–28.* New York: Bloomsbury.
Davis, A., B. Gardner, and M.R. Gardner. 1941. *Deep South: A Social Anthropological Study of Caste and Class.* Chicago: University of Chicago Press.
Davis, Lennard J. (ed.). 2017. *The Disability Studies Reader.* New York: Routledge.
De Genova, Nicholas. 2013. "'We are of the connections': Migration, methodological nationalism, and 'militant research.'" *Postcolonial Studies* 16.3: 250–58.
De La Torre, Miguel A. 2002. *Reading the Bible from the Margins.* Maryknoll: Orbis.
De Silva, David A. 1993. "The Parable of the Prudent Steward and Its Lucan Context." *Criswell Theological Review* 6.2: 255–68.
Deifelt, Wanda. 2020. "Bodies, Identities, and Empire." In Havea, Jione (ed.), *Vulnerability and Resistance: Body and Liberating Theologies*, 107–122. New York: Lexington Books/Fortress Academic.
Derrett, J.D.M. 1960–61. "Fresh Light on St. Luke XVI. I. The Parable of the Unjust Servant." *New Testament Studies* 7: 198–219.
Derrida, Jacques. 1993. *Aporias.* Translated by Thomas Dutoit. Stanford: Stanford University Press.
Derrida, Jacques. 2005. *The Animal That Therefore I Am.* Translated by David Wills. New York: Fordham University Press.
Derrida, Jacques. 2009–2011. *The Beast and the Sovereign.* 2 volumes. Edited by Michel Lisse, Marie-Louise Mallet, and Ginette Michaud. Translated by Geoffrey Bennington. Chicago: University of Chicago Press.
Donahue, John R. 1988. *The Gospel in Parable: Metaphor, Narrative, and Theology in the Synoptic Gospels.* New York: Fortress.
Donaldson, Laura E. 2007. "Gospel Hauntings: The Postcolonial Demons of New Testament Criticism." In *Postcolonial Biblical Criticism: Interdisciplinary Intersections*, edited by Fernando F. Segovia and Stephen D. Moore, 97–113. London: Bloomsbury.
Dube, Musa W. 2000. *Postcolonial Feminist Interpretation of the Bible.* St. Louis: Chalice.
Dube, Musa. 2014. "Boundaries and Bridges: Journeys of a Postcolonial Feminist in Biblical Studies." *Journal of the European Society of Women in Theological Research* 22: 139–156. doi: 10.2143/ESWTR.22.0.3040795.
Eiesland, Nancy L. 1994. *The Disabled God: Toward a Liberatory Theology of Disability.* Nashville: Abingdon.
Elden, Stuart. 2006. "Heidegger's Animals." *Continental Philosophy Review* 39: 273–91.

Fabella, Virginia, and Sergio Torres, eds. 1985. *Doing Theology in a Divided World*. Maryknoll: Orbis.
Fanon, Frantz. 1963. *The Wretched of the Earth*. Translated by Constance Farrington. New York, NY: Grove.
Fitzmyer, Joseph A. 1964. "The Story of the Dishonest Manager." *Theological Studies* 25: 23–42.
Fitzmyer, Joseph A. 1985. "The Parable of the Dishonest Manager (Lk 16:1–8a)." In *The Gospel According to Luke X-XXIV.* The Anchor Bible. New York: Doubleday.
Fontanari, Rodrigo. 2015. "A noção de punctum de Roland Barthes, uma abertura da imagem?" *Paralaxe* 3.1: 61–74.
Fox, Diana J. 2020. *Cultural DNA: Gender at the Root of Everyday Life in Rural Jamaica*. Kingston, Jamaica: University of the West Indies Press.
Fox, Diana J., and Jillian M. Smith. 2016. "Stewards of their island: Rastafari Women's Activism for the Forests and Waters in Trinidad and Tobago-Social Movement Perspectives." *Resilience: A Journal of the Environmental Humanities* 3: 142–168.
Garnsey, Peter. 1999. *Food and Society in Classical Antiquity*. Cambridge: Cambridge University Press.
Gebara, Ivone. 2002. "Caminho da torre, caminho das aldeias." *Tempo e Presença* 322 (março/abril): 28–29.
Geertz, Clifford. 2008. *A interpretação das culturas*. Rio de Janeiro: LTC.
Glancy, Jennifer A. 2022. *Slavery in Early. Christianity*. Oxford, UK: Oxford University Press.
Gonzaga Jayme, Juliana, and Magda Almeida Neves. 2010. "Cidade e Espaço Público: política de revitalização urbana em Belo Horizonte." *Caderno CRH Salvador* 23.60 (Sep-Dec 2010): 605–617.
Graham, David John. 1997. "The use of film in theology." In *Explorations in Theology and Film: Movies and Meaning*, ed. Clive Marsh and Gaye Williams Ortiz, 35–44. Maiden: Wiley-Blackwell.
Guardiola-Sáenz, Leticia A. 1997. "Borderless Women and Borderless Texts: A Cultural Reading of Matthew 15:21–28." *Semeia* 78: 69–81.
Gullotta, Daniel. 2014. "Among Dogs and Disciples: An Examination of the Story of the Canaanite Woman (Matthew 15:21–28) and the Question of the Gentile Mission within the Matthean Community." *Neotestamentica* 48: 325–340.
Gutiérrez, Gustavo. 1991. *On Job: God-Talk and the Suffering of the Innocent*. Maryknoll: Orbis.
Halberstam, Jack. 2005. *In a Queer Time and Place: Transgender Bodies, Subcultural Lives*. New York: New York University Press.
Handasyde, Kerrie, Rebekah Pryor, and Cathryn McKinney, eds. 2021. *Contemporary Feminist Theologies: Power, Authority, Love*. New York: Routledge.
Haraway, Donna. 1991. *Simians, Cyborgs, Women: The Reinvention of Nature*. New York: Routledge.
Harris, Max. 2019. *Christ on a Donkey: Palm Sunday, Triumphal Entries, and Blasphemous Pageants*. Leeds: Arc Humanities.

Haslam, Molly C. 2012. *A Constructive Theology of Intellectual Disability: Human Being as Mutuality and Response*. New York: Fordham University Press.

Havea, Jione. 2011. "Lazarus troubles." In Ken Stone and Holly Toensing (eds.), *Bible Trouble: Queer Reading at the Boundaries of Biblical Scholarship*, 157–73. Atlanta: SBL.

Hegde, Radha. 1996. "Narratives of Silence: Rethinking Gender, Agency, and Power from the Communication Experiences of Battered Women in South India." *Communication Studies* 47.4: 303–317. DOI: 10.1080/10510979609368485.

Heidegger, Martin. 1962. *Being and Time*. Translated by John Macquarrie and Edward Robinson. Oxford: Blackwell.

Heidegger, Martin. 1995. *The Fundamental Concepts of Metaphysics: World, Finitude, Solitude*. Translated by William McNeil and Nicholas Walker. Bloomington: Indiana University Press.

Heinlein, Robert A. 1984. *Job, a Comedy of Justice*. New York: Ballantine.

"Helping Kopino Kids Fight Poverty, Prejudice." 2011. *The Korean Herald* (August 14; http://www.koreaherald.com/view.php?ud=20110814000224; accessed April 28, 2021).

Henry, Roland. 2006. "Female biology dictates family life in Rasta camp." *Sunday Observer* (July 17).

Hepner, Tricia Redeker, and Randall L. Hepner. 2001. "Gender, Community and Change among the Rastafarl of New York." In *New York glory: Religions in the city*, edited by Tony Carnes and Anna Karpathakis, 333–356. New York: New York University Press.

Herzog II, William R. 1994. *Jesus as Pedagogue of the Oppressed*. Louisville: Westminster John Knox.

Herzog II, William R. 1994. *Parables as Subversive Speech*. Grand Rapids: Westminster John Knox.

Homiak, John P. 1998. "Dub History: Soundings on Rastafari Livity and Language." In *Rastafarl and Other African-Caribbean Worldviews*, edited by Barry Chevannes, 127–181. New Jersey: Rutgers University Press.

Hong, Grace Kyungwon. 2015. *Death beyond Disavowal: The Impossible Politics of Difference*. Minneapolis: University of Minnesota Press.

Hopkins, Keith. 1978. *Conquerors and Slaves*. Cambridge, UK: Cambridge University Press.

Horrell, David G. 2005. *Solidarity and Difference: A Contemporary Reading of Paul's Ethics*. London: T&T Clark.

Huberman, Leo, and Paul M. Sweezy. 1989. "The Revolutionary Heritage." In *The Cuba Reader: The Making of a Revolutionary Society*, ed. by Philip Brenner, et al. New York: Grove.

Ireland, Dennis. 1992. *Stewardship and the Kingdom of God: An Historical, Exegetical, and Contextual Study of the Parable of the Unjust Steward in Luke 16:1–13*. Netherlands, Brill.

Isasi-Diaz, Ada María. 2009. "A Mujerista Hermeneutics of Justice and Human Flourishing." In *The Bible and The Hermeneutics of Liberation*, edited by Alejandro F. Botta and Pablo R. Andiñach, 181–95. Atlanta: SBL.

Jackson, Moana. 2020. "Where to next? Decolonisation and the stories in the Land." In *Imagining Decolonisation*, 133–155. Auckland: Bridget Williams.

Jeremias, Jeremiah. 1963. *The Parables of Jesus.* London: SCM.

Jones, Scott C. 2013. "Corporeal Discourse in the Book of Job." *Journal of Biblical Literature* 132: 845–63.

Jones, Serene. 2009. *Trauma and Grace: Theology in a Ruptured World.* Louisville: Westminster John Knox.

Jorgerseon, Kiara A., and Padgett, Alan G. (eds). 2020. *Ecotheology: A Christian Conversation.* Grand Rapids: William B. Eerdmans.

Kadish, Rachel. 2017. *The Weight of Ink.* Boston: Houghton Mifflin Harcourt.

Kafer, Alison. 2013. *Feminist, Queer, Crip.* Bloomington: Indiana University Press.

Kampen, Melanie. 2014. "Unsettling Theology: Decolonising Western Interpretations of Original Sin." Master of Theological Studies Thesis, University of Waterloo and Conrad Grebel University College (https://uwspace.uwaterloo.ca/bitstream/handle/10012/8368/Kampen_Melanie.pdf).

Kandiyoti, Deniz. 1998. "Bargaining with Patriarchy." *Gender and Society* 3.3: 274–290.

Kayatekin, Serap, A. 2001. "Sharecropping and Feudal Class Process in the Postbellum Mississippi Delta." In *Re/Presenting Class: Essays in Postmodern Marxism,* edited by J.K. Gibson-Graham, S. Resnick, and R. Wolff, 227–46. Durham, NC: Duke University Press.

Kayatekin, Serap, A. 2004. "Hegemony, Ambivalence, and Class Subjectivity: Southern Planters in Sharecropping Relations in the Post-Bellum United States." In *Postcolonialism Meets Economics,* edited by Eiman O. Zein-Elabdin and S. Charusheela, 235–52. London; New York: Routledge.

Kim, Nami. 2016. *The Gendered Politics of the Korean Protestant Right: Hegemonic Masculinity.* New York: Palgrave Macmillan.

King, Fergus J. 2018. "A Funny Thing Happened on The Way to the Parable: The Steward, Tricksters and (Non)Sense in Luke 16:1–8." *Biblical Theology Bulletin* 48.1: 18–25.

Kloppenborg, John. 1989. "The Dishonoured Master (Luke 16:1–8a)." *Biblica* 70.4: 474–495.

Knight, Franklin W. 1990. *The Caribbean: The Genesis of a Fragmented Nationalism.* 2nd edition. New York: Oxford University Press.

Kolbert, Elizabeth. 2015. *Field Notes from a Catastrophe: Man, Nature, and Climate Change.* New York: Bloomsbury.

Krell, David Farrell. 2013. *Derrida and Our Animal Others: Derrida's Final Seminar, The Beast and the Sovereign.* Bloomington: Indiana University Press.

Kumar, Ruchi. 2022. "In Afghanistan, 'people selling babies, young girls to survive.'" *Aljazeera* (31 March) https://www.aljazeera.com/news/2022/3/31/afghanistan-faces-hunger-crisis-of-unparalleled-proportions.

Kuperus, Gerard. 2007. "Attunement, Deprivation, and Drive: Heidegger and Animality." In *Phenomenology and the Non-Human Animal: At the Limits of Experience,* edited by Corinne Painter and Christian Lotz, 13–28. Dordrecht: Springer.

Lacan, Jacques. 1966. *Écrits*. Paris: Seuil.
Lake, Obiagele. 2008. "The Culturalization of African Female Pollution: Rastafarī Adaptations." In *Rastafari*, edited by Rex Nettleford and Veronica Salter, 231–254. Caribbean Quarterly: The University of the West Indies.
Lake, Obiagele. 2014. "Cultural Ideology and Rastafarī Women." In *Rastafarī in the New Millennium: A Rastafarī Reader*, edited by Michael Barnett, 222–238. New York: Syracuse University Press.
Landfair, Valerie Ranee. 2020. "Complicity and Silence: How Lament Could Lead us to a Better Place," in "Womanist Theology: Unravelling the Double Bind of Racism and Sexism." *Mutuality Magazine* (September 05): 24–30, https://www.cbeinternational.org/resource/article/mutuality-blogmagazine/complicity-and-silence-how-lament-could-lead-us-toward.
Latner, Teishan A. 2018. *Cuban Revolution in America: Havana and the Making of a United States Left, 1968–1992*. Chapel Hill: University of North Carolina.
Latour, Bruno. 2004. *Politics of Nature: How to Bring the Sciences into Democracy*. Translated by Catherine Porter. Cambridge, MA: Harvard University Press.
Latour, Bruno. 2005. *Reassembling the Social: An Introduction to Actor-Network-Theory*. Oxford: Oxford University Press.
Lawrence, Louise Joy. 2009. "'Crumb Trails and Puppy-dog Tales': Reading Afterlives of a Canaanite Woman." In *From the Margins: Women of the New Testament and their Afterlives*, edited by Peter S. Hawkins, Lesleigh Cushing Stahlberg, 262–278. Sheffield: Sheffield Phoenix.
Lawrence, Louise Joy. 2013. "Reading Matthew's Gospel with Deaf Culture," in *Matthew: Texts @ Contexts Series*, edited by Nicole Wilkinson Duran and James F. Grimshaw, 155–174. Minneapolis: Fortress.
Lee, Jin-Kyung. 2010. *Service Economies: Militarism, Sex Work, and Migrant Labor in South Korea*. Minneapolis: University of Minnesota Press.
Lewis, Jovan Scott. 2017. "Rights, Indigeneity, and the Market of Rastafari." *International Journal of Cultural Property* 24: 57–77 (doi:10.1017/S0940739116000400).
Lewis, Sehon M. 2013. *From Mythology to Reality: Moving Beyond Rastafari*. Raleigh, NC: Lulu Enterprises.
Linfield, Susie. 2010. *The Cruel Radiance: Photography and Political Violence*. Chicago, IL: The University of Chicago Press.
Luz, Ulrich. 1992. "The Son of Man in Matthew: Heavenly Judge or Human Christ." *Journal for the Study of the New Testament* 48: 3–21.
Lyons-Pardue, Kara J. 2019. "A Syrophoenician Becomes a Canaanite: Jesus Exegetes the Canaanite Woman in Matthew." *Journal of Theological Interpretation* 13.2: 235–250. Doi: 10.5325/jtheointe.13.2.0235.
Macdonald, Erik. 1993. *Theater at the Margins: Text and the post-structured stage*. Ann Arbor: University of Michigan Press.
Maluleke, Tinyko. 2021. "Beyond the Graveyard and the Prison, a New World is Being Born." In Jione Havea (ed), *Doing Theology in the New Normal*, 327–343. London: SCM.
Manson, T.W. 1949. *The Sayings of Jesus*. London: SCM.

Marboeuf, Olivier. 2021. "Towards a de-speaking cinema [1] (A Caribbean Hypothesis)." *Non-Fiction: The Living Journal* 3 (2021). https://opencitylondon.com/non-fiction/issue-3-space/towards-a-de-speaking-cinema1-a-caribbean-hypothesis/.

"Marcha contra a LGBTfobia percorre centro de Belo Horzonte." *O Tempo* (May 14, 2016). http: //www.otempo.com.br/cidades/marcha-contra-a-lgbtfobia-percorre-centro-de-belo-horizonte-1.1299752.

Martí, José. 1895. *Obras Completas.* Volume 4. La Habana: Editorial Nacional de Cuba.

Martínez, Jessica, and Gregory A. Smith. 2016. "How the Faithful Voted: A Preliminary 2016 Analysis." *Pew Research Center* (November 9; https://www.pewresearch.org/fact-tank/2016/11/09/how-the-faithful-voted-a-preliminary-2016-analysis/).

Mbembe, Achille. 2008. "What is Postcolonial Thinking? An Interview with Achille Mbembe." *Eurozine* (September 1; http://www.eurozine.com/articles/2008-01-09-mbembe-en.html).

Mbembe, Achille. 2019. *Necropolitics.* Durham, NC: Duke University Press.

Meier, John P. 1979. *The Vision of Matthew: Christ, Church, and Morality in the First Gospel.* New York: Paulist.

Mello, Luiz; Braz, Camilo; Almeida De Freitas, Fátima Regina; Rezende De Avelar, Bruno. 2012. "Questões LGBT em debate: Sobre desafios e conquistas." *Sociedade e Cultura* 15.1 (Jan-Jul): 151–161.

Mercier, Ocean Ripeka. 2020. "What is Decolonisation?" In *Imagining Decolonisation*, 40–82. Auckland: Bridget Williams.

Metzger, James A., and James P. Grimshaw. 2013. "Reading Matthew's Healing Narratives from the Perspectives of the Caregiver and the Disabled." In *Matthew: Texts @ Contexts Series*, edited by Nicole Wilkinson Duran and James F. Grimshaw, 133–154. Minneapolis: Fortress.

Mignolo, Walter. 2007. "Introduction." *Cultural Studies* 21.2–3: 156. (DOI: 10.1080/09502380601162498).

Monro, Anita. 1994. "Alterity and the Canaanite Woman: A Postmodern Feminist Theological Reflection on Political Action." *Colloquium* 26.1 (May): 32–43.

Montlouis, Nathalie. 2013. *Lords and Empresses in and out of Babylon: The EABIC community and the dialectic of female subordination.* PhD Thesis, in African Languages and Cultures. Department of the Languages and Cultures of Africa School of Oriental and African Studies, University of London.

Moore, Stephen D. 2017. *Gospel Jesuses and Other Nonhumans: Biblical Criticism, Post-Poststructuralism.* Atlanta: SBL.

Morley, N. 2001. "The Transformation of Italy, 225–28 B.C." *Journal of Roman Studies* 91: 50–62.

Naas, Michael. 2015. *The End of the World and Other Teachable Moments: Jacques Derrida's Final Seminar.* New York: Fordham University Press.

Nandy, Ashis. 2009. "Open Pasts, Open Futures." *Monsoon* 4 (https://static1.squarespace.com/static/612b5c38a84af13ad0a05fe2/t/6198e09d49dabd2b10dcf097/1637408925938/china.pdf).

Nangwaya, Ajamu. 2007. "Rastafari as a Catalytic Force in Ecotourism Development in Jamaica: Development as Economic and Social Justice." Paper presented at The University of the West Indies conference series (http://sta.uwi.edu/conferences/salises/documents/Nangwaya%20%20A%20.pdf).

Newman, Philip C. 1965. *Cuba Before Castro: An Economic Appraisal.* New Delhi, India: Prentice Hall.

Newmyer, Stephen. 2020. *Plutarch's Three Treatises on Animals: A Translation with Introductions and Commentary.* Milton: Taylor and Francis.

Newsom, Carol A. 2003. *The Book of Job: A Contest of Moral Imaginations.* Oxford: Oxford University Press.

Ngugi wa Thiong'o. 1987. *Devil on the Cross.* Portsmouth: Heinemann.

Ngwa, Kenneth Numfor. 2005. *The Hermeneutics of the "Happy Ending" in Job 42:7–17.* Berlin and New York: Walter de Gruyter.

Oesterley, W.O.E. 1936. *The Gospel Parables in the Light of the Jewish Background.* New York: MacMillan.

Patte, Daniel. 2000. "The Canaanite Woman and Jesus: Surprising Models of Discipleship (Matt. 15:21–28)." In T*ransformative Encounters: Jesus and Women Re-viewed,* edited by Ingrid R. Kitzberger, 33–53. Leiden: Brill.

Perdue, Leo G. 1991. *Wisdom in Revolt: Metaphorical Theology in the Book of Job.* Sheffield: Almond.

Perkins, Anna Kasafi. 2018. "Blood clot, ras clot and bun bow clot: Lovindeer takes on female bodily taboos in Jamaica." In *Breaking Down Binaries: Tidal shifts in the study of the languages, literatures and cultures of the Greater Caribbean and beyond*, edited by Nicholas Faraclas, et al., 63–78. Puerto Rico/Curacao: University of Curacao.

Perrin, Norman. 1967. *Rediscovering the Teaching of Jesus.* New York: Harper & Row.

Perry, Troy. 2007. *Call me Troy.* YouTube. Scott Bloom.

Ras Dizzy I. 2008. "I wants no part with you" (poem by the poet). In *Rastafari*, edited by Rex Nettleford and Veronica Salter, 104. Kingston, Jamaica: Caribbean Quarterly.

Reddie, Anthony G. 2021. "Not Returning to the Old Normal." In Jione Havea (ed), *Doing Theology in the New Normal*, 243–257. London: SCM.

Rivera, Mayra. 2015. *Poetics of the Flesh.* Durham: Duke University Press.

Rosa, João Guimarães. 1988. *Grande Sertão: Veredas.* 30th ed. Rio de Janeiro: Editora Nova Fornteira.

Rosendahl, Zeny. 1996. "O Sagrado e o urbano: Gênese e função das cidades." *Espaço e Cultura* 1.1: 26–40.

Ross, Mike. 2020. "The Throat of Parata." In *Imagining Decolonisation*, 21–39. Auckland: Bridget Williams.

Rossetti, Léo (Org.). 2016. *Borboletas tropicais: O caminho brasileiro das Igrejas da Comunidade Metropolitana.* Rio de Janeiro: Metanoia.

Roy, Arundhati. 2002. *The Algebra of Infinite Justice.* London: Flamingo.

Roy, Arundhati. 2997. *The God of Small Things.* New York: Random House.

Royal commission into Violence. N.d. *Abuse, Neglect, and Exploitation of Peoples with a Disability.* https://disability.royalcommission.gov.au/system/files/exhibit/EXP.0020.0001.0001.pdf.
Royal, Charles Te Ahukaramu (ed.). 2003. *The Woven Universe—Selected Writings of Rev. Māori Marsden.* Masterton: The Estate of Māori Marsden.
Rubano, Craig Anthony. 2016. "Where Do the Mermaids Stand? Toward a 'Gender-Creative' Pastoral Sensibility." *Pastoral Psychology* 65.6 (Dec): 821–834.
Rubino, Silvana. 2009. "Enobrecimento Urbano." In *Plural de Cidades: Novos léxicos urbanos,* edited by C. Leite; R. P Fortuna. Coimbra: Edições Almedina.
Runions, Erin. 2014. *The Babylon Complex: Theopolitical Fantasies of War, Sex, and Sovereignty.* New York: Fordham University Press.
Said, Edward W. 1982. "Opponents, Audiences, Constituencies, and Community." *Critical Inquiry* 9.1: 1–26.
Said, Edward W. 1991. "The Politics of Knowledge." *Raritan: A Quarterly Review* 11.1: 17–31.
Sankara, Thomas. 2007. Thomas Sankara Speaks. New York: Pathfinder.
Schipani, Daniel S. 2001. "Transformation in the Borderlands: A Study of Matthew 15:21–28." *Vision* 2.2 (Fall): 13–24.
Schreiner, Susan E. 1989. "Exegesis and Double Justice in Calvin's Sermons on Job." *Church history* 58.3: 322–38.
Schüssler Fiorenza, Elisabeth. 2001. *Wisdom Ways: Introducing Feminist Biblical Interpretation.* Maryknoll: Orbis.
Scott, Bernard Brandon. 1983. "A Master's Praise: Luke 16,1–8a." *Biblica* 64:2: 173–183.
Scott, J. Martin C. 1997. "Matthew 15:21–28: A Test-Case for Jesus' Manners." *Journal for the Study of the New Testament* 19.63 (Jan): 21–44.
Scott, James C. 1985. *Weapons of the Weak: Everyday Forms of Peasant Resistance.* New Haven: Yale University Press.
Shanks, Andrew. 2011. *Hegel and Religious Faith: Divided Brain, Atoning Spirit.* London and New York: Bloomsbury T&T Clark.
Shanks, Andrew. 2015. *Hegel versus 'Inter-Faith Dialogue': A General Theory of True Xenophilia.* New York: Cambridge University Press.
Silberman, Steve. 2015. *NeuroTribes: The Legacy of Autism and the Future of Neurodiversity.* New York: Avery/Penguin Random House.
Sim, David C. 1996. *Apocalyptic Eschatology in the Gospel of Matthew.* New York: Cambridge University Press.
Smith, Mitzi. 2016. "Race, Gender, and the Politics of 'Sass': Reading Mark 7: 24–30 through a Womanist Lens of Intersectionality and Inter(con)textuality." In *Womanist Interpretations of the Bible: Expanding the Discourse,* edited by Gay L. Byron, and Vanessa Lovelace, 95–112. Semeia Studies 85. Atlanta: SBL.
Soelle, Dorothee. 1975. *Suffering.* Translated by Everitt R. Kalin. Philadelphia: Fortress.
Sontag, Susan. 2003. *Regarding the Pain of Others.* New York, NY: Farrar, Straus and Giroux.

Spies, Miriam. Forthcoming. "Cripping the Failes Body of Christ." In *Decolonizing Church, Theology, and Ethics in Canada*, edited by Néstor Medina and Becca Whitla. Montréal: McGill/Queen's University Press.

Still, Judith. 2015. *Derrida and Other Animals: The Boundaries of the Human*. Edinburgh: Edinburgh University Press.

Strauss Swanson, Charlotte & Dawn Szymanski. 2020. "From Pain to Power: An Exploration of Activism, the #Metoo Movement, and Healing from Sexual Assault Trauma." *Journal of Counselling Psychology* 67.6: 653–668.

Tafari Ama, Imani. 2014. "Resistance Within and Without: Reasonings on Gender Relations." In *Rastafari in the New Millennium: A RastafarI Reader*, edited by Michael Barnett, 190–221. New York: Syracuse University Press.

Tavares Natividade, Marcelo. 2010. "Uma homossexualidade santificada? Etnografia de uma comunidade inclusiva pentecostal." *Religião & Sociedade* 30: 90–120.

Taylor, Richard. 1868. *The Past and Present of New Zealand: With its Prospects for the Future*. Wanganui: Henry Ireson Jones.

The Bacchus Lady (Korean title: *Jugyeojuneun Yeoja*). 2016. Directed by E J-yong.

The Care Collective. 2020. *The Care Manifesto*. Brooklyn: Verso (Kindle Edition).

Theije, Marjo de. 2006. "Religião e Transformações Urbanas em Recife, Brasil." *Ciências Sociais e Religião* 8.8 (Out): 63–84.

Thomas, Deborah A. 2011. *Exceptional Violence: Embodied Citizenship in Transnational Jamaica*. Durham and London: Duke University Press.

Thomas, Hugh. 1971. *Cuba: The Pursuit of Freedom*. New York: Harper & Row.

Turner, Terisa E. 1991. "Women, RastafarI and the New Society: Caribbean and East African roots of a popular movement against structural adjustment." *Labour, Capital and Society/Travail, capital et société* 24.1 (April/Avril): 66–89. (https://www.jstor.org/stable/43157919).

Tutu, Desmond. 2011. *God is not a Christian: Speaking Truth in Times of Crisis*. Ed. John Allen. London: Random House.

Ukpong, Justin S. 1996. "The Parable of the Shrewd Manager (Luke 16:1–13): An Essay in Inculturation Biblical Hermeneutic." *Semeia* 73: 189–210.

Valencia, Sayak. 2018. *Gore Capitalism*. South Pasadena, CA: Semiotext.

van Wolde, Ellen. 1994. "Job 42,1–6: The Reversal of Job." In *The Book of Job*, edited by W.A.M. Beuken, 223–50. Leuven: Leuven University Press.

Varakukalayil CST, Jojo. 2020. "Small Goodness (la petite bonté) as Human Flourishing: Overcoming Structural Goodness through Ethical Transcendence." *Jnanadeepa* (24/2 July-December 2020): 42–60.

Wainwright, Elaine M. 1991. *Towards a Feminist Critical Reading of the Gospel According to Matthew*. New York: De Gruyter.

Wainwright, Elaine M. 1995. "A Voice from the Margin: Reading Matthew 15:21–28 in an Australian Feminist Key." In *Reading from this Place, Vol. 2: Social Location and Biblical Interpretation in Global Perspective*. Edited by Fernando F. Segovia & Mary Ann Tolbert, 132–153. Minneapolis: Fortress.

Wainwright, Elaine M. 2013. "Of Dogs and Women: Ethology and Gender in Ancient Healing." In *Miracles Revisited: New Testament Miracle Stories and Their*

Concepts of Reality, edited by Stefan Alkies, and Annette Weissenrieder, 55–69. Berlin/Boston: De Gruyter.
Walck, Leslie W. 2011. *The Son of Man in the Parables of Enoch and in Matthew*. New York: Bloomsbury.
Ward, Graham. 2017. "Decolonizing theology." *Stellenbosch Theological Journal* 3.2: 561–584.
Ward, Judith. 2016. "The Invention of Papahurihia." PhD Thesis, Massey University (https://mro.massey.ac.nz/bitstream/handle/10179/9988/01_front.pdf?sequence=1&isAllowed=y).
West, Gerald O. 2000. "Kairos 2000: Moving Beyond Church Theology." *Journal of Theology for Southern Africa* 108: 55–78.
West, Gerald O. 2016. "Between Text and Trauma: Reading Job with People Living with HIV." In *Bible through the Lens of Trauma*, edited by Elizabeth C. Boase and Frechette Christopher G., 209–30. Atlanta: SBL.
West, Gerald O. 2017. "Senzeni Na? Speaking of God 'What Is Right' and the 'Re-Turn' of the Stigmatising Community in the Context of HIV." *Scriptura* 116.2: 260–77.
West, Gerald O. 2017. "The Co-Optation of the Bible by 'Church Theology' in Post-Liberation South Africa: Returning to the Bible as a 'Site of Struggle.'" *Journal of Theology for Southern Africa* 157: 185–98.
West, Gerald O. 2021. "Reopening the Churches and/as Reopening the Economy: Covid's Uncovering of the Contours of 'Church Theology.'" In *Doing Theology in the New Normal*, edited by Jione Havea, 79–98. London: SCM.
Wignall, Mark. 2013. "Religion, menstruation and mass ignorance." *Jamaica Observer*. (Sunday, February 24).
Witte, Brendon Robert. 2016. "'Who Do You, Matthew, Say the Son of Man Is?' Son of Man and Conflict in the First Gospel." PhD dissert., University of Edinburgh.
World Population Review. 2021. "Obesity Rates by Country 2021." (https://worldpopulationreview.com/country-rankings/obesity-rates-by-country).
World Population Review. nd. "CO2 Emissions by Country." (https://worldpopulationreview.com/country-rankings/co2-emissions-by-country).
Yee, Gale A. 2020. "Thinking Intersectionally: Gender, Race, Class, and the Etceteras of Our Discipline." *Journal of Biblical Literature* 139.1: 7–26.
Zacharias, H. Daniel. 2011. "Old Greek Daniel 7:13–14 and Matthew's Son of Man." *Bulletin for Biblical Research* 21.4: 453–61.

Index

abilities, 167, 168, 170, 171, 185, 188
abject bodies, 145, 148
actant(s), 44, 49, 51, 52
activism, 65, 66, 110, 113, 141, 149, 203
agony, 97
altar, 132
altruism, 205
ambivalence, xi, 45–48, 52, 167, 168
ancestor(s), 94, 109, 117, 194, 209
animal(s), x, 2, 6, 12, 27–37, 49, 58, 73–76
anomalies, 60
apartheid, 204
asylum, 1, 100, 102, 15

basileia, 58, 59
beast(ly), x, 4, 10, 27, 29, 31–35, 37, 90
belonging(s), xii, 84, 87, 89
blah-blah-blah, 203, 204
border(s), x, xii, 2, 8, 76, 84, 86, 90, 97, 98, 100, 102, 103, 118, 141, 161
borderland(s), 59, 100, 104
bread(crumbs), 58, 61, 79, 80, 101
breadwinner, 130, 134

capitalism, 125, 130, 162, 206, 209
carpenter, 84
chaos, xii, xv, 14, 173–77, 178

child(ren), xi, xiii, xiv, xv, 2, 15, 17, 18, 20, 28, 31, 32, 41, 46, 47, 55, 58, 61, 62, 64, 66, 77, 84, 88, 92, 93, 94, 102, 105, 125, 128, 130, 132, 133, 134, 153, 154, 157, 158, 161, 168, 173, 174, 176, 177, 184, 186, 188, 195, 196
chronic, 185
classism, 64, 92
coal, 101
complexity theory, 174
conflict, 20, 73, 109
congenital, 185
conquest, 57, 99, 101, 102, 104
consumerism, 97, 126, 181
crisis, xi, 44, 71, 204
crush(ing), 15, 23, 92, 136

debt(s), 43, 47, 48, 50, 206
defiance, xiii, 109, 110, 112, 113, 115, 119, 173, 177, 178
deficit(s), xv, 60, 169, 170, 171, 172, 173, 175, 176, 185
defilement, 12
dementia, 20, 159, 168, 170, 173, 176, 177
demon, 55, 56, 59, 60
diabetes, 195

225

dignity, xv, 15, 44, 59, 60, 63, 132, 156, 158, 163, 169, 186, 187
dirt, 11, 19, 84
disability, xvi, 17, 55–66, 154, 158, 163, 181–88
dis/ability, 167–78
disdain, 46, 47
dishonest (manager), x, 43
displacement, xii, 60, 86, 87, 187
dissonant, 142, 143
distress(ing), 14, 58, 62, 85
dog(s), 30, 32, 36, 58
domination, 20, 21, 64, 104, 125, 129, 136, 152, 154
dreadlocks, 126, 131, 133
drink, xiv, 21, 23, 51, 92, 136, 151, 153

economic, xi, xiii, xv, 21, 41–52, 56, 79, 87, 90, 91, 93, 127, 144, 145, 151, 155, 159, 163, 170, 171, 177, 184, 195
emancipation, xiv, 206
embodiment, xvi, 56, 75, 181, 182–87, 226
empathy, 162, 175
epistemology, epistemologies, 172, 209
equality, 62, 79, 129, 134, 144, 182
eunuch, 32
euthanasia, 152, 159, 162
exclusion, 33, 56, 94, 127, 131, 145, 168, 172, 185, 187, 204
exile, xii, 83, 84, 85, 86, 87, 88
exploitation, 19, 44, 47, 97, 112, 126, 152, 153, 154, 155, 156

fatherhood, 132, 133
fear, 14, 16, 21, 23, 32, 34, 35, 46, 65, 90, 131, 170, 199
fertility, 134, 151
filth(y), xiv, 11, 12, 19, 159
finance, 49
food, 2, 15, 18, 28, 29, 32, 48, 58, 101, 105, 113, 131, 132, 156, 159, 160, 205
fool(s), 160

foreigners, xii, 28, 82, 85, 158
forest, xiii, 111
fragility, 10, 11, 16, 23
freedom, xiii, 18, 29, 66, 100, 111, 127, 130, 132, 144, 182, 196, 207
from below, xii, 72–80

garbage, 20
genealogy, 27, 57
Gentile(s), 57, 58

haka, 109–10, 112–13
haunting, xii, 34, 42
healing, xi, xv, 16, 21, 56, 57, 59–61, 62, 63, 65, 66, 89, 97, 106, 117, 175, 188, 197, 206
homeland, 84, 85, 87, 89, 90, 104
homeless(ness), 20, 27
homophobia, 142, 43, 156
honor, 18, 50, 51, 77, 79
hunger, 14, 18, 29, 87, 92, 105
hungry, 58, 73, 92, 101

idealism, 205
illusion, 16, 86, 88, 116, 177, 193
impurity, 60
inchstone(s), 170, 174, 176
inclusion, 32, 33, 57, 60, 62, 66, 79, 142, 185
indecent, xv, 154, 163
injustice, xi, xii, 13, 21, 48, 58, 71, 73, 74, 75, 77, 80, 168, 207, 209
interpellation, 46
intimacy, 49, 187
invasion(s), 1, 2, 11, 90, 91, 104, 110
iTaukei, 193, 194

justice, xii, xiii, 2, 13, 15, 43, 44, 59, 60, 64, 71–72, 79, 80, 93, 142, 149, 169, 177, 204, 206, 207

kill(er), 47, 101, 152, 153, 167

Index

labor/labour, xiii, xiv, 45, 46, 74, 90, 94, 105, 125, 126, 127, 128, 134, 154–56, 161, 162, 184
lament, xi, xii, 56, 63, 65, 73, 77, 99, 102, 106
landowner(s), x, 42, 45, 46, 47, 48, 51
laughing, 50, 51, 146, 204
lesbophobia, 142
LGBT, 142, 143, 147
liberation, 59, 79, 87, 93, 94, 111, 130, 134, 206
linear, 194
liturgy, xiv, 148
looking back, 88, 194, 199
loopholes, 204

machine(s), xvi, 19, 105, 119, 185, 187
madness, 195, 206
malaria, 195
mammon, 41, 42, 43, 49, 52
marginalisation, xi, 55, 65, 133
menses, xiv, 128, 133
mental (illness, disorder, issue), 60, 170, 184, 186
militarism, 162
mimicry, 46, 47
mobility, 168, 169
money, 1, 41, 42, 43, 44, 46–49, 51, 52, 79, 80, 94, 157, 158, 159, 162, 171, 172, 174, 183
motherhood, 132, 161
mourning, 77, 78, 99–106
myth, 22, 130, 152, 182

nakedness, 29
narcissism, 97
native(s), x, xii, xiii, 7, 8, 10, 11, 84, 101, 103, 110, 111, 115, 195
necropolitical labor, 154, 155
necropolitics, 15
necropower, xii, 97, 100, 101, 104
negotiation, 134, 136

occupation, 2, 85, 155

oil, xi, 6, 44, 47, 48, 49, 51, 91, 203, 204
othering, xi, 46
outlaw, 33

parable(s), 32, 42–44, 48–51, 151–52, 156, 158, 160–63
paradise, 88, 92, 203
passion, 16, 103, 182
performativity, 144, 149
pigs, 36
pillar of salt, 194, 195
poison, 203
pollution, 130, 131
polygamy, 133
poor, 15, 27, 44, 84, 158, 163, 183, 209
poverty, 14, 92, 152, 159, 162, 163
power-with, 21, 71
predator(s), 43, 62, 73
prey(ing), 16, 27, 29, 33, 73
prison(er), 6, 98, 156, 159, 161, 162, 195, 207, 208
prosthetic labor, 154–56, 162
public assembly, 144
purification, 132, 134

queer(ing), xiv, xv, 10, 94, 141, 148, 159, 160, 177

racism, xiii, 64, 87, 92, 110, 116, 117, 198
refugee(s), xii, 2, 10, 84, 85, 86, 87, 88, 90, 93, 100, 102, 104, 161
reincarnation, 12
remembering, 86, 163, 194
resilience, 21, 172, 187, 188, 207
resonance box, 145
restoration, 58, 64, 79, 109, 118, 119, 199
resurrection, 34, 35, 36, 37, 194, 197, 198, 200, 208
revolution(ary), 11, 44, 50, 84, 90, 92, 119, 173, 206, 208
ringleader, 73

sacred, xii, 11, 19, 20, 87, 101, 102–5, 145, 158
saliva, 175, 182
sanitary pad, 19, 131
sass, xii, 66
savage(s), 1, 2, 28, 113, 114
savvy, xi, 45
sea, xiii, 2, 3, 9, 12, 14, 20, 35, 74, 75, 76, 89, 102, 111, 195
secular(ism, isation), xiii, 93, 126, 147
settlers, 104, 119
sexism, 64, 92, 125
sex worker(s), xv, 148, 152, 154, 155, 156, 162, 163
shame, 3, 9, 29, 50, 51, 86, 187
silence, xi, 15, 21, 55, 56, 61, 63–66, 101
silenced, 2, 56, 64, 66
sin, 60
skin, 1, 17, 28, 101, 103
slave(s), 6, 8, 11, 31, 42, 44, 45, 74, 207
solidarity, 65, 66, 145, 149, 154, 162, 167, 177, 178, 184, 205, 206
sovereignty, x, 28, 29, 30, 32, 33, 34, 35, 36, 37, 85, 90, 91, 92, 93, 206
special [military] operation, 2, 3, 4, 6, 9
stones, 2, 3, 4, 5, 10, 186, 187
stupidity, 35, 204
suicide, 100, 102, 152, 154, 156, 157, 159, 161, 162
surrogate, 154, 155, 156, 161, 162
symbolic universe, 51

tears, 4, 11, 14, 65, 172, 182
testify, xiii, 3, 13–16, 98, 100, 208
testimony time, 14
theodicy, 85

therapy, xii, 103, 186
trajectory, 80, 194
transphobia, 142, 156, 162
transvestites, 145
trauma(s), xii, 14, 75, 88, 89, 99, 103
travesti, 148
trees, xv, 82, 175–78, 187
truth telling, xiii, 63, 171

ubuntu, 21
unclean spirits, 60
unholy, 154
untouchables, 12
uprising, 9, 13, 19–20
urban, 141, 148

victim(s), 1, 2, 8, 15, 64, 66, 98, 99, 101, 102, 105, 195, 205
virility, 77

water(s), 9, 14–16, 18, 20, 29, 83, 105, 207
wealth, x, xi, 15, 42, 42, 48, 49, 52, 90, 174
wheelchair, 168, 182
whiteness, 2
white supremacy, xiii
wilderness, 28, 29, 30
worker(s), xv, 42, 45–47, 51, 74, 84, 148, 152, 154, 155, 156, 161, 162, 163, 168, 183

xenophobia, 162

youth, 19, 132, 181

zealot, 47

About the Editor and Contributors

Jione Havea is co-parent for an eight-year-old daughter, native pastor (Methodist Church in Tonga), migrant to the unceded Wurundjeri lands and waters, and research fellow with Trinity Methodist Theological College (Aotearoa New Zealand) and with Australian Center for Christianity and Culture (Charles Sturt University, Australia). An activist-in-training, on the ground and in the classroom, and easily irritated by bullies and suckers, Jione authored *Jonah: An Earth Bible Commentary* (2020) and *Losing Ground: Reading Ruth in the Pacific* (2021); and edited *Bordered Bodies, Bothered Voices: Native and Migrant Theologies* (2022).

* * *

Graham Adams is a theological educator, specializing in missiology. He teaches for Northern College (United Reformed and Congregational), a constituent college of Luther King Centre for Theology and Ministry (Manchester, UK), and with the Congregational Institute of Practical Theology. Previously, he was in local ministry in Manchester, while also working nationally in lay training. His research interests are theologies of solidarity, mission in the context of empire, theologies of religious diversity, childlikeness, and "chaos." His publications include *Christ and the Other* (2010) and *Theology of Religions: Through the Lens of 'Truth-as-Openness'* (2019), and contributions to *The Spirit of Dissent* (2015), *Bible and Theology from the underside of Empire* (2016), *Scripture and Resistance* (2019), and *Hymns of Hope and Healing* (2017).

Gregory L. Cuéllar is Associate Professor of Old Testament at Austin Presbyterian Theological Seminary. Currently, he is a Visiting Academic at the Centre for Criminology at the University of Oxford. Cuéllar is interested in counterintuitive ways of reading biblical texts, especially those that are rooted in a decolonizing discourse of liberation. He has written on topics related to the U.S. Mexico Borderlands, Latinx immigration, race, Bible museums, and empire. His current research focuses on the carceral geographies of immigration detention facilities at the intersections of religion, migratory aesthetics, borderlands, and postcolonial trauma. His most recent books are *Resacralizing the Other at the US-Mexico Border* (2020) and *Empire, the British Museum, and the Making of the Biblical Scholar in the Nineteenth Century Archival Criticism* (2019).

Wanda Deifelt is a Brazilian theologian serving as professor of religion at Luther College in Decorah, Iowa. She is an ordained Lutheran pastor and has served as theological advisor to many ecumenical organizations (World Council of Churches, Lutheran World Federation, Latin American Council of Churches, etc.). Her publications are on embodiment, feminist and liberation theologies, ecumenism and inter-faith dialogue, religious pluralism in Latin America and the Caribbean, as well as the encounter of religion with literature and art.

Miguel A. De La Torre is a scholar-activist who deals with social ethics in contemporary U.S. thought, specifically how religion affects race, class, and gender oppression. He has authored over a hundred articles and published forty-one books. He presently serves as Professor of Social Ethics and Latinx Studies at Iliff School of Theology in Denver. A Fulbright scholar, he has taught in Indonesia, Mexico, South Africa, Costa Rica, Cuba, and Germany. Within his guild he served as the 2012 President of the Society of Christian Ethics. He is the recipient of the 2020 AAR Excellence in Teaching Award and the 2021 Martin E. Marty Public Understand of Religion Award. Within the academy, he is past director to the American Academy of Religion.

Maxime de Palm has been drawing from a very young age. Drawing was her form of self-expression and self-therapy. Born in 1992 on the Caribbean island of Curaçao she was always drawn to vivid colors. She moved to the Netherlands for her studies at age 19 and for the past five years she has been refining her signature within contemporary art. Maxime's sources are the arts and cultures of Curaçao, and holistic life practices in the Caribbean. She is an activist, and she portrays the worth of Black people through photography. Maxime is currently based in Rotterdam where she works as a creative professional at The Niteshop, a bodega research center for Urban Culture/Neighborhood Embassy. A big theme in Maxime's work is mental health in a Black body.

Wendy Elson is an ordained minister in the Uniting Church in Australia, currently in placement in South Gippsland, Victoria. Elson has background in school chaplaincy in government schools. She has a heart for community engagement and ministry to those on the margins, with a focus on the intersections of feminism, disability, and faith. Mother to three sons, Elson draws on her experience as the mother of a child with a disability.

Ana Ester Pádua Freire holds degrees from Pontifícia Universidade Católica de Minas Gerais (PUC Minas); Instituto Metodista Izabela Hendrix; and the Centro Universitário de Belo Horizonte. She works with themes related to religion and sexuality, feminist theology, lesbian feminist theology, queer theology, artivism, and theopoetics. She is an independent researcher of the theological work of Marcella Althaus-Reid and a columnist at *Revista Senso* (Senso Magazine—Contemporary Religious Sense).

Emmanuel Garibay is a Filipino artist who studied at the University of the Philippines and at Union Theological Seminary (Cavite, Philippines). His experiences and studies coalesce in his works which show a stunning combination of social realism and avant-garde figurative expression, seriousness and humor, sharp social critique, and humane character depiction. What is achieved through his carefully crafted work is an effective storytelling of people in scenes of social, political, and religious complexity. A prolific and internationally established painter, he spearheaded art projects in Asia and beyond. He is the current chairperson of Artletics Foundation, a non-stock, non-profit organization that empowers young artists to transform communities through art education. Garibay believes that art can be an effective medium for awakening consciousness and empowering people to bring positive change.

Aruna Gogulamanda hails from Andhra Pradesh, India, and studied at Hyderabad Central University. In India, wherever you go your Caste follows and people take great pride in belonging to certain, upper Castes; but Gogulmanda hails from an oppressed Caste and identity. Because of the same identity, her mother discarded the Hindutva that she used to like, and embraced Christ, who loved humanity as a whole without discrimination. Presently in India, Dalit Christians face attacks for their choice of Christianity over other religions. At this crucial juncture, it is important to come together. For the same reason, she is using her pen as a weapon.

Michael N. Jagessar, CWM's Mission Secretary for the Caribbean, is from Guyana where the natives kept Eldorado out of the reach of the Colonials by spinning excitingly deceptive stories. After 'pirates plundered the Caribbean' extracting most of the Region's wealth and the IMF became a new form of piracy, Michael decided to follow the trail of the wealth which finally landed him in Britain (1999). Michael's religious heritages include Islam, Hinduism, and Christianity—Caribbean style: meaning poly-doxy and multiple religious impulses! Michael lives in the UK, while he 'dwells' the Caribbean and gets excited over cricket, Caribbean spirit-filled punch, creolised Caribbean curry, and the ever-elusive Anancy/Anansi (patron saint of the Caribbean). He writes (eclectic, interdisciplinary and Caribbean at heart), teaches, and preaches, among other callings.

Dong Hyeon Jeong is the Assistant Professor of New Testament Interpretation at Garrett-Evangelical Theological Seminary. He served as a missionary in the Philippines for two years with his parents, who are missionaries themselves since 1987. He is an ordained elder of the United Methodist Church. His forthcoming book is *With the Wild Beasts, Learning from the Trees: Animality, Vegetality, and (Colonized) Ethnicity in the Gospel of Mark*.

Sainimili Kata Rockett currently works for the Council for World Mission as the Programme Associate for Europe region. She is an indigenous iTaukei woman from Fiji and was raised between Fiji and England. She has a background in Anthropology of Development and Transformation and has particular interests in development studies, the anthropology of food, and the Pacific region. Sai currently lives in the southeast of England with her husband Mana, and son, Levi. And there is a gift on the way.

Nami Kim is professor of religious studies and chair of the Department of Philosophy and Religious Studies at Spelman College in Atlanta, U.S.A. She is the author of *The Gendered Politics of the Korean Protestant Right: Hegemonic Masculinity* (2016) and the co-editor of *Feminist Praxis against U.S. Militarism* (2016) and *Critical Theology against U.S. Militarism in Asia: Decolonization and Deimperialization* (2020). She serves on the editorial board of the *Journal of Feminist Studies in Religion* and *Journal of Race, Ethnicity, and Religion*.

Anna Jane Lagi is a student at the University of the South Pacific, Fiji. She has shared and sharpened her craft for writing and speaking through NGOs, local and international and published poems in *Poetry Anthology Collection: Rising Tide* (2020). The issues of suicide prevention, ending domestic violence, and helping sexual abuse victims, are fragments of her own story. She is no longer a product of whatever "culture" she has been raised or lived in; she chooses to be a culture maker.

John Robert Lee is a St. Lucian writer and poet. His short stories, poems, essays, and reviews can be found in journals (print and online), newspapers and anthologies. Lee's latest publications are *Pierrot* (2020), *Saint Lucian Writers and Writing* (2019) and *Collected Poems 1975–2015* (2017). He is a teacher, librarian, radio and TV broadcaster, literary journalist, reviewer, newspaper columnist, actor, and director. He presently manages an email list serve for Caribbean writers at home and abroad, and he is committed to Caribbean Community. He is an Elder with the Calvary Baptist Church, Saint Lucia, and has been involved with preaching, Bible teaching, broadcasting, writing Christian columns from 1978.

Tat-siong Benny Liew is Class of 1956 Professor in New Testament Studies at the College of the Holy Cross, Worcester, MA. He is the author of *Politics of Parousia* (1999), and *What Is Asian American Biblical Hermeneutics?* (2008). The works he edited include *The Bible in Asian America* (with Gale Yee; 2002), *Postcolonial Interventions* (2009), *Psychoanalytical Mediations between Marxist and Postcolonial Readings of the Bible* (with Erin Runions; 2016), *Present and Future of Biblical Studies* (2018), and *Colonialism and the Bible* (with Fernando Segovia; 2018). Liew has served on the Board of Directors of the American Academy of Religion, and is currently Chair of the Council of the Society of Biblical Literature and of the Wabash Center for Teaching and Learning in Theology and Religion.

Anna Kasafi Perkins is a Senior Programme Officer with the Quality Assurance Unit in The University of the West Indies's (UWI) Office of the Board for Undergraduate Studies, and adjunct faculty at St. Michael's Theological College. She teaches and researches in ethics, justice, popular culture, sexuality, theology, scripture, and quality assurance. She serves the community as a Commissioner of the Broadcasting Commission of Jamaica (BCJ); member of the National Bioethics Committee of Jamaica; and the Jamaica Council of Churches' representation on the Legal Aid Council of Jamaica. Her recent publications are *Ethics Amidst COVID-19: A Brief Ethics Handbook for Caribbean Policymakers and Leaders* (2020, co-authored with Professor R. Clive Landis), and *Rough Riding: Tanya Stephens and the Power of Music to Transform Society* (2021, co-edited with Adwoa Onuora and Ajamu Nangwaya).

Chad Rimmer is the Program Executive for Lutheran Theology and Practice at the Lutheran World Federation (Geneva, Switzerland). He is the author of several articles, the book *Greening the Children of God: Thomas Traherne and Nature's Role in the Ecological Formation of Children* and a collection of poetry, *Yellow: Chemopoetry from a Caretaker's Journey*. His works are at the intersection of faith and ecology, focusing on the role that nature plays in the ecological formation of children. He advocates for a constructive theo-poetic approach to theology, which is a method of theological reflection and meaning making that reconnects Beauty with Truth and Goodness. Through the beauty of poetry (and other arts), we can open new ways to access theological discourse.

Te Aroha Rountree (Ngai Tuteāuru, Ngā Puhi) is Senior Lecturer in Māori/Moana Studies at Trinity Methodist Theological College (Auckland, NZ). *He uri ahau no te hapu o Ngai Tuteāuru, no te iwi o Ngā Puhi. Ko Puhanga Tohorā te maunga, Ko Mangatawa me Otaua ngā awa e rerenei, Ko Pukerata te marae e tū ake nei, Ko Rahiri te Rangatira, te tupuna.* She has worked as an academic researcher for the University of Auckland with a focus on Māori language and oral traditions, and as a consultant on Te Tiriti o Waitangi, Te Reo Māori and Tikanga Māori for government organisations in the education and health sectors. Her current research focuses on *tangata whenua* theology, and native wisdoms and scripture as a means of healing.

Karen Georgia A. Thompson is the Associate General Minister (AGM) for Wider Church Ministries (WCM) and Operations in the United Church of Christ and Co-Executive for Global Ministries with the United Church of Christ and the Christian Church (Disciples of Christ). She is an inspiring preacher and theologian, often using her poetry as a part of her ministry. Her ecumenical and interreligious commitments overlap with her interest and implementation of global consultations on multiple religious belonging. She is a gifted writer and poet. Her forthcoming *Drums in Our Veins* is a compilation of poems that focus on the injustices facing people of African Descent and the fight for racial justice globally.

Neil Thorogood is a minister in the United Reformed Church, who develops his art alongside ministry. His dissertation was an art installation exploring the Lord's Prayer as a call to mission. In 2005 he was appointed Director of Pastoral Studies at the URC's Westminster College, Cambridge. In 2014 he became Principal of Westminster College, and in 2020 he moved to Bristol as minister to a reasonably large suburban congregation and also to a smaller congregation about 12 miles away in the market town of Thornbury. He more recently reflected on empire, colonialism, missionary movements, and the legacies of slavery. He has also been looking at theologies of aging, and of ways in which older age is understood within and beyond the Church.

Gerald O. West is Professor Emeritus in the School of Religion, Philosophy, and Classics in the University of KwaZulu-Natal, South Africa. He has worked extensively with the Ujamaa Centre for Community Development and Research for the past thirty years, a project in which socially engaged biblical scholars and ordinary African readers of the Bible from poor, working-class, and marginalised communities collaborate for social transformation. His most recent book is *The Stolen Bible: From Tool of Imperialism to African Icon* (2016).

www.ingramcontent.com/pod-product-compliance
Lightning Source LLC
Chambersburg PA
CBHW020742020526
44115CB00030B/840